LIFE IN BRITAIN AND GERMANY
ON THE ROAD
TO WAR

LIFE IN BRITAIN AND GERMANY
ON THE ROAD TO WAR
Keeping an Eye on Hitler

Anton Rippon and Nicola Rippon

PEN & SWORD HISTORY

AN IMPRINT OF PEN & SWORD BOOKS LTD.
YORKSHIRE – PHILADELPHIA

First published in Great Britain in 2024 by
PEN AND SWORD HISTORY
An imprint of
Pen & Sword Books Ltd
Yorkshire – Philadelphia

Copyright © Anton Rippon and Nicola Rippon, 2024

ISBN 978 1 39904 716 6

The right of Anton Rippon and Nicola Rippon to be identified as Authors of this work has been asserted by them in accordance with the Copyright, Designs and Patents Act 1988.

A CIP catalogue record for this book is available from the British Library.

All rights reserved. No part of this book may be reproduced or transmitted in any form or by any means, electronic or mechanical including photocopying, recording or by any information storage and retrieval system, without permission from the Publisher in writing.

Typeset in Times New Roman 11.5/14 by
SJmagic DESIGN SERVICES, India.
Printed and bound in the UK by CPI Group (UK) Ltd.

Pen & Sword Books Limited incorporates the imprints of Atlas, Archaeology, Aviation, Discovery, Family History, Fiction, History, Maritime, Military, Military Classics, Politics, Select, Transport, True Crime, Air World, Frontline Publishing, Leo Cooper, Remember When, Seaforth Publishing, The Praetorian Press, Wharncliffe Local History, Wharncliffe Transport, Wharncliffe True Crime and White Owl.

For a complete list of Pen & Sword titles please contact
PEN & SWORD BOOKS LIMITED
George House, Units 12 & 13, Beevor Street, Off Pontefract Road, Barnsley, South Yorkshire, S71 1HN, England
E-mail: enquiries@pen-and-sword.co.uk
Website: www.pen-and-sword.co.uk

Or
PEN AND SWORD BOOKS
1950 Lawrence Rd, Havertown, PA 19083, USA
E-mail: Uspen-and-sword@casematepublishers.com
Website: www.penandswordbooks.com

Contents

Prelude: So, Keep Your Eye on Hitler   vi

Chapter 1	Uninhibited by Convention	1
Chapter 2	A Great Wave of Reaction	11
Chapter 3	A New and Stronger Spirit?	20
Chapter 4	Political Upheavals	28
Chapter 5	Statesman or Showman?	34
Chapter 6	The Good Old English Fist	41
Chapter 7	Rowdy Streets	50
Chapter 8	One of the World's Most Evil Places	64
Chapter 9	Hitler's Games	75
Chapter 10	Pharaohs and a Führer	89
Chapter 11	Flags Flying, Bands Playing…	95
Chapter 12	A Most Inconvenient Dilemma	100
Chapter 13	The Man Who Leaked the Budget	107
Chapter 14	An Affront to the National Conscience	114
Chapter 15	The Empty Hell of War	120
Chapter 16	God Save the King!	127
Chapter 17	Voting Only for Peace or War	141
Chapter 18	A Terrible Transformation	148
Chapter 19	Asylum and Sanctuary on Our Doorsteps	158
Chapter 20	A Period of Danger More Acute…	165
Chapter 21	Adolf Hitler Stepped In, Didn't He?	175

Bibliography   181
Index   183

Prelude

So, Keep Your Eye on Hitler

'For years after the war, we looked like the fellow in the advertisement headed: "Have you got that tired feeling?" Well, we most certainly had.'

'The Man Next Door',
Sunday Illustrated

On New Year's Day 1922, Horatio Bottomley MP, writing in the *Sunday Illustrated*, looked back on the previous twelve months:

Just reflect on what a year we have gone through. Unemployment has been rampant, but it has been bravely borne – the ex-Serviceman has been as patient as he was valiant in war; Ireland has been a land of civil war; taxation has been crushing; our coal mines have stood silent; the iron moulders and ship joiners have been on strike ... Still, we have survived it all; but there is a limit to even national endurance, and I am afraid that we are perilously near to it.

The years immediately following the First World War – the Great War, as everyone called it – were difficult ones for the victors as well as for the vanquished. Between 1915 and 1918, Britain had spent 25 per cent of her GDP on the war effort, triggering her decline as the world's greatest economic power, a mantle now being assumed by the United States. Britain's empire was at its largest extent, covering one-quarter of the world and governing one in every four people on Earth, a stark contrast to Germany, which had emerged broken from the war. Yet, after the initial joyous celebrations of victory, David Lloyd George's target of a 'land fit for heroes' seemed a dream as distant as ever.

The nation's mental scars ran deep. There were more than 900,000 dead British servicemen to mourn. A further 2.2 million men – most of them in what should have been the prime of their lives – had returned to Blighty suffering from physical and psychological wounds. No city, town, village, or hamlet had escaped the effects of the 'Great War for Civilisation', as it was described on the Victory Medal awarded to 5.7 million men and women who had served.

There were indirect casualties of the war, too. In December 1922, the Newcastle *Sunday Sun* reported the case of the 10-year-old daughter of a Bradford mill worker who had burned to death while her parents were out. Her school was closed for Christmas, and when the coroner asked the mother if she thought it right that the girl should have been left alone, the woman replied, 'I have to consider the future. My husband was gassed in the war ... If I leave my work and my husband falls away, who is going to keep us?'

After the Armistice, life was indeed still far from trouble-free, especially on the island of Ireland. The Irish War of Independence fought between the Irish Republican Army and the British Army raged until a ceasefire in July 1921, and the creation of the Irish Free State and a separate Northern Ireland. But then disagreement among republicans over the terms of the Anglo-Irish Treaty led to the start of the eleven-month-long Irish Civil War.

On the mainland, in 1920, strikes on the railways, in the docks, the Yorkshire coalfield, in munitions factories, and even the police, had seen the average number of workers involved in strikes and lockouts top 2 million. In 1921, coal rationing was introduced after the government returned the mines – temporarily nationalised during the war – to their private owners, who then demanded that the miners accept wage cuts. The working class had become more organised during the war, but when the Miners' Federation of Great Britain called on its partners in the workers' Triple Alliance – the National Union of Railwaymen and the National Transport Workers' Federation – to join it in strike action, the railway and transport unions decided not to call out their members.

It was a day that would be long remembered by many trades unionists and socialists as 'Black Friday', and it saw the break-up of the Alliance. When the miners went it alone, Lloyd George declared a state of emergency, called up 80,000 special constables, and deployed armed troops to some pitheads. After three months, the miners were forced to return to work, accepting bigger pay cuts and no national bargaining, worse terms than they could have had at the start.

The labour force in general was having to accept lower wages. The *Sunday Illustrated* columnist 'The Man Next Door' claimed that the speed of bricklaying 'is only about half what it was before the war ... the notion has got about that the men do less than half on purpose because they think that's all their wages are worth, or so that there may be more work to go round'.

By 1922, unemployment in Britain had fallen from well over 2 million the previous year (at 11.3 per cent the highest since records began) but was still around 1.5 million. The 1918 Representation of the People Act had extended the franchise to all men aged 21 and over (subject to a six-month residency) and to women aged 30 and over, and after the disintegration of Lloyd George's wartime coalition (the Liberal Party itself had been torn apart by the bitter personal rivalry between Lloyd George and Herbert Asquith, and a division between right and left), the United Kingdom had a new Conservative government led by Bonar Law. An influenza epidemic killed more than 800 Britons in January alone. The BBC was formed, although even if you could afford a wireless set, there was another ten shillings to find for an annual licence fee. Huddersfield Town won the last FA Cup Final before the showpiece game moved to the newly opened Wembley Stadium, and five months after his article looking back at 1921 appeared, Horatio Bottomley was sentenced to seven years' penal servitude when an Old Bailey jury found him guilty of fraud on an industrial scale.

Thus, four years after the end of 'the war to end all wars', there was already much to engage the average citizen. But, as Britain got ready to celebrate Christmas 1922, tucked away on an inside page of the *Westminster Gazette*, alongside a report of a Nottingham football spectator being fined for attacking a player, and an advertisement for Debenham & Freebody's 'sound and reliable furs', there was a story headlined 'Swashbuckler Gangs in Munich'. It related 'extraordinary information' about the activities of 'the Bavarian Fascista under the leadership of an Austrian called Hitler'. According to the report, the gangs appeared to be well supplied with funds, and had been touring various towns in motor-lorries. They were generally 'armed to the teeth' with clubs and knuckledusters, spreading a 'reign of terror against which the police are powerless'. They plastered railway stations and other public places with inflammatory posters, attacked workmen who opposed them, and in the beer halls of Munich their collecting boxes, labelled 'Jewish Massacre Fund', were a common sight. One young man who protested at the boxes was 'violently assaulted and carried out insensible'. In the hope of appealing to Germany's working classes, said the newspaper, they called themselves National Socialists, a term strongly resented by republicans.

On the same day, the London-based *Daily News*, also carrying the story deep inside the paper, reported that Bavaria was being 'overrun by terrorising gangs led by an Austrian named Hitler'. A 'Labour party' had attached itself to 'this strangest of all "Labour" programmes'. Orthodox socialists had shrugged their shoulders at what they saw simply as paid mercenaries. But then, on the streets of Munich, there appeared young men wearing armlets of red, white, and black – the colours of the old German Empire, and bearing the 'Hakenkreuz', the swastika, a hitherto spiritual symbol but now, in Germany, the new symbol of antisemitism. The young men who wore it appeared to be some form of 'Hitler Guard', and when, one day, these young men marched through the streets of Munich, the more stolid of its citizens were surprised to see that they were some 10,000 strong.

Disaffection in post-war Germany was inevitable. More than 2 million German soldiers had lost their lives in the conflict, a social and economic catastrophe. The geography of Europe was redrawn as Germany was made to suffer large territorial losses. In all, 2.6 million square kilometres of land were lost – 28,000 of them in Europe – and 6 million subjects. Many of the victors wanted every last drop of blood – or was it lemon juice? Speaking at a rally before the 1918 General Election, Sir Eric Geddes, the MP for Cambridge, said:

> If I am returned, Germany is going to pay – restitution, reparation, and indemnity – and I have personally no doubt we will get everything out of her that you can squeeze out of a lemon, and a bit more. But there are some things I would not take from Germany, because they would hurt our industries. I propose that every bit of property, movable and immovable, in Allied and neutral countries, whether State property or private property of Germans, should be surrendered to the Allies, and that Germany should pay her precious citizens in her precious paper money. No German should be allowed to own anything in this country. If Germany has got anything to buy with, she can pay that in indemnities. I propose that not only all the gold Germany has got, but all the silver and jewels she has got, shall be handed over. All her pictures and libraries and everything

of that kind should be sold to the neutral and Allied world, and the proceeds given to pay the indemnity. I would strip Germany as she has stripped Belgium.

His speech was met with resounding cheers.

Sir Eric would doubtless have been pleased with the Treaty of Versailles that was signed on 28 June 1919. It put the blame for the war squarely on Germany and dictated that reparations, eventually set at £6.6 billion, would be paid in monthly instalments. In addition, although the Germans had to rebuild their economy, the loss of colonies, and land ceded to other countries, deprived them of rich sources of raw materials.

Also incorporated into the Treaty of Versailles was the Charter of the League of Nations, which, it was hoped, would once and for all provide a legal order that would see the end of a Europe where armed sovereign states with widely differing self-interests – not to mention mutual distrust – posed a perennial threat. Now an attack on one member of the League would be regarded as an attack on all. Collective security would deliver peace. Europe felt able to relax – even though Germany had not been invited to join this mutual protection society. Instead, the German army was to be reduced to no more than 100,000 men, the German navy to 15,000 sailors, and there could be no armour and no air force. Safeguards in the Treaty ensured that the Germans could not build up a military reserve by stealth.

Europe could never again be threatened by German militarism. At least, that was the theory. Others thought differently, not least in Britain. Lloyd George said the Treaty was too harsh: 'We shall have to fight another war again in 25 years' time.' And a cartoon that appeared in the *Daily Herald* depicted three men looking back at a naked child weeping behind a pillar in a corner. They are shown to be leaving a building, possibly the Palace of Versailles where the Treaty was signed. Beside the feet of the young boy is the peace treaty. Above his head are the words, '1940 Class'. One man, possibly meant to be Georges Clemenceau, the Prime Minister of France, says, 'Curious! I seem to hear a child weeping.' The cartoon is entitled 'Peace and Future Cannon Fodder'.

The German newspaper *Deutsche Zeitung* commented, 'Today ... the disgraceful Treaty is being signed ... The German people will ... reconquer the place among the nations to which it is entitled.' In his diary for Saturday, 10 January 1920, Count Harry Kessler, a French-born German (with Irish ancestry) diplomat and author, wrote:

> Today the Peace Treaty was ratified at Paris; the War is over. A terrible era begins for Europe, like the gathering of clouds before a storm, and it will end in an explosion probably more terrible than that of the World War. In Germany there are all the signs of a continuing growth of nationalism.

The political impact in Germany itself was indeed enormous. The government of the day refused to sign the Versailles Treaty and resigned. The incoming administration had no choice but to agree. And as the economy collapsed – and many old soldiers wondered how Germany could have lost the war when they had still held French territory taken at the very outset in 1914 – the argument that it was the politicians, not the military, who had been responsible for national humiliation gained huge support. It would not be long before millions of Germans distrusted the Weimar Republic – named after the town where Germany's new government was formed by a national assembly after the abdication of Kaiser Wilhelm II – in all its manifestations, with devastating consequences not only for Germany but also for the entire civilised world.

Conditions were perfect for the rise of a man like Adolf Hitler. Third son of a local customs inspector, he was born on 20 April 1889, in Braunau am Inn, a town on the border between the Austro-Hungarian Empire and the German Empire. When he was 14, his father died. Five years later, his mother also passed away and Hitler moved to Vienna, where he made two failed attempts to enter the Academy for Art, instead being forced to move from one mundane job to another: copying and peddling picture postcards, producing advertisements, and painting and decorating houses. In 1913, he moved again, to Munich, where he joined the Bavarian Army.

During the Great War, in which he was awarded the Iron Cross, Hitler was wounded in the leg near Bapaume in October 1916, and temporarily blinded by a British gas attack in the Ypres Salient in October 1918. In the summer of 1919, he joined a handful of other restless young men in the German Workers' Party. They had no properly worked out programme, but their broad ideals fitted perfectly with the racism he had first digested as a disaffected youth in Vienna. He climbed swiftly up the party ladder and, by 1921, was leader of what had now become the National Socialist German Workers' Party – the *Nationalsozialistische Deutsche Arbeiterpartei*, the NSDAP, or the Nazi Party, the popular abbreviation that would be most familiar to readers of British newspapers from 1930 onwards.

Despite his comical appearance – a lock of hair falling over his forehead, a square little moustache seemingly capable of independent movement on his pallid, sombre face, often sweating – Hitler proved a mesmeric, rabble-rousing speaker, a natural skill he first discovered in the back room of a Munich café. The Treaty of Versailles was his main obsession, but his targets were manifold: Jews, capitalists, democrats, communists. The German people were looking for someone – anyone – to blame. Hitler provided them with plenty of targets and they were drawn to him. As well as workers, the Nazis recruited doctors, lawyers, teachers, scientists, and members of the upper class. The movement utilised crude symbols of power. Hitler's early followers were called *Sturm Abteilung* (SA) or Storm Section – popularly, 'stormtroopers' – who wore a uniform of ski caps, brown shirts, knee breeches and combat boots and, of course, those swastika armbands. Hitler created a Nazi flag, a red banner with a swastika on a white circle. His stormtroopers disrupted the meetings of political opponents, and physically attacked people whose race, religion, or political persuasion appeared on Hitler's growing list of perceived enemies of Germany. At militaristic rallies they saluted their leader with cries of 'Heil Hitler!'

Hitler dashed by motorcar from meeting to meeting, talking about Versailles as a 'Treaty of Shame', and blaming Jews and profiteers for Germany's woes. With his message of hate, the leader travelled all over Bavaria, although not always freely. On one occasion, workers refused to let the special train on which he was travelling proceed. Traditional socialists called on the Bavarian government to break up the National Socialist Party as a danger to the maintenance of the Republic. They referred to the new party as 'the Gravediggers of Germany' and they called five meetings in Munich to protest. Hitler quickly arranged ten simultaneous meetings. While the socialists struggled to fill their halls, more than 30,000 answered Hitler's call to hear him give a five-minute speech at each meeting.

Writing in the *Daily Chronicle* in December 1922, the distinguished foreign correspondent Leonard Spray said, 'You have never heard of Hitler – Adolf Hitler? ... A few months ago, you would have asked in vain ... ask today and anyone in Bavaria will tell you ... keep your eye on Hitler...'

Hitler was, said Spray, forging for himself a reputation as 'the German Mussolini': 'Six months ago, you had never heard of Mussolini. But now Mussolini is Premier of Italy and sits in conference with statesmen whose European reputation was assured long before his name was known even in his own country.' Spray pointed out that 'Bavaria is not Germany', but it was, he said,

> the new Prussia of Germany ... and in this new Prussia, reactionary and militarist Hitler is taking the leadership ... his followers have passed a resolution against everything and everybody from the Versailles Treaty to Berlin's politicians, from 'Internationalism' to the Jews.
>
> The affirmative programme of this great new host?
>
> Well, that is the secret of its leader.
>
> So, keep your eye on Hitler.

It was a warning that few heeded. With all that was happening in their own lives, events in the beer halls of Munich were supremely irrelevant to most Britons. As in Germany, the poor were focused on surviving; the better-off on enjoying themselves. Few were keeping an eye on Adolf Hitler.

Chapter 1

Uninhibited by Convention

'We ... disported ourselves with an abandon that was all the fiercer because we knew that the press was watching – and watching with a very disapproving eye.'

Beverley Nichols,
All I Could Never Be

In 1922, the London *Daily News* reported that police in Berlin had begun a campaign against some of the Kabaretts. It cited the story of two detectives who had attended a performance organised by the 'Friends of Art' and been 'so shocked at what they witnessed that they urged the police president to institute the prosecution, in the interests of public morals, of Fraulein Lola Bach and other dancers'. Of particular offence were performances named 'The Nun', 'The New Hat', and 'Champagne Delerium'.

Since the nineteenth century, Berlin's Kabaretts had each offered its own type of entertainment which catered to a specific demographic. Prior to the Great War, however, heavy censorship had limited the type and themes of entertainment. The overthrow of the authoritarian Kaiser in 1918, foreign investment, and a burgeoning youthful Berlin population, changed that. Kabaretts began to feature acts that involved progressive arts, political satire, jazz, and performances that revolved around sexual innuendo with most bills including at least some naked dancers. At Der Weiss Maus (The White Mouse), guests wore masks while a naked dancer, often supposedly interpreting the tale of *Salome*, performed before them. Some performances dabbled in sado-masochistic themes.

Whatever the authorities' concerns, Berlin was becoming a hotspot for visitors. In April 1929, *The Clarion* weekly newspaper featured the observations of a visiting businessman who wrote about a venue called The Jockey, just off Kurfurstendamm: 'tables crowded uncomfortably close ... an atmosphere of smoke, liquor, conversation and bad jazz ... here a masculine woman and there an effeminate man'. And yet he warned that despite the superficial appearance to the contrary, Germany today is a poverty-stricken nation ... Germany is struggling to overcome the burden of reparations, high taxation and shortage of capital ... tenements approached through dirty alleyways ... houses rickety with age and unsafe through lack of repair ... all the characteristics of the worst London slums.

The author noted that he had been told that the very worst poverty was among the older middle classes, whose savings had been 'swept away'.

In contrast, Hannen Swaffer, writing in *The Bystander*, described his experience of Berlin's nightlife and, upon watching the scene in one location, that an American friend had said, 'I want you to tell me who the hell won the war!'

Swaffer wrote, 'Everywhere ... the lights were full on. Everywhere the tango was danced, syncopation committed sin upon the floor, and the popping of champagne corks almost kept pace with the band.'

One of the most famous dancers working in Berlin was Anita Berber, a bisexual classically trained performer, and eventual cocaine addict, who appeared in more than twenty films, modelled for artists and was a Kabarett sensation. On stage and in public, Berber dressed provocatively, in revealing or barely-there outfits, or conversely in man's tuxedo and sporting a monocle. Out on the town, she 'wore' her pet monkey draped around her neck and reputedly ate in restaurants wearing nothing but a short sable coat. Berber was not alone in grasping this hedonistic and cultural expression, in a population perhaps aware that this abundance, if not liberty, might well be rather short-lived. The new liberal view allowed homosexuals, lesbians, and transvestites to openly display their lives, at least within the confines of the Kabarett. And this was something that did not sit at all happily with the more traditional members of society. Austrian-born Jewish writer Stefan Zweig called Berlin 'the Babel of the world'. He wrote that 'made-up boys with artificial waistlines promenaded along the Kurfurstendamm' and declared that 'even Rome had not known orgies like the Berlin transvestite balls where hundreds of men in women's clothes and women in men's clothes danced under the benevolent eyes of the police'.

In Germany, as in Britain, such decadence was frowned upon. German socialists hated that it highlighted the extravagance of capitalism, while those on the political right were apt to suggest it revealed moral weakness and political corruption.

Uninhibited by Convention

The Nazis, in particular, made clear their disgust at bars, clubs, and restaurants where people of different racial and ethnic groups, or sexual preferences, could gather unhindered. Both political wings became the target of the biting satire so popular in the Kabaretts which, as well as poking fun at the rotund body of the Weimar's first president, Friedrich Ebert, or the Chaplinesque appearance of Adolf Hitler, regularly shone a critical light on their policies.

Inevitably, when the Nazis came to power in 1933, it spelt the death knell for Kabaretts. By their very liberal nature, many of the performers were left-wing, and many of them were Jewish. Those who were able to do so fled the country entirely. Those who felt able to remain, thanks to their 'Aryan' qualifications, found their material was strictly controlled. Kabaretts like the Catacombs and the Tingel-Tangel, that persisted in openly questioning the Third Reich, were closed down. The German government tried first to reframe the whole concept, so that the acts performing there were supportive of the Nazi Party, and critical only of their opposition. It failed utterly and, in 1937, Joseph Goebbels, the Minister of Public Enlightenment and Propaganda, would ban all political themes from German stages, effectively turning them back into old-fashioned music-halls which, by 1939, featured only female casts. On the eve of another world war, the widespread mobilisation of the male population would see to that.

The war had left Europe scarred, bereft, and on its knees in 1918. On both sides of the Channel, the majority faced the hard grind of poverty. For others, however, it was time to break out from normality, to grasp new freedoms and reject convention. Just as citizens of post-war Berlin were exercising their own new-found freedoms of expression, never solely intending to be decadent but nevertheless uninhibited by convention, so, too, in Britain there was a group whose behaviour scandalised polite society. The tone might have been different in Weimar Germany, the participation wider, but in Britain the purpose was the same. Throughout the 1920s and early 1930s, a group of aristocrats, socialites, aspiring members of the middle class, and avant garde artists became known for their bohemian ways and hedonistic celebrations. They revelled in the nickname given to them by the *Daily Mail* in 1924 – 'Bright Young People'.

They were members of a group who expressed their identities through their tastes in music, fashion, recreational activity, and sexual proclivity. They also courted sections of the media who enthusiastically reported on their regular shenanigans – effectively heralding the beginnings of what we have come to know as the paparazzi. The press would pursue them as they either sped through London's streets in fast cars, or disrupted other passengers on public transport, on their way to an adventure – a treasure hunt, or a party. It was a relationship that seems surprisingly modern and would ultimately end rather acrimoniously. For their part, the British public at large initially admired their beauty, their style, their modernity, but despised their wantonness and ill-behaviour, despairing of their often outrageous activities: drinking to excess, using drugs, and partying until dawn being the most mundane. They – women and several of the men – decorated their faces in heavy make-up. The twist on their soubriquet – 'Bright Young Things' – became increasingly used, and perhaps better suited the wider public's increasing perception of the set as a group of wealthy, over-indulged, and unruly revellers with no understanding of the problems suffered by the rest of society.

Understandably, after the years that had gone before, anything daring, cutting-edge, and seemingly independent-minded became desirable. More fashion-conscious British women did their best to follow trends, to adopt some of the latest styles – shortened skirt and dress hems – some even rouging their knees to draw attention to them. They adopted new boyish haircuts like the bob and the even more avant garde shingle and Eton crop. This so-called 'Flapper fashion' was certainly not limited to the upper, or celebrity, classes. Ordinary young women right across the country were doing their best to keep up to date with London's latest in fashion and beauty.

Even as far away as Aberdeen, a journalist from the *Press & Journal* reported in December 1923 that although 'I have not yet observed the fashion [for the shingle] in Aberdeen, doubtless a few flappers are premeditating a further shearing of their locks as they have tired of bobbing'. The shingle, with its ultra-short back with sides left longer, was regarded as universally flattering, particularly to those older women whose locks had become less luxuriant as they had aged. It was predicted that the style would soon be ubiquitous. Indeed, in 1927, the *West Bridgford Advertiser*, in Nottingham, featured an advertisement for F. H. Redmonds of Trent Boulevard, whose services included a Shingle Trim or Semi-shingle for a shilling (5p) and a Bob Trim for 8 or 9 pence (less than 4p). By the end of the decade, it seemed, dramatically short hair was losing popularity. According to information supplied by an 'annual hairdressing fair of fashion' at London's White City in October

1928, and as reported in the *Northampton Chronicle & Echo*, some 'twelve million women in the British Isles have their hair regularly and permanently waved every six months'. Hairdressers reported that many of their clients were now thinking about growing out their hair, while the hairdressers were warning them that long hair would not yet be in fashion, and tried to persuade them to opt for something 'just a leetle longer' and, perhaps, with soft curls and waves.

The report stated that the

> average Society women spends from four to six hours each week at her beauty salon where they have their hair, their faces, their eyebrows and lips and arms treated and now the latest craze is to have beauty treatment for their legs, because of the fine net stockings which are being worn in the evening.

For those whose only 'society' concerns were the prices in the local Co-op, constrained circumstances prevented avid adherence to high fashion. That was the preserve of the very wealthy. And the 'Bright Young' set were certainly that. The average person could either choose to rely upon vicarious pleasure, or tutting disapproval, from the pages of the newspapers.

While, in the early years, even members of the royal family – the Prince of Wales, Prince George, Duke of Kent, and even the Duchess of York, a future queen – were reported to have joined in some of the more dignified occasions, the corps of the Bright Young did not come from the very highest echelons of the nobility. They did include the likes of Robert Byron, Rex Whistler, William Walton, and Cecil Beaton – all of whom would eventually find long-lasting professional fame as a travel writer and historian, artist, composer, and photographer respectively. It was Beaton's recording of the group that lead to his career as a Society photographer. The heart of the set became best known purely for their social lives – individuals like siblings Nancy and Diana Mitford (Diana would later marry Oswald Mosley) and David and Stephen Tennant, the sons of Baron Glenconner. David founded the Gargoyle Club, a private members' club in Soho's Dean Street, while Stephen was the inspiration for Evelyn Waugh's Sebastian Flyte in *Brideshead Revisited*.

The press may have found these antics provided good copy, but not everyone in their social circle was so enamoured. English writer

Lytton Strachey, a prominent member of the Bloomsbury Group circle of artists, writers, and intellectuals, and himself no stranger to living outside of societal norms, wrote on meeting them, 'I saw these marvellous people, they were absolutely beautiful, but they had feathers where brains should be.'

A keener member of the set was author and playwright Beverley Nichols, who wrote in his memoir of those days:

> It was an age of 'parties'. There were 'white' parties in which we shot down to the country in fleets of cars, dressed in white from head to foot, and danced on a white floor laid in the orchard, with the moonlight turning all the apples to silver, and then – in a pale pink dawn – playing races with champagne corks on the surface of the stream. There were Mozart parties in which, powdered and peruked, we danced by candlelight and then – suddenly bored – rushed out into the street to join a gang excavating the gas mains at Hyde Park Corner.

Ironically, given the social origins of many of the set, they embraced anything they deemed anti-establishment. Together they adopted their own slang, and had a fondness for using words like 'divine' and 'darling'. Unusually for the time, they accepted and approved of same-sex relationships. They were utterly uninhibited.

When partying, whether out in town, or at one of the group's country homes, flamboyant and even fancy dress was often worn. Many of them travelled with the ready-made costume of a sailor suit in their regular luggage, just in case the opportunity to don it arose. By the late 1920s, newspapers were regularly featuring photographs and reports of the latest themed party. In 1927, *Tatler* gave over two pages to a feature and photographs of the 'Impersonation Party' held in Mayfair by Captain Neil MacEachean. Guests like Cecil Beaton and Tallulah Bankhead dressed as living celebrities. Stephen Tennant went in drag as Queen Marie of Roumania. In June 1928 came the notorious 'Bath and Bottle Party', which took place at St George's Baths on Buckingham Palace Road. Guests arrived at 11.00 pm wearing bathing costumes. Each brought along a bottle of alcohol, although a special cocktail was created to match the colour of the water at the baths, and a jazz orchestra played.

In January 1929, the *Sheffield Daily Telegraph* reported that 'after a period of quiet, Society's "bright young people" have burst out again with one of their eccentric stunts which they fondly believe are the outward and visible sign of their superior intelligence'.

The venue this time was the Five Hundred Club in Mayfair. Elizabeth Ponsonby, daughter of Arthur Ponsonby, the peace campaigner and Labour MP for Sheffield Brightside, hosted her own 'mock wedding' to John Rayner. As her father's constituency newspaper reported, 'The guests who wore somewhat strange attire for a wedding, paraded their inanities at a restaurant in Piccadilly where they celebrated the "wedding breakfast".' Guests arrived dressed in over-the-top outfits – hats adorned with dangling cherries and the like. They posed before the invited press photographers for faux wedding photographs. Elizabeth and John were not even romantically involved, and the 'bride' married for real later in the year.

Fashion designer Norman Hartnell boasted a clientele of Society folk, up-and-coming actresses and Bright Young People. In July 1929, at his Bruton Street property, he hosted one of the most extraordinary celebrations – the Circus Party. *The Sketch* called it 'admittedly, the most wonderful, magnificent, and amazing gathering of the season'. The house was 'most cleverly transformed into the likeness of a circus'. There was a ring, 'genuine performing bears', hoop-la, a hurdy-gurdy, coconut shies, and even a fortune teller. Guests included the likes of Mrs Ernest De Winton Wills, Princess Lalita of Burdwan, actress Brenda Dean-Paul, and the Marchioness of Carisbrooke. Some guests came straight from political receptions but many of those who didn't dressed up in circus costumes. Hartnell was the ringmaster, one guest arrived with two snakes draped around her neck, Ivor Novello wore the ubiquitous sailor suit, while Eleanor Smith – daughter of F. E Smith, 1st Earl of Birkenhead, former Secretary of State for India, and who, as attorney general, had prosecuted some of the best-known British trials – brought her own pony and rode it up the stairs.

If these excesses did not play well with the rest of the country, the Bright Young People did hatch at least one hoax that earned them grudging admiration – if only because their targets were just as disliked as the set themselves. In 1929, Bryan Guinness and his wife, Diana Mitford, held an art exhibition in London of modern work by an apparently unknown self-taught painter named Bruno Hat. German-born Hat had been discovered working in a village shop in Clymping, West

Sussex. At the opening, attended by art enthusiasts, several paintings, among them *Still Life With Pears*, were exhibited and the wheelchair-using artist himself was introduced to his public. When one of the guests helpfully asked him a question in German, Hat denounced his homeland and insisted on speaking only in English. In truth, the artist barely spoke German. Hat was a fake and was really another Mitford sibling – this time Tom – wearing dark glasses and a false moustache. Bryan Howard, who happened to be the son of the chairman of the National Portrait Gallery and a reasonably talented artist, had dashed off most of the artwork in a couple of days.

Although the pranksters' usual sniggering japes met with little admiration, this time, several newspapers and magazines approved. The 'Town and County' gossip column of the *Sporting Times* declared it had 'administered a hefty kick in the stomach to some of the bone-headed humbugs who pretend to admire whatever they think is "newest" in Art', while *The Bystander* noted, 'Many of the guests felt it incumbent upon them to fall into ecstasies over his work on the assumption, apparently, that anything you can't understand must be clever.'

Generally, though, it was the Bright Young Things themselves who were roundly mocked. One 1929 issue of the *Daily Herald* published a poem by 'Tomfool' that included the lines:

> They suck their comforters, pout and yowl,
> Talk infant jargon and romp and howl.

Public derision, though, was about to turn to exasperation and condemnation. While once there had been an idle fascination with the profligate lifestyles of these supposed Bright Young Things, this had begun to turn to boredom. And, as the country fell further into economic strife, it inevitably morphed into something more powerful – resentment.

By the autumn of 1931, the financial crisis had brought an emergency National Government to power, leaving little public patience for bright young anythings. Just about the last thing newspaper readers wanted to see was a report of yet another outrageous shindig. The 'Red and White Party' that took place on 21 November 1931 proved a party too far for the patience of Depression Britain and the stomachs of the newspapers and magazines that had, to that point, enthusiastically reported every last show of decadence.

Uninhibited by Convention

The party was held by a rich playboy, Arthur Jeffress, at the Regent's Park home of fading star of dance, Maud Allan. Allan had unsuccessfully sued the MP for Hertford, Noel Pemberton Billing, for libel after he accused her of being a lesbian associate of German wartime conspirators who were attempting to 'exterminate the manhood of Britain' by luring men into homosexuality. One of the women that Allan had been close to was Margot Asquith, the wife of Britain's prime minister at the outbreak of war in 1914, and it was Margot who, for many years, paid the rent on Allan's luxurious apartment in the west wing of Holford House. It was a most suitable venue for a party. And what a party it was. Every guest arrived dressed in red or white or a combination of the two, many bedecked in rubies and diamonds, topped off with feathers, flowers, and furs. Everything that could be themed was – from the lobsters and strawberries on the menu to the cigarettes they smoked.

But Britain was staring austerity in the face. The number of registered unemployed topped 3.5 million. Men in the north were going on hunger marches to London to draw attention to their plight. Seldom could such a party have been so ill-timed. The public may, at one time, have been dazzled by the Bright Young set's lavish excesses. Now they were simply disgusted. It helped little that there were fights between guests – one woman pulling out a chunk of another woman's hair – and arrests for drug possession. *The Bystander* labelled the scene 'ill-bred extravagance'. It was to prove the last public exhibition of outrageous partying. The parties might have continued, but they did so behind closed doors; the set's fall from grace was not yet complete. Then, in 1932, one of the brightest of all, 28-year-old actress and socialite Elvira Barney, was tried for murder. According to newspaper reports, in the early hours of 31 May, Elvira, who was separated from her husband, returned home to Knightsbridge, together with her bisexual lover, 24-year-old Michael Scott Stephen. A neighbour reported being woken by an argument between the pair during which Elvira had been heard to shout, 'Get out of my house! I hate you! Get out! Get out! I will shoot you!'

Shortly after Stephen apparently agreed to leave, a gunshot was heard. Elvira screamed. Stephen shouted, 'Oh God, God, what have you done?'

Elvira then called, 'Chicken, Chicken, I am so sorry. Come back to me. I will do anything you ask me.'

After a few minutes, the neighbour heard Elvira calling out to Stephen, then all had fallen silent. The alarm was raised only when

Elvira telephoned her doctor to report a 'terrible accident'. When the doctor arrived, he found Michael Stephen's lifeless body at the bottom of the stairs. He had been shot at close range in the chest. The police were called. Elvira confirmed that there had been a row, but that this had been nothing unusual. On this occasion, her lover had threatened to leave her, and Elvira had promised to kill herself. Stephen had grabbed her gun to prevent this, a struggle had followed, and the weapon had gone off accidentally. Rather than being taken to a police station, Elvira was allowed to accompany her parents to the family home in Belgrave Square.

But she was charged. At her Old Bailey trial, Elvira was defended by Sir Patrick Hastings, a former attorney general and associate of her father. It paid off – the judge said that Sir Patrick's final address to the jury was the best he had ever heard. The jury were impressed, too – and found Elvira not guilty. She died four years later, in a Paris hotel room.

The Bright Young Things had passed on, too. Theirs had been a bizarre distraction while events in Germany had begun to take a worrying turn as Adolf Hitler marched into a Munich beer hall.

Chapter 2

A Great Wave of Reaction

> 'When one goes into Germany one encounters plenty of residual swashbuckling spirit ... but it is very hard to find any Germans who seem to be steadily busy upon the reconstruction of Europe upon broad modern lines.'
>
> H. G. Wells

On Friday, 9 November 1923, two stories shared equal billing on the front page of *The Daily News*. One told of the howls of protest that greeted the British government's plan to impose taxes on some foodstuffs – the housewives of Britain were apparently 'amazed at tinned salmon duty'. The other reported on 'Revolution in Bavaria ... all-German dictatorship proclaimed ... Berlin cut off.'

While in London, the managing director of a firm of produce merchants complained that the imposition of 10s (50p) duty per hundredweight (50.8 kilograms) of tinned salmon was 'about the silliest economic proposal I have heard for many a year', in Bavaria 'a military dictatorship proclaimed ... the Minister of the Interior has been arrested ... Munich is in the hands of thousands of Hitler's troops'. If the British public had hitherto ignored Leonard Spray's advice to keep their eyes on Adolf Hitler, they would soon become uncomfortably familiar with the name. For the moment, though, it was still events much closer to home that diverted their attention, not least that the purchaser of 'a favourite little luxury for the poorest in the land' would now have to pay one penny more for a 1lb (0.45 kilograms) tin.

While Hitler was attempting to overthrow the government of Bavaria, in Britain there was also political upheaval. In May 1923, the Prime Minister, Bonar Law, seriously ill with throat cancer, resigned after only 209 days in office. Stanley Baldwin, the Chancellor of the Exchequer, replaced him as premier. The Labour Party also had a new leader in 57-year-old Ramsay MacDonald. In October, Baldwin announced that the Conservative government would seek a mandate to introduce protectionist tariffs and 'imperial preference' to stem the flow of what he saw as unfair competition from imports. By offering home-manufactured goods a fair playing field and greater economic stability, it would, argued Baldwin, tackle Britain's still unacceptable level of unemployment.

Baldwin did not receive his mandate. In the December 1923 General Election, the Conservatives won most seats, 258, but not enough to gain an overall majority. Labour, together with Herbert Asquith's reunited Liberal Party, gained sufficient to produce a hung parliament. Asquith announced that the Liberals, with 158 MPs, would not keep the Tories in power. Labour had won 191 seats, and Asquith declared that if a Labour government were ever to be tried in Britain, 'it could hardly be tried under safer conditions'. On 22 January 1924, Baldwin resigned. At midday, Ramsay MacDonald was driven to Buckingham Palace to be appointed Prime Minister of a Labour government supported by those champions of free trade, the Liberals, who had joined them in voting down the King's Speech prepared by Baldwin. The Conservatives were left to reflect that the election had not been necessary. In 1922, Bonar Law's Tories had been returned with an overall majority. Now Baldwin's call for the unpopular pre-war policy of tariff reform had sunk them.

Ramsay MacDonald's elevation had not been achieved by the overwhelming consent of the British people, but it had still been delivered by the democratic process. Adolf Hitler, meanwhile, was about to stand trial for his failed attempt to seize power by force, his 'Munich beer hall putsch', as history would remember it, inspired by Benito Mussolini's October 1922 march on Rome that had succeeded in overthrowing a liberal government of Italy.

Germany had hit rock bottom. The country was behind on the swingeing reparations imposed on it for, according to the victorious Allies, being solely responsible for the Great War. Germany's failure to maintain payments had provoked retaliatory French-Belgian military occupation of the industrial district in the Ruhr valley in order to use its resources to make up for the unpaid reparations. This affected the livelihoods of millions of Germans who might otherwise have provided a stabilising influence at a time when the country was riven by strikes and by unrest on the streets. Local citizen militias were formed to keep the peace and combat looters. And then there was the rampant hyperinflation; a measure of this can be seen in the cost of a simple postage stamp. In 1920, the highest-valued stamp issued was 4 marks;

three years later, it was 50 billion marks. By December 1923, the exchange rate was 6.7 trillion marks for one US dollar. In August, the German journalist Friedrich Kroner had written, 'It pounds daily on the nerves: the insanity of numbers, the uncertain future ... An epidemic of fear and naked need...' In October, Robert Clive, the British consul-general in Munich, had described the scene in the Bavarian capital:

> Few families can afford meat more than once a week, eggs are unprocurable, milk terribly scarce and bread already sixteen times the price of a few days ago ... No one expects political disturbances, but hunger riots are another matter ... and the cold, no one can afford central heating.

By 1923, hyperinflation had radically redistributed the wealth of Germany. If the poor had little to lose in the first place, and if the very richest segment of society had managed to convert their wealth into forms untouched by the problem of hyperinflation, then the people that were hardest hit were the middle and upper-middle classes. They were Hitler's target, and Bavaria was where he decided to begin his revolution. Early in 1923, he and Ernst Röhm, who had been disfigured after being shot in the face while serving near Verdun in 1916, formed pacts with the right-wing Patriotic Leagues against the liberal Bavarian government. After seizing power there, Hitler planned that the Nazi Party would launch a revolution against the Weimar Republic itself, with the right-wing wartime general Erich Ludendorff a figurehead who would lead the Nazis' march on Berlin.

Hitler had initially thought of using the conservative state commissioner of Bavaria, Gustav von Kahr, in that role, but von Kahr backed away from the idea. When Hitler learned that von Kahr was to address a crowd of around 3,000 at the Bürgerbräukeller, one of Munich's largest beer halls, on 8 November 1923, he surrounded the hall with his followers. Von Kahr had been speaking for three-quarters of an hour when Hitler and his men forced their way in. In his book *The Rise and Fall of the Third Reich*, William L. Shirer quotes the German-American businessman Ernst Hanfstaengel, a confidant of Hitler:

> Hitler began to plough his way towards the platform and the rest of us surged forward behind him. Tables overturned with their jugs of beer. On the way we passed a major

named Mucksel, one of the heads of the intelligence section at army headquarters, who started to draw his pistol as soon as he saw Hitler approach, but the bodyguard had covered him with theirs and there was no shooting. Hitler clambered on a chair and fired a round at the ceiling.

According to a Reuters correspondent,

> As he could not make himself heard, due to the uproar, his two escorters fired their revolvers into the air and Herr Hitler shouted, 'We are not against Herr von Kahr.' A staff officer of Hitler's troops then announced to the assembly, 'Today begins the national revolution which is solely directed against the Berlin Jewish Government.' The remark was greeted with tremendous enthusiasm, and the singing of *Deutschland über alles*, Herr Hitler then stepped forward and, after having fired his revolver in the air in order to obtain silence, announced that the Knilling Cabinet [Eugen Ritter von Knilling was the Prime Minister of Bavaria from 1922 to 1924; on this night he was arrested by Rudolf Hess, one of Hitler's closest allies] had been deposed and the Bavarian Government would be formed of a state administrator and premier with full dictatorial powers. As the former, Dr von Kahr was proposed, and as the latter Herr von *Pöhner*, formerly the police president in Munich.

Von Kahr and two others – General Otto von Lossow (commander of the military region that covered Bavaria) and Colonel Hans Ritter von Seisser (head of the Bavarian police) – had been bundled into a back room, where, under threat of death, the trio agreed to Hitler's demand for the march on Berlin.

Hitler told the meeting that he had just hijacked,

> The November government of criminals in Berlin is declared deposed, as also President Ebert [Friedrich Ebert, a Social Democrat, had been appointed Germany's first president in 1919]. The national army is hereby immediately created, and I propose that I assume direction of this provisional national government until the treaties which are today the ruin of

Germany are torn up. General Ludendorff takes charge of the national army, General von Lossow becomes German minister of defence, and Colonel von Seisser minister of police. The task of the provisional government is to begin the march against the den of iniquity in Berlin. Tomorrow there will be either a national government in Germany, or we shall be dead.

Ludendorff was brought to the beer hall. As the man who had directed Germany's wartime military strategy, he had found Hitler's claims that the war had been lost, not by the army but by Jews, communists, and a weak German government, most attractive. He was, however, annoyed that Hitler had apparently started a revolution in his name without telling him, and even less pleased with Hitler's distribution of roles that made a former Austrian corporal into a dictator and gave a wartime general charge of an army that did not exist.

Ludendorff's displeasure aside, according to Reuters,

> Herr Hitler's speech was greeted with thunderous applause by the assemblage, which was renewed when Dr von Kahr said that he was ready to take charge of Bavaria's fate and considered himself to be the upholder of monarchy. The proceedings ended with Dr von Kahr and Herr Hitler shaking hands amidst scenes of tremendous enthusiasm.

Along with von Knilling, Bavaria's Minister of the Interior and other prominent local politicians who had attended the meeting were also arrested. At midnight, all telephonic communication with Berlin was cut off. In the German capital, Gustav Stresemann, the recently appointed Chancellor and Foreign Minister of a grand coalition government, called a cabinet meeting, while the Prussian government issued a statement that 'traitors in Munich have attempted to overthrow the Bavarian Government. The unity of the empire and the constitution are menaced ... Prussian citizens support your government and help it to maintain the unity of the Reich.'

Hitler left Bürgerbräukeller to deal with events unfolding elsewhere, and von Kahr, von Seisser, and von Lossow were allowed to leave, whereupon they immediately renounced their support for Hitler. Von Kahr declared the Nazi Party a banned organisation and ordered the authorities to 'exercise extreme care in examining passports, and all members of the National Socialist Association and of the Bund Oberland [a voluntary paramilitary organisation that became the core of the brownshirt Sturm Abteilung in Bavaria] are to be arrested no matter where they may be caught'. For his opposition, von Kahr would meet a grizzly end, at Dachau concentration camp after the 'Night of the Long Knives' in June 1934.

The following morning, a dull, grey start to the new day, Hitler and Ludendorff led some 3,000 supporters towards the Bavarian Defence Ministry, but the march was blocked by state police officers. Shots were exchanged, and four policemen and fourteen Nazis were killed. Two more Nazis perished elsewhere. In the melee, Hitler fell to the pavement and damaged his shoulder. Leaving his followers to face armed police, he fled to the house of a friend, Ernst Hanfstaengl, where depressed and allegedly suicidal, he hid in an attic for two days before being arrested. The Central News Agency reported:

> The sensational Bavarian coup collapsed with dramatic suddenness. After heavy fighting, in which severe losses were sustained on both sides, the War Ministry in Munich was occupied and General Ludendorff and his chancellor, Herr Hitler, have been arrested. The new government of all Germany, which was proclaimed at ten o'clock last night, lasted sixteen hours.

Accused of high treason, Hitler faced a twenty-five-day trial in a makeshift courtroom on the second floor of the Reichswehr Infantry School, an old red-brick building in Munich's suburbs. It began on 26 February 1924, and it was a farce that only provided a showcase for his extreme views. He dazzled those present with his oratory, and in his closing argument declared that he would ignore the court's verdict because the 'eternal court of history' would acquit him and his co-conspirators.

Hitler and three of his co-defendants were found guilty but sentenced to only five years' imprisonment, the minimum that could be handed out for their convictions. They were never going to serve even five years: each would be eligible for parole in six months' time with a further reduction for time served. Five other defendants were placed on probation after being found guilty of aiding and abetting high treason. Ludendorff was acquitted of all charges. The NSDAP's funds were impounded, its literature seized, and the party newspaper *Völkischer Beobachter* (*People's Observer*) banned.

The presiding judge, the right-leaning Georg Neithardt, told the court that the lenient sentences were justified because the defendants' motives had been 'patriotic', 'noble', and 'unselfish'. The law mandated that all foreigners found guilty of treason must be deported. But Hitler, who at this time was still an Austrian, not German, citizen, would not face that because he 'considers himself to be German' and he had served in the German army during the Great War. The decision brought cheers from spectators. Then Hitler was taken to a second-floor room to await transport to a relatively comfortable jail at Landsberg am Lech, a town about 65 kilometres from Munich. In 1924, it was a facility certainly not intended for dangerous criminals. It was more a sanatorium that housed people while they saw the error of their ways. In 1944, more than 200 of the Nazis' enemies would die there, either through mistreatment or execution.

Hitler walked to a window and waved to the crowd below. They returned his gesture with cries of 'Heil Hitler!' Before being released on 20 December 1924, assisted by Rudolf Hess, he had begun work on his political autobiography, *Mein Kampf* (*My Struggle*), a turgid autobiographical exposition of his political theories, ideas that would later culminate in the Second World War. Prominent throughout this rambling work is the violent antisemitism of Hitler and his acolytes. There was a 'Jewish peril', a Jewish conspiracy to gain world leadership. The international language, Esperanto, was part of that Jewish plot. There were also many arguments in favour of the old German nationalist idea of *Drang nach Osten*: the necessity to gain *Lebensraum* (living space) eastwards, especially in Russia. But always there were the Jews to blame. It is a truly boring book that one critic called 'a queer *mélange* of half-truths and nonsense combined with an almost uncanny insight into the mind of the mob'. *Mein Kampf* certainly achieved the latter. Its recurring theme was, 'I am the only one who is right, so shut up and listen,' and millions did so. In the 1930s, it became a bestseller in Germany.

In Britain, *The Daily News* summed up the views of most people to the remarkably light sentences that Hitler and his henchmen had received:

> Two extracts from leading Nationalist newspapers this evening serve to reveal the astonishing state of mind of a large and influential class in Germany at this moment. The *Deutsche Tageszeitung* says: 'For Germans it is a satisfaction that the man whose services to Germany are

inscribed among the stars should come out unaffected by the ordeal.' Another newspaper expresses the hope that the 'first act of the new Reichstag will be to release Hitler and other heroes from the prison to which the Munich court has reluctantly sent them'. The Munich judgement means, of course, that the judges either felt unable to run counter to the great wave of reaction now sweeping through Germany or went willingly with it.

In April 1924, in a syndicated column that appeared in several British newspapers, the author H. G. Wells commented:

> the acquittal of that foolish old monarchist blunderer, Ludendorff, the ridiculous mitigated sentences of Hitler and the other conspirators against the German Republic, and, above all, the public demonstrations of sympathy with these second-rate nationalist reactionaries, come as a real shock to our hopes of an approaching European reconstruction.

Wells wrote:

> One may recognise the stream of injustices and disappointments that have been inflicted on Germany in the last five years, one may be willing to concede the right of Germans to a considerable resentment, and yet one may find it hard to forgive these sentimental dangerous reversions towards monarchism in uniform, and above all, that petty and provocative folly in Washington.

The German flag in in the US capital had remained flying high when all others had been lowered upon the death of President Woodrow Wilson.

Wells felt that Germany had been 'divided anatomically between the right and the left': 'When the German displays will, he does something stupid and violent, and when he displays intelligence, he does nothing at all.' The impression that Wells now had was of 'an unhelpful and uncreative and irresponsive Germany, cheated it is true, and disappointed, but lapsing far too readily into a sullen unhelpfulness'.

The putsch might have failed but it had elevated Hitler to national prominence. The deaths of sixteen Nazi Party members had created political martyrs, and Hitler now saw that his way to power was not by armed force but by the manipulation of Weimar Germany's political system.

Meanwhile, the matter of tinned salmon continued to engage the British. When Miss Deakin addressed the local Women's Conservative and Constitutional Association at Horsham in West Sussex in July 1924 – 'heavy rain accompanied by gusts of wind obliged all to adjourn to the large garage in the gardens of Compton's Lea' – she told the meeting that 'the big rivers of Canada produce the finest salmon … yet we spend £6 million on foreign tinned salmon and only one and a half million on that produced within the Empire'.

Miss Deakin begged those present that, whenever the next General Election came, they must 'give their votes to those who helped trade and unity within the Empire'. Three months later, after Conservative and Liberal MPs (the always stormy Labour–Liberal pact had soon fallen apart) combined to pass a motion of no confidence in Ramsay MacDonald's government, a General Election – the third in less than two years – was called for 29 October 1924.

Labour lost forty seats, the Liberals lost 118 of their 158, and the Conservatives, now reverting to a policy of free trade, swept back to power with a parliamentary majority of 209. They were helped in no small measure by the so-called 'Zinoviev letter', a document published in the *Daily Mail* only four days before polling day. Purporting to be from Grigori Zinoviev, president of the Comintern, the Soviet-controlled international communist organisation, it called on British communists to mobilise 'sympathetic forces' in the Labour Party to support an Anglo-Soviet treaty and to encourage 'agitation-propaganda' in Britain's armed forces. 'Civil War Plot by Socialists' ran the headline. The article described the alleged letter from Zinoviev ('whose real name is Apfelbaum') as revealing 'a great Bolshevik plot to paralyse the British Army and Navy and to plunge the country into civil war', and the Communist Party as 'masters of Mr Ramsay MacDonald's Government'. *Punch* magazine published a cartoon depicting a caricatured Bolshevik wearing a sandwich board bearing the slogan, 'Vote for MacDonald and me'.

In 1999, an official report concluded that the Zinoviev letter was forged by an MI6 agent's source and leaked by MI5 or MI6 officers to the Conservative Party. Historians had long agreed that the letter was almost certainly a forgery, but, in 1924, it meant that Britain was keeping her eyes on Russia, not on Hitler.

Chapter 3

A New and Stronger Spirit?

> 'When after the first few months of the war, Germany had lost a high percentage of her officer class, she had no means of replacing it. That could never happen in Britain.'
>
> Kennedy Graeme

In March 1925, the *Belfast News Letter* speculated on who would succeed Fredrich Ebert. The first president of the Weimar Republic had died a month earlier, at the age of 54, from septic shock following an emergency appendectomy. Two months before his death, a German court had ruled that Ebert, a moderate socialist and trades unionist, had, in a strictly legal sense at least, committed high treason during the war when he supported a munition workers' strike. Nonetheless, opined the Belfast newspaper, Ebert's contribution 'during six of the most eventful years in that country's chequered history could hardly be over-estimated'.

The Weimar Republic, set up in 1919, was a democratic state that was governed by two houses of parliament, an upper house called the Reichsrat, and the lower house, the Reichstag, which was headed by the Chancellor. No one could ever obtain a working majority in the Reichstag because Germany had more than twenty political parties seeking seats. Elections were held often, but the deadlock was never broken.

Germany's president served for seven years, and in 1925 much hung on who would be Germany's next president. Would they also be a safe pair of hands? Could Germany be no longer regarded as a threat to peace in Europe? The *Belfast News Letter* again: 'When the verdict of the German people has been made public, the Allies should have no difficulty in determining whether or not it is possible to evacuate Cologne and surrender the safeguards provided by the retention of the Rhine bridgeheads.'

More spectacular figures had, from time to time, featured on the Berlin stage, but none could compare to Ebert, 'who had remained quietly in the background, steering a moderate course and retaining real power throughout'. Those figures, said the newspaper, included the chancellors, the Junkers (the landowning aristocracy of Prussia and eastern Germany) generals, the communist plotters – and 'the ludicrous Hitler'.

After an inconclusive first vote, the overwhelming decision, in what was to prove a pivotal moment in the history of the Weimar Republic, was that 78-year-old Paul von Hindenburg, the field marshal who had led the German army during the Great War, would be Germany's next president. Hindenburg had stood before, in the 1920 election that was cancelled by the Reichstag after a failed coup by army officers, members of the Freikorps paramilitary units sympathetic to right-wing causes, and by right-wing nationalists. Save for making the occasional political comment in the German press, he was living in retirement in Hanover when he was eventually persuaded by right-wing parties to stand as a presidential candidate in 1925. In his only public address of the election campaign, Hindenburg said:

> I do not consider the form of government of principal importance but the spirit that pervades that form. I stretch out my hand to every German who thinks nationally, who protects the dignity of the German name at home and abroad, who desires freedom of worship and class understanding, and put to him the request: Help me to work for the resurrection of the Fatherland.

During the final few days of the campaign, the *Belfast Telegraph* reproduced a report from the *Chicago Tribune*:

> That the last vestige of Germany's famed military discipline has gone was proved today when all the officers of the German National Association turned against General Ludendorff, their chief during the four years' world war. They requested him to withdraw his presidential candidacy to 'save the National cause'. Ludendorff was deaf to their plea, and deaf to his war chief, Hindenburg. Ludendorff has now only one man left on his side – Adolf Hitler, who was recently released from prison after serving his sentence for high treason against the German Republic. But Ludendorff is still living in the dream that he is still master of Germany's

fate, and that one day he will be recognised as the saviour of the country. According to Hitler, who is acting as adjutant to General Ludendorff in his campaign, the Nationalists even tried to bribe the general to withdraw his campaign. 'The general will not withdraw from the fight for the presidential post, even if the mountains of gold were moved to tempt him,' declared Hitler.

He may as well have withdrawn. In the first round of voting, Ludendorff, standing for the German Völkisch Freedom Party, which had been founded in 1922 after breaking away from the German National People's Party, polled only 1.06 per cent of the votes cast. None of the candidates attained the required majority and so a second round was held in April. This time, Hindenburg was persuaded to stand, and he secured 904,000 more votes than his nearest opponent, the Centre Party candidate Wilhelm Marx.

The result was met with varied reaction. In Britain, David Lloyd George attributed it to France's policy of 'pin pricks which have caused a spirit of resentment in Germany'. The former prime minster expressed the opinion that Hindenburg was 'a steady old man' who was unlikely to do anything rash. James Gerard, who was the US ambassador in Berlin from 1913 to 1917, felt that while Hindenburg 'will secretly create an able and effective war machinery, the German masses will not revolt, much less permit a new war'. One Herbert Smith, described by the *Yorkshire Post* as a 'bluff, plain-spoken, plain-thinking Yorkshireman', was less sure. President of the Miners' International Committee, Mr Smith opened his speech to the committee's meeting in Brussels by regretting Hindenburg's election, although his local newspaper wondered 'how it came to be Mr Smith's business to pass adverse judgement upon the decision of the German people'. Whatever his objections to the new president, eight years later, Herbert Smith would have been able to say, 'I told you so,' when Hindenburg appointed Adolf Hitler as Germany's Chancellor.

The attempted coup in Munich had taught Hitler a valuable lesson. There would be no more armed uprisings. To gain control of Germany, he would instead use the rights that were guaranteed by the Weimar constitution. For the moment, Hitler set aside guns and cudgels. Freedom of speech, the right to assemble, the freedom of the press would be his weapons now.

In February 1925, Hitler had persuaded the Bavarian government to lift the ban on the NSDAP, and, as its undisputed leader, he began to mould the Nazi Party into an effective, financially sound organisation. A party secretary and a party treasurer were appointed, and, thinking it would add an air of respectability, Hitler allowed women to join. NSDAP membership was divided between a 'Leadership Corps', which was appointed by Hitler, and the general membership. The SA, Hitler's 'stormtroopers', were kept separate, although they had to be NSDAP members, and so were the Schutzstaffel (the SS) that began as Saal-Schutz ('Hall Security'), a small paramilitary unit of volunteers who provided security at party meetings, but which would grow into one of the most powerful and feared organisations in Nazi Germany.

Hitler now began to expand the NSDAP beyond its Bavarian base. He found support in the rural Protestant areas of East Prussia, Schleswig-Holstein, Pomerania and Mecklenburg, and in depressed working-class areas such as Thuringia. Owners of small businesses, who blamed Jewish big business for their economic woes, were particularly receptive to the Nazis' antisemitic message, while crippling hyperinflation drove the lower-middle classes into his arms. Students, too young to have served Germany during the Great War, were attracted to Hitler's call for extreme social change, a call delivered with effective rhetoric. Nazi Party rallies had first been held in Munich in 1923, and then in Weimar in 1926. In Weimar, Joseph Goebbels, a brilliant orator, addressed the rally. Goebbels was developing propaganda techniques that would be vital to the Nazis when the impending economic disaster finally engulfed Germany. In 1927, the rallies moved exclusively to Nuremburg. By 1930, the NSDAP's membership had grown to 130,000. The Great Depression was under way, and the economic collapse that had begun in the United States saw Germany suffering as badly as any country in the world. Perhaps more so. It was American loans that had eventually saved the German economy when the vengeance wreaked upon her at Versailles was making it impossible for her to meet her dues. It had become obvious that the best way to rehabilitate Germany and reintegrate her into the European community was to allow her to support herself. Now, thanks to the Wall Street Crash and all it brought down with it, there were more crashing business failures and mass unemployment in Germany. The conditions for Hitler to finally take total control would soon be in place.

Britain, though, could still not keep a watchful eye on him. While Hitler's mounting presence began to overshadow Hindenburg's presidency, Stanley Baldwin's premiership was beset by a labour dispute that would soon see 1.7 million workers on strike. Just as in 1921, the nation's coalmines were at the centre of the problem. The huge demand caused by the Great War had depleted Britain's coal stocks, and, when the mines were returned to their private owners, they fell behind other countries, such as Poland and, ironically, Germany, in modernisation. As Germany began supplying 'free' coal to other Allied nations as part of the reparation plans, so falling coal prices had a negative effect on Britain. And Chancellor of the Exchequer Winston Churchill's 1925 Gold Standard Act had made the British pound too strong against foreign currencies, thus adversely affecting the export market. Mine owners, reluctant to see their profit margins shrink, instead decided to cut wages and increase working hours. At the coalface, mining was as difficult and dangerous as it had ever been. Miners were being injured and some suffered fatal accidents, all with little or no support from the industry. 'Not one penny off the pay, not one minute on the day,' became the miners' clarion call.

Anxious to resolve the issue that was threatening the economy still further, Baldwin sought to provide a subsidy that would maintain the miners' wages at their current level. In March 1926, a Royal Commission recommended a reorganisation of the mining industry that would make improvements 'where necessary'. It also recommended ending the government subsidy and the reduction of miners' wages by 13.5 per cent. Unsurprisingly, the Miners' Federation refused to accept these new terms of employment, and the Trades Union Congress (TUC) supported the calling of a General Strike for the beginning of May 1926. The intervention of King George V failed to stem the miners' anger, and an Emergency Powers Act was passed that used the armed forces and volunteers to maintain basic essential services. According to *The Daily News*, the cost of these emergency services was between £1 million (£68 million today) and £1.5 million (£102 million) a day. The general secretary of the Transport and General Workers Union, Ernest Bevin, had little enthusiasm for the strike, and thought that, behind the scenes, the government was 'mobilising forces for war'.

By 4 May 1926, 1.5 million workers – the TUC initially restricted the call-out to miners, iron and steel workers, transport workers, and printers – had withdrawn their labour. More would soon follow. The General Strike lasted nine days before the miners were left to fight on alone once more. They saw Walter Citrine, the TUC general secretary, as their betrayer. Citrine had been desperate to end the dispute because strike pay was draining union funds.

Arthur J. Cook, the general secretary of the Miners' Federation of Great Britain, and a founder member of the Communist Party of Great Britain, appealed for support in the struggle against the Mine Owners' Association:

> We still continue, believing that the whole rank and file will help us all they can. We appeal for financial help wherever possible, and that comrades will still refuse to handle coal so that we may yet secure victory for the miners' wives and children who will live to thank the rank and file of the unions of Great Britain.

Railwaymen all over the country, including in Sheffield, Grimsby, Bradford, Derby, Ilford, Merthyr Tydfil, Cardiff, Southampton, Hereford, Edinburgh, Liverpool, Salford, Peterborough, Carlisle, and Doncaster, refused to return to work, although that was less to do with supporting the miners and more to do with the fact that it was railwaymen now who faced the most ferocious anti-union backlash after the General Strike ended. On 14 May, *The Daily News* reported: 'Railway Strike Continues. Chaos All Over the Country. Men Will Not Work Under Conditions. TUC Deplores Breach of Premier's Goodwill Spirit.'

The newspaper said:

> There was a good deal of propaganda on both sides last week. One piece of it told men on the railway that an attack on their wages was to come. 'So far as I know,' added Mr Baldwin, 'there is not a word of truth in that.' Then the Premier went on, 'I will countenance no attempt on the part of any employer to use the present occasion for trying to get a reduction of wages in force before the strike, or an increase in hours.'

Workers in London's Victoria, Albert, and King George V docks and at Manchester docks also refused to return. In Newcastle, however, the position was almost normal on the railways; the only factor preventing steelworkers from returning was that furnaces had been damped down. Shipbuilding firms were working as normal as men there had refused to strike.

Eventually, though, hardship forced a return to work everywhere, and even the miners began to drift back to their pits. By the end of November, most had reported for work again. In 1927, the government passed the Trade Dispute and Trade Union Act that made all sympathetic strikes and mass picketing illegal, forbade Civil Service unions to affiliate to the TUC, and ensured that members of a trade union had to voluntarily 'contract in' to pay the political levy to the Labour Party.

Writing in the *Sunday Pictorial* in May 1926, columnist Kennedy Graeme laid into 'the wild men of the Labour movement':

> They thought they had reckoned with everything, but they had not reckoned with the indomitable spirit of the great middle classes ... When I speak of the middle classes, I speak of something that exists in no other nation. Our middle class is not really a class at all ... they are more alike in their temperament and outlook than in material property ... We had, and still have, an inexhaustible supply of men of good breeding and intellectual capacity who can quickly adapt themselves to whatever work a crisis demands ... Now that the General Strike is over, the time has come when a new and stronger spirit of co-operation is called for from every class. By that alone can England be saved.

The German industrialist Arnold Reichberg suggested that the General Strike had been planned by Moscow several months earlier, but British newspapers were now already concerned with other matters. Not all of them were of great import, such as the news that Erich von Ludendorff was being divorced. Reuters reported:

> Frau Ludendorff claimed that her husband was so concerned in politics that he had neglected his domestic duties. Since the Armistice, Ludendorff, once described as the 'brains of Hindenburg' and the 'organiser of victory', had played a farcical part in German politics. Identified with the extreme Monarchist faction, he took a prominent part in Hitler's opera-bouffe 'beer garden putsch.'

A New and Stronger Spirit?

The Munich court granted Frau Ludendorff her divorce, although declaring that both she and General Ludendorff were to blame.

Few people in Britain, however, cared what was happening in Germany, and in May 1926, as Stanley Baldwin had grappled with the General Strike, Adolf Hitler, now the Führer, the supreme leader, of the Nazi Party, had been spending his days in Bavaria, in a small cabin in Obersalzburg, gazing over the mountains above the market town of Berchtesgaden.

The years between 1926 and 1929 were his 'quiet years', which he later described as 'one of the happiest times of my life'. Then again, he is reported to have also thus described wandering around the Austrian city of Linz in his late teens, and his time in the German army during the Great War. In Linz, he had dreamed of becoming a famous artist. In Obersalzburg, he dreamt of the glory for himself and his German Reich that lay ahead.

Chapter 4

Political Upheavals

> 'Hitler is not just a hard-shell reactionary ... he has the keenest of political noses to scent out success, the bravest of workaday hands to construct it, and an ear tuned to receive the chaotic atmospherics of public opinion and translate them into harmonies.'
> Commander Oliver Locker-Lampson, DSO

In 1929, Stanley Baldwin's Conservative government came to the end of its five-year term, struggling to stem the flow of unemployment. The Roaring Twenties? The latter half of the decade may have been booming for some fortunate souls, but for millions more, it signalled the beginning of a poverty brought about by the most severe economic downturn in history.

Speaking during the General Election campaign, the Labour leader, Ramsay MacDonald, summed up: 'Consider what it is that worries the lives of our people. First and foremost, that is the dread of an ever-overhanging poverty ... The way by which most of our dreaded poverty comes is unemployment.' A few days later, MacDonald was the UK's new Prime Minister, again the leader of a minority government, this time after the 'Flapper election' – the first in which women aged between 21 and 29 joined those aged 30 or over in the right to vote – produced a hung parliament.

Labour had enjoyed its best-ever result. For the first time, it became the largest grouping in the House of Commons. But it was not enough to govern effectively. Twenty-one seats short of an overall majority, to pass legislation Labour, as it had in 1924, was forced to depend on the Liberals, something that the more radical members of the Labour movement could not abide.

Two years later, the minority government collapsed under the weight of fighting what would become known as the 'Great Depression'. Following the US stock market crash of 1929, almost every nation in the world had been affected, the UK and Germany included. Many of them attempted to protect their domestic markets by taxing imports. World trade slumped, prices fell, credit dried up. In Britain, taxes were raised, and public spending was cut, 'cures' that led only to the economy being further depressed and unemployment rising still further. Northern England and Wales suffered most, but even in London, where cheap interest rates encouraged a building boom, the poor seemed to be everywhere.

By the late summer of 1931, MacDonald found several influential members of his Cabinet unwilling to support his budget proposals. Chancellor of the Exchequer Philip Snowden was against imposing tariffs or introducing deficit spending – simply put, where spending exceeds revenue – while Foreign Secretary Arthur Henderson, who was immersed in trying to reduce rising tensions in Europe, was also firmly opposed to budget cuts. The value of the pound sterling and its place on the gold standard was under threat. To remain in the gold standard would have required a loan from the USA, but New York's bankers first insisted on an austerity programme that would have included a cut in unemployment benefit. The Cabinet voted twelve to nine for a 10 per cent cut but soon realised that the parliamentary Labour Party would savage them for it.

On 24 August 1931, MacDonald resigned as Prime Minister. King George V asked him to form another government, this time an interim 'National' administration with ministers from the Labour, Liberal, and Conservative parties. It was intended that, after a few weeks, this would be dissolved and that traditional party politics would resume, but the Labour Party expelled all those of its MPs who supported the idea.

MacDonald called a General Election for Tuesday, 27 October 1931, seeking a 'doctor's mandate' to fix the economy. What had been planned as a temporary emergency administration remained together, and the National Government won by a landslide, taking 554 seats out of 615. It was a bizarre turn of events. The Labour Party lost four out of every five seats it had won in 1929, including that of its leader, Arthur Henderson. David Lloyd George opposed the calling of the election and urged his colleagues to withdraw from the National Government. In fact, the Liberals returned more MPs than the combined total of mainstream Labour and National Labour, but they were now split three ways, and although it was the Conservatives who won most seats (470), Ramsay MacDonald, who had stood for National Labour, which won only thirteen seats, continued as the UK's prime minster.

On election day, the Labour-supporting *Daily Herald* inevitably had gone full throttle after MacDonald:

> Today is the day. Today the electors of Britain have their opportunity to turn out this Government of wage-cutters and food-taxers ... We have not only to give poor old Mac a 'doctor's mandate,' but we daren't even risk getting his prescription made up when he has written it ... Since poor old Mac takes his orders from the bankers, you know what to expect...

In an election night message to the nation from 10 Downing Street, MacDonald said:

> The majority, as unique as it is gratifying, must convince the whole world that when this country calls for assistance, willing hands and devoted minds will always respond heartily. The very emphasis of the response is embarrassing, but I appeal for forbearance as well as confidence. To my political friends who have suffered such unusual reverses, and especially to those of them who, with splendid faith and courage, backed our appeal and helped to swell our victory, I give the assurance that our triumph will in no way mean that either the interests or the point of view of the working classes will be overlooked in our performance of the task which is before us.

MacDonald's first Cabinet of the new National Government consisted of eleven Tories (there was no place for Winston Churchill, who was now in his 'wilderness years'), five Liberals, and four former members of the Labour Party. MacDonald's already tarnished reputation, so far as trade unions and the Labour Party (of which he had been one of the three principal founders, but which had now expelled him) were concerned, worsened still further when he gave the former Conservative Prime Minister Stanley Baldwin, now Lord President of the Council, the responsibility for most of the UK's domestic policies. The left now reviled the man who, in 1924, had become the first Labour Prime Minister in the UK's history. To them, he was now a traitor to the Labour movement.

The National Government's approach to dealing with the Great Depression was largely to wait it out, with little direct intervention. There were certain things that the citizenry could do to help themselves, without the government interfering. In November 1931, British housewives were being reminded that 'bread is the cheapest food'. Ramsay MacDonald's words topped one advertisement for home-milled flour: 'I hope that everyone will be vigilant in making demands for British labour and its products, so that we do not have to import one shilling's worth of goods more than is necessary.'

The American historian John A. Garraty wrote that in neither the UK nor in Germany was there 'any consistently held theory about either the causes of the Depression or how to end it'. There was, however, one man who was beginning to convince many Germans that he could fix everything. In September 1930, Germany held a parliamentary election in which the Nazi Party won 18 per cent of the vote. The *Daily Mirror* reported, 'The German Fascists, who favour a dictatorship, have had an astonishing success, winning 197 seats as against 12 in the old Reichstag.'

At a time when, over the winter of 1929–1930, unemployment in their country had risen from 1.4 million to over 2 million, Adolf Hitler's promises appealed to many Germans: he would fix the economy and get people back to work; regain the territory lost at the end of the Great War; return Germany to its rightful status as a great European power; and create a strong government that would right the ills caused by the Jews and communists.

Many Germans were beginning to lose faith in democracy, and extreme parties were gaining support. In March 1930, Chancellor Hermann Müller, of the Social Democratic Party, had resigned after his government failed to agree on how to reduce high government spending that had been caused by the rise in unemployment. Müller's successor, Heinrich Brüning, the leader of the German Centre Party, fared no better. As unemployment continued to rise, the new Chancellor feared social disorder caused by the despair felt by millions of Germans over the economic depression. But his plan – to cut government spending, including unemployment pay – would serve only to make the unemployed even poorer. The Reichstag did not support Brüning's ideas, and so President Paul von Hindenburg used Article 48 of the Weimar constitution to give himself powers to pass laws by decree. At a stroke, this weakened the Reichstag – and strengthened the hand of

Adolf Hitler, whose growing influence was now interesting the British press.

In July 1930, under the headline 'Secret Arsenal, Dead Policeman and a Plot', the *News Chronicle* carried a report from Berlin:

> Police today raided a secret arsenal, alleged to belong to the National Socialists. Machine-guns and munitions were seized, and twelve persons were arrested. Behind the raid is a remarkable story (told by Reuter) of how a motor accident led to the discovery of munitions. It was a collision between a motorcar and a motorcycle ridden by an officer of the Potsdam Criminal Police, who was killed together with a young woman who was riding pillion behind him, which led to the revelations. It transpired that the officer, whose name was Doerre, was an active member of the National Socialist Party and had been engaged as military instructor for members of that Party. Letters found upon his body disclosed the fact that a large number of weapons, including a machine gun, were in the possession of National Socialists. The revelations show how followers of Adolf Hitler of Putsch fame, have crept into every branch of official service, even the police.

Writing in the *Daily Mirror* in September 1930, the splendidly named Commander Oliver Stillingfleet Locker-Lampson, a former Royal Naval officer who had become entangled in Russian politics during the Bolshevik Revolution and who was now the Conservative MP for Birmingham Handsworth, told how he had met Hitler around the time of the attempted Munich putsch. The introduction came through a group of British officers who had been prisoners of war in a German hospital during the Great War. They said that they had been approached by Hitler, a fellow patient. The future Führer asked them to explain the game of cricket. He returned a few days later to say that he had a team in training and would like to arrange a friendly match. Hitler also apparently told them that he had been cogitating over the laws of the game and had rewritten them, including banning pads, considering these 'artificial boosters as un-German'. He also thought that a bigger and harder ball should be employed, and that the game could then be used to 'train troops in times of peace'.

Of his own meeting with Hitler, Locker-Lampson said that

> long before today's fame, he had been an arresting personality ... toothbrush moustache in the latest military style, a soft collar always united with a pin shaped like a swastika, and eyes hidden behind loaded lids – suggestive of hidden fire and fury.
>
> Even when he spoke in his deep guttural voice, we were not necessarily thrilled. But after a few hours in his company any honest observer must admit that folk became electrified. The temperature of the room rises in his presence. He enhances the value of life. He makes the humblest follower feel twice the man. And he does it with no bluster or mock heroics. He achieves it by a sincerity which is sun-clear, and which almost reaches fanaticism. By a patience, too, that is Germanic in its plodding persistence. This man will never stop working, will never give in ... the Munich fiasco with which he is associated would never have failed but for Ludendorff's bungling.

Hitler, wrote Locker-Lampson, meant to 'ride off on the patriotic ticket, and play for a tear-up of the treaties and a rip-up of reparations ... I doubt his ability to wait – or his country's wish that he should'.

Hitler, though, was still not a German citizen – he was effectively stateless since renouncing his Austrian citizenship in 1925 – and to enable him to stand in the 1932 presidential election, he was appointed by a fellow member of the Nazi Party to the post of Regierungsrat (government councillor) in the office of State Culture and Measurement in Braunschweig (Brunswick) in Lower Saxony and as a state representative in Berlin. This effectively gave him German citizenship. In the event, Paul von Hindenburg was elected with 18.65 million votes. Hitler came runner-up with 11.33 million.

Britain was now beginning to keep an eye on Adolf Hitler.

Chapter 5

Statesman or Showman?

'Herr Hitler, former house painter, wartime lance-corporal, now leader of the German National Socialists, or Nazis, and hailed as the German Mussolini, achieved his ambition yesterday.'

Western Daily Press

In April 1931, the London-based weekly illustrated magazine *The Sketch*'s regular 'We Take Our Hat Off To...' page featured a variety of characters. There was Miss Catherine Doret, a Los Angeles dentist's assistant who spent her spare time making miniature skeletons from gold, silver, hard rubber, and dental plaster; Lister Hartley, a golfer who, during the Sidgwick Cup tournament at the Royal St George Championship course at Sandwich, drove onto the green at the tenth hole, 'a startling shot' of 380 yards, slightly uphill; Ellen Wilkinson, the Labour MP for Middlesbrough East, who suggested that sunray apparatus be provided in the House of Commons 'because it had such a marvellous effect on the inhabitants of the monkey house at the zoo'; and Miss Marion Duckham, who was helping to build her own house in Surrey and who admitted that after laying 4,000 bricks in a day, she was 'a little tired'.

There was also Heinrich Aloysius Maria Elisabeth Brüning, 'the most economical and ascetic Chancellor that Germany has ever known'. According to *The Sketch*, 'He occupies only two rooms in the Chancellor's residence and had turned the rest over to the public as a Bismarck museum, and he finds his salary so large that he is able to return an unused balance to the treasury!'

Two months later, Reuters reported:

> Nazi hooliganism greeted the German Chancellor [Brüning] and Dr Curtius [Julius Curtius, the Weimar Republic's Foreign Affairs Minister] when, in their special train, they

traversed the harbour district here [Bremerhaven] today. Demonstrators with unfolded Nazi banners had taken up a position by the railway and they shouted abuse at the ministers as their train went by ... Four arrests were made, including the editor of a Nazi journal ... The police had already seized a boat occupied by Nazis who had a megaphone with them for the purpose of regaling the disembarking ministers with Nazi propaganda. Overnight, the Nazis had covered the walls of the pier and the sides of the steamer *Columbus* with inscriptions as follows: 'Down with the Hunger Dictator' and 'Wake up, Germany.'

After Brüning had succeeded Hermann Müller as Chancellor in March 1930, the British Conservative MP Robert Boothby described him as

Snowden's [Philip Snowden, the Chancellor of the Exchequer] German counterpart – a puritanical ascetic and a bit of a masochist, with considerable charm ... He was a willing listener to the deplorable advice tendered to him by Dr Sprague, the emissary of the Bank of England [Oliver Sprague was the first American to be appointed as an advisor to the Bank of England]. This, of course, was to continue his policy of deflation at all costs; and was designed primarily to maintain the value of the fantastic investments made by the City to Germany ... Brüning was a lonely, saintly man, upon whom the burden of responsibility bore heavily.

It seemed so. In December 1931, the *Larne Times and Weekly Telegraph* reported, 'According to those who know him best, Dr Heinrich Brüning, the German Chancellor, feels his responsibility so keenly that his hair has gone from dark to white within the space of a single year.'

As unemployment soared in Germany, Brüning's plans to halt it – the increased taxation, tariffs on imports, and the lowering of unemployment benefit that were all so familiar to British voters – failed, and he came under attack from the extreme left and from the extreme right. Communists and National Socialists had one thing in common: they all hated Heinrich Aloysius Maria Elisabeth Brüning.

In January 1932, diplomat and diarist Harold Nicolson felt that Hitler had 'missed the boat'. There had been a moment, wrote

Nicolson, that Hitler had stood at the crest of national emotion, and he could then have made either a coup, or forced a coalition with Brüning, but now, 'I have the impression that the whole of the Nazi movement has been a catastrophe for this country. It has mobilised the discontented into an expectant group. Hitlerism can never satisfy these expectations...'

In May 1932, writing in the *News Chronicle*, Henry Wilson Harris, who was active in the League of Nations that had been formed in 1918 to promote permanent international peace, said, 'Dr Brüning is the only man who can save Germany from anarchy, bankruptcy and external embroilments.' But Harris also had to concede, 'He has the narrowest of parliamentary majorities ... the president is having poisoned and insidious attacks on his chancellor every day.'

The *News Chronicle*'s editorial writer agreed:

> There could hardly be a greater blow to confidence in Europe today than the disappearance at this moment from the head of affairs in Germany of the only German statesman since the war who has won and held the complete trust (not excepting France) both in the honesty of his policy and in his ability to carry it out.

But disappear he did, from German politics at least. Germany's unemployment figure reached 6 million, and although the Chancellor had vigorously campaigned for the president to be re-elected, Brüning gradually lost Hindenburg's support. On 30 May 1932, exactly two years after he was appointed Chancellor, the man with a PhD on the implications of nationalising Britain's railways announced the resignation of his cabinet, and was relieved of his office. In 1934, aware that he was in danger of being sent by the Nazis to a concentration camp, he emigrated to the USA, and from 1937 to 1951 was professor of political science at Harvard University.

Brüning's successor was the Centre Party's Franz von Papen, a right-winger, wealthy landowner, and former army officer with a somewhat notorious reputation. In 1915, he had been forced to leave the USA, where he was serving as a military attaché, after being accused of attempting to sabotage American armament production intended for the Allies. He was also accused of trying to provoke a war between the USA and Mexico. There followed undercover work, allegedly planning rebellions in Ireland and in India, and sabotage in the USA before he was elected to the Reichstag in 1921.

Von Papen's political following was relatively small and his appointment something of a shock, and not just in Germany. The *Yorkshire Post* commented:

> Hindenburg has shown clearly that the time has not yet come for a return to constructional government in Germany. The name of von Papen ... will certainly recall not very friendly memories on both sides of the Atlantic ... More important is the fact that soldiers have triumphed over the civilians in Germany. The new Cabinet, judged by the names cabled from Berlin tonight, represents a victory for what has been called the Generals' camarilla.

The *Sheffield Daily Telegraph* ran the story under the headline 'Hitler Snubbed', repeating Reuters's view that the main interest was that Hindenburg had not turned to Adolf Hitler for his next Chancellor. In fact, Hindenburg, now 84 years old, was looking to form a coalition Cabinet from the right wing of German politics, and with the Nazis in their present mood, securing their cooperation seemed highly doubtful.

Von Papen's tenure lasted for only seven months before he was replaced by a former German army officer, General Kurt von Schleicher, who had been instrumental in toppling Hermann Müller's government in 1930. Schleicher also organised von Papen's downfall, succeeding him in December 1932. His was also a short reign, all of fifty-seven days. In a bid to form a coalition of the centre parties, Schleicher tried to moderate the excesses of the Nazi party. German politics was a veritable web of intrigue, fear, and rumour. Government by parliamentary consent had ended, and Hitler now joined forces with von Papen to oust Schleicher. The German federal election of 31 July 1932 had already provided Hitler with a remarkable triumph when the Nazi Party took 37.27 per cent of the vote to become the largest party in German history. The Social Democrats polled 21.58 per cent, the Centre Party 12.44 per cent. The communists achieved 14.32. There could be no coalitions without including either the Nazis or the communists. Four months later, another election was held. The Nazis saw their share of the votes drop to 33.09 per cent, but, despite losing thirty-four seats, they were still the largest party in the Reichstag.

On 30 January 1933, Hindenburg removed Schleicher as Chancellor and was persuaded by von Papen to ask Adolf Hitler to assume the post. True, Hitler was loud and unsophisticated. But millions of Germans were now beginning to believe in him. Von Papen was sure that Hitler could be restrained. And the alternative was that Germany might fall into civil war. Hindenburg was reluctant but could see no other way. So, Hitler led the Reichstag, and his fellow Nazi, Wilhelm Frick, was appointed Reichminister of the Interior, and another Nazi, Hermann Göring, a fighter pilot ace during the Great War, and since the July 1932 federal election the president of the Reichstag, was given Minister Without Portfolio. Göring immediately set about forming the Gestapo, the secret state police. The rest of the Cabinet positions went mostly to the conservative German National People's Party. With von Papen as Vice Chancellor, the plan was that, between them, they could control the Nazis. It was a forlorn hope. Hitler was about to do away with politics and, anyway, parliamentary democracy in Germany was already dead.

In Britain, everyone was now keeping their eyes on Adolf Hitler. The *News Chronicle* asked, 'Will Adolf Hitler, the statesman, be as successful as Adolf Hitler the agitator?' The mood among organised German labour was 'morose', the newspaper said, although trades unionists had declined to respond to the communists' call for a General Strike, and copies of the *Red Flag*, Berlin's communist newspaper, and handbills circulated by the Communist Party were being confiscated by police.

In the *Daily Herald*, the journalist and author Gordon Beckles recalled seeing Hitler land at Berlin's Tempelhof airport some eight months earlier. He thought of a line in a book he had been reading, Tennyson's 'By blood a king, in heart a clown'. Beckles passed the book to a fellow traveller, remarking, 'There's a lot more, but it might be about your flying friend, Adolf.' The young man seated next to Beckles had just returned from an air tour with 'the little Austrian ex-corporal'.

'Adolf Hitler!' wrote Beckles. 'A stubby little Austrian with a flabby handshake, shifty brown eyes, and a Charlie Chaplain moustache. What sort of man is this to head a great nation?' Beckles pondered on Hitler's delivery:

> He has discovered that some trick in his voice, some vibrant nuance, gave him an almost hypnotic power over his listeners. It was a discovery comparable to that of a

man who finds that he can make a thimble disappear, or by looking at someone with a glazed stare assert his will. It was a trick. And Adolf Hitler's whole career had been one vast and surprising (most of all to himself) illusion.

Another early discovery that Hitler had made, said Beckles, was that any reference to the Jewish influence on German affairs – 'The Jew is a parasite; The Jew has no artistic impulse' – was greeted with enthusiastic applause. 'But,' wrote Beckles, 'I honestly believe that he cannot have had any deep-seated grudge against the Jews. It was simply that he had discovered a powerful new weapon. Like a baby who finds that constant yelling on a high-pitched note will bring him immediate response from the maternal powers.'

A *Birmingham Gazette* leader opined that Hitler did indeed hate the Jews, and went into detail as to how Hitler – 'a Mussolini without Mussolini's genius', who had a 'bitter hatred of the Versailles Treaty and the Jews' – would 'sentence Jewish people to a cruel network of medieval purging'. The newspaper explained that all Jews would have to be specially registered; Jewish doctors would only be allowed to treat Jewish patients; taxes on Jews would be twice the amount paid by Christians; the Jewish Sabbath would have to be celebrated on the Christian Sunday; and there would be 'no less than five years' imprisonment for any Jew conveying information of any intended raising or depressing of security prices by secret sign or by word of mouth, and this would be the prelude to the confiscation of all their possessions'. 'Hitler,' said the *Birmingham Gazette*, 'first learned his bloodthirsty hatred of the Jews in Vienna where he is supposed to have found them ringleaders of both Socialism and Capitalism.'

Although the Birmingham newspaper regarded Hitler as a poor man's Mussolini, the *Daily Mirror* felt he could be compared to only one man, and that was the Italian dictator: 'Their careers have had many points in common, for both have forced their way to power from lowly beginnings and have built up armies to follow them.' Reuters reported that 'the man who in 1923 had, at the most, a couple of thousand followers, in 1932 had 13 million'.

The *Leicester Evening Mail* thought that 'Great Britain, with reasonable prospects for a speedy return to normal conditions of trade and industry, can observe with some air of detachment, the political events of recent days in other parts of the world', although it allowed that 'the attainment of Adolf Hitler to the Chancellorship of Germany is as startling an adventure as any related in the volumes of history'.

The *Halifax Courier* carried a comment from its Berlin correspondent: 'The future will show whether Hitler is, as his enthusiastic followers declare, "The greatest statesman since Bismarck," or whether, as his enemies say, "Merely a showman and a beater of the big drum."'

One thing was clear: Europe was now dealing with a different kind of Germany to the one that it had tried to rehabilitate in the 1920s.

Chapter 6

The Good Old English Fist

'We are going to defend the right of free speech in this country and will not tamely submit to methods of violence and intimidation. Those who begin things must be careful where they end.'

Sir Oswald Mosley

When the journalist and future Labour – and then Conservative – MP Ivor Bulmer-Thomas described the 1931 UK General Election as 'the most astonishing in the history of the British party system', he was referring to the result. But it was also remarkable for the number of disparate figures who fought the campaign, among them hopefuls from parties such as the Liverpool Protestant, Scottish Prohibition, Agricultural, and Commonwealth Land.

There was another new party dipping its toe into the sea of British politics. It was called, quite simply, the New Party. It contested twenty-four seats and won none of them. Among its disappointed candidates was the New Party's founder, a man who had already also served in the House of Commons for both the Conservative and Labour Parties. Oswald Mosley was the eldest of three sons of the fifth baronet of a complicated line of descent that had seen the baronetcy twice recreated by other branches of the family after being extinguished through lack of heirs. Mosley was indeed well connected: his father was a third cousin of the father of the woman who would become Queen Elizabeth, the wife of King George VI; his first father-in-law was the Foreign Secretary and a former Viceroy of India.

Mosley entered Parliament after a varied wartime career. Despite being expelled from the Royal Military College at Sandhurst in 1914, for 'a riotous act of retaliation' against a fellow student during a row over some 'misplaced' polo ponies, when war was declared he was commissioned into the 16th The Queen's Lancers. Transferring to the Royal Flying Corps as an observer, he was one of the first British airmen to fly over enemy lines. He was training as a pilot when, in 1915, he crashed at Shoreham while demonstrating his flying skills – or perhaps the lack of them – to his mother and sister.

Despite suffering a severe leg injury in the crash, before it had healed Mosley was recalled to his regiment and remained in the line at the Battle of Loos before collapsing with pain from the injury. He almost lost the leg – it ended up three inches (7.62 centimetres) shorter than the other, leaving him with a permanent limp – and in April 1916, he was invalided out of the army, and spent the rest of the war behind a desk, working as a temporary civil servant at the Ministry of Munitions and at the Foreign Office.

Mosley was still only 22 years of age when, in the General Election of 1918, he entered the House of Commons for the first time. A man of his background would naturally choose the Conservative Party, and it was happy to select him for the safe seat of Harrow. He took his place as the youngest MP in Parliament (Joseph Sweeney, an abolitionist Sinn Féin member, was seven months younger but did not take his seat).

Mosley, though, was not a 'natural' Conservative. His experience on the Western Front had left him with a conviction that he had to use his wealth and social privilege to build a better world for the youth that had fought the war. In November 1918, in a speech accepting the freedom of the borough of Wolverhampton, Prime Minister David Lloyd George implored voters in the imminent General Election to help him to 'cleanse this noble land' of 'poverty, wretchedness and squalor'. Lloyd George promised to light the road 'along which England shall march to a nobler and grander future'.

The young Oswald Mosley was inspired. In his election campaign, he advanced bold ideas: higher wages and shorter hours for industrial workers; the nationalisation of electricity and transport; slum clearance; better health provision; better education and child welfare programmes. It was hardly a Conservative programme, but then Mosley was standing for a coalition government of Conservatives and those Liberals who supported coalition. In fact, Lieutenant Mosley was described in local newspapers as 'the Coalition candidate', and Mosley rarely spoke of himself as a Conservative.

He certainly had it in for the Germans. Speaking at an election meeting in Wembley a few days before polling day, Mosley drew thunderous applause when he said that the first thing to do was to bring the Kaiser to justice, and not only the Kaiser but all the German leaders and socialists who had supported him throughout the war. If a man murdered another, he was hanged for it. 'Why should the man who has murdered millions of men, who has committed the greatest crimes the world has ever known, escape without punishment?' Mosley asked his audience. He said that 'Germany must also pay the fullest indemnity, and it would not take many years to pay. They must make full payment for all damages. All enemy aliens must be deported from this country and must not be allowed to enter again. They abused our hospitality and therefore must not be offered it again.'

It was what a war-weary electorate wanted to hear. Mosley comprehensively defeated the only other candidate, Arthur Chamberlayne, a local man who had defected from the Conservatives and stood as an Independent Coalitionist, by 13,959 votes to 3,007. It was a bitter, often silly, campaign, with Chamberlayne calling Mosley 'a bit of a boy', and a dog decorated with Mosley's colours wandering into Chamberlayne's committee room in Wealdstone and being 'incontinently ejected'.

Once installed as an MP, Mosley attempted to form a 'New Members' Association' that would counter the influence of MPs who had done rather well out of the Great War. When Baldwin semi-anonymously donated to the nation one-fifth of the profits that his family's iron and steel works had made during the war, Mosley urged that all 'war profiteers' should be taxed retrospectively back to 1914.

Mosley also clashed with Winston Churchill, notably on injustices served on men who had fought the war but who now struggled to find work, and also on Mosley's belief that the aviation industry must be developed. In his maiden speech to the Commons, in February 1919, during the second reading of the Aerial Navigation Bill, he told the House that while aerial progress in the next decade should be as great as in the last, 'if one, however, may judge our expectations from officialdom ... then British manufacturers will embark upon this great new stage of their business with a millstone around their necks'. Mosley continued:

> No great exercise of the imaginative faculty should be required to foresee the day when the aviation tank and the aeroplane will have driven the infantry and other similar units from the battlefield, whilst the furious speed and mobility of the aerially-armed plane, with a weight-lifting capacity which will enable it to carry heavy armaments, will have banished the battleship and the merchant ship from the ocean.

Disarmament was another issue that engaged Mosley. In February 1920, he was asking,

> What actual steps were taken by the Prime Minister and the Peace Conference to give effect to the pledge to abolish conscript armies not only in this country but on the Continent? ... Repulsive as the suggestion is ... the moment has come to exercise our financial powers to bring the less enlightened members of the European continent to a state of peace.

In August 1920, Mosley married Lady Cynthia Curzon, the beautiful daughter of the Foreign Secretary. Two months later, he horrified his new father-in-law by crossing the floor to sit on the back row of the Labour benches as an Independent. Mosley had become out of tune with the coalition, but it was the Conservatives' Irish policy that finally drove him away. As secretary of the Peace with Ireland Council, which he had formed with a group of left-wing political figures, he wanted to send a commission to Ireland to investigate atrocities committed by the Black and Tans, a force of temporary constables, mostly jobless ex-servicemen, recruited into the Royal Irish Constabulary. They soon acquired a reputation for carrying out extrajudicial killings, looting, and arson. Mosley regarded them as 'worse than the Germans in Belgium'.

Harrow Conservative Association pressed Mosley to support the government in the Commons. He wrote back:

> I cannot enter Parliament unless I am free to take any action of opposition or association, irrespective of labels, that is compatible with my principles and is conductive to their success. My first consideration must always be the triumph of the causes for which I stand and in the present condition of politics, or in any situation likely to arise in the near future, such freedom of action is necessary to that end.

In the 1922 General Election, Mosley again stood in Harrow, this time as an Independent. The Labour and Liberal Parties did not contest the seat, and Mosley beat the Conservative candidate, Major Charles Ward-Jackson, by 15,290 votes to 7,868. After the campaign, Mosley sued Ward-Jackson for slander after the latter referred to something

Mosley was alleged to have said two years earlier when speaking to the Cambridge Union. Ward-Jackson alleged that Mosley had incited Indian students to rebel against the existence of the British Raj. Mosley won a retraction as well as his legal costs of £200.

Mosley, the Independent, now intensely disliked by the Conservatives, was aligned more with the Liberals, and steadily drifting towards Labour, while openly talking about 'the old parties'. The Liberal *Westminster Gazette* regarded Mosley as 'the most polished speaker in the Commons', while Beatrice Webb, a senior Labour Party figure, wrote in her diary for 8 June 1923, 'We have made the acquaintance of the most brilliant man in the House of Commons – Oswald Mosley ... this young person would make his way in the world without his adventitious advantages, which are many – birth, wealth and a beautiful aristocratic wife.'

In his opening speech of the 1923 General Election campaign, at St Mark's School in Hanwell, Mosley (who arrived, with Cynthia, halfway through the meeting) called Baldwin's protectionist plans 'the last gambler's throw of a bankrupt and discredited party'. Mosley again retained the seat, this time polling 14,079 votes against the Conservative Hugh Morris's 9,433. It was to be the last time that he asked the people of Harrow for their votes. On 27 March 1924, Mosley applied to join the Labour Party, which pleased Ramsay MacDonald, who thought that Mosley's aristocratic background would help Labour appear more respectable. But it angered the Liberals' Margot Asquith, who wrote to Mosley to tell him that she thought he had done 'an unwise thing at a foolish time'.

Mosley first joined the Independent Labour Party and applied for the Labour Party whip. In April 1924, a German journalist, Egon Ranshofen-Wertheimer, the London correspondent of the Social Democratic newspaper *Vorwärts*, who was born in Braunau am Inn, the birthplace of Adolf Hitler, saw Mosley speaking at the New Cross Empire, at a Labour Party meeting arranged to introduce the new recruit:

> Suddenly there was a movement in the crowd, and a young man, with the face of the ruling class in Great Britain, but the gait of a Douglas Fairbanks, thrust himself forward through the throng to the platform, followed by a lady in heavy, costly furs. There stood Oswald Mosley ... a new recruit to the Socialist movement at his first London meeting. He was introduced to the audience, and even at that time,

> I remember, the song 'For he's a jolly good fellow' greeted the young man from two thousand throats.

Harrow now left behind, in the 1924 General Election Mosley stood in Neville Chamberlain's constituency of Birmingham Ladywood. The newcomer to Labour's ranks might have stood a good chance of winning, had it not been for the publication, four days before polling, of the so-called 'Zinoviev letter' that purported to show that British Communists had infiltrated the Labour Party. It was close, Chamberlain winning by a majority of seventy-seven votes after four recounts.

Mosley, now fully embracing socialism, called for the nationalisation of the banking system. 'Let us to our cry for the minimum wage, the battle cry "banks for the people",' he told an Independent Labour Party meeting at Gloucester. In May 1925, the 2,500-capacity Birmingham Town Hall turned away as many again, such was the desire to hear Oswald Mosley speak. Introducing his 'unauthorised economic programme', he argued that increasing workers' wages would stimulate growth.

He fully supported the miners in the General Strike, and in December 1926, he returned to Parliament, winning a by-election for Smethwick after the sitting MP, Labour's John Davison, a railwayman, was forced to retire due to ill-health.

The idea of a rich aristocrat soliciting working-class votes had captured the attention of right-wing newspapers. During the election campaign, descriptions and photographs of the Mosleys' lavish lifestyle – top European hotels, holidays on sun-kissed beaches, Cynthia Mosley's furs and jewels – were just what their editors, or at least their owners, wanted. The *Daily Herald* said that Mosley was 'a victim in the capitalist Press of a great deal of coarse and vulgar comment', and that 'a great deal of amazement was caused by a remarkable letter from his father to the Press in which he hoped that the working class of Smethwick would not be deluded into voting for his son who had "never done an honest day's work in his life ... For many years I paid out of my own pocket for his education and upkeep."' Mosley's response was stinging: 'I was removed from the care of my father when I was five years of age by a court of law, and so far as I am aware, he has contributed nothing to my education and upbringing except in the form of alimony which he was compelled to contribute.' Mosley's father died in September 1928, and although the son succeeded to the title, and inherited the family estates, he was excluded from his father's personal will.

In 1927, Mosley was elected to the constituency section of Labour's national executive. He was re-elected in 1928, and in June 1929, after Labour took office again, in the minority government he was made Chancellor of the Duchy of Lancaster. It was a post just outside the Cabinet, but MacDonald gave Mosley special responsibility for tackling unemployment. He was still only 32 years old. In the 1929 General Election, Cynthia Mosley, who three years earlier had joined her husband on visits to India and the USA to study labour conditions, gained the Stoke-on-Trent seat for Labour, ousting the sitting Liberal, John Ward, by 7,850 votes. By now, Cynthia was in poor health and shortly after her election, she suffered a miscarriage.

Discontent began to ripple through the Labour movement, not least because its traditional supporters from the working classes suspected that aristocrats and intellectuals were taking over. That manifested itself in the 1929 election for the national executive when Mosley and his fellow Labour baronet, Sir Charles Trevelyan, the MP for Newcastle Central, were voted off. Chancellor of the Exchequer Philip Snowden urged Labour 'not to degenerate into an instrument for the ambitions of wealthy men'.

In January 1930, Mosley presented a set of proposals that became known as the Mosley Memorandum. They called for the nationalisation of key industries, high tariffs to protect British industries from foreign imports (in 1923 he had opposed this but now refined it to provide protection only for equivalent British goods that were efficiently produced and which provided fair wages for those workers), the transformation of the British Empire into a self-sufficient trading bloc, a programme of public works, a higher school leaving age, and state retirement pensions at the age of 60 to also help reduce the unemployment figures, which then stood at 1.7 million and would grow until, in July, it was 2 million.

A committee chaired by Philip Snowden looked at Mosley's ideas and rejected them, arguing that state action to reduce unemployment 'would be to plunge the country into ruin'. In May 1930, Mosley resigned his ministerial position. He could no longer support a government that he saw as doing nothing but sit around waiting for something better to turn up. The Liberal-leaning *The Nation* weekly newspaper felt that 'Sir Oswald has acted rightly – as he has certainly acted courageously – in declining to share any longer in the responsibility for inertia'.

That October, Mosley attempted to persuade the Labour Party conference to accept his Memorandum, but again he was defeated.

The same month, the *Manchester Guardian* commented, 'In Sir Oswald Mosley, British Labour may yet find its Hitler. The parallel is not so absurd as it sounds, for ... resemblance might be found between the crude aspirations of the "Nazis" and the new Socialist Imperialism to its own imperative needs, to which Sir Oswald Mosley is drifting.'

On 20 February 1931, Mosley, together with Cynthia and four other MPs, resigned from the Labour Party. The previous month, Sir William Morris (later Lord Nuffield) had funded Mosley to the tune of £50,000 to help him form a new political party. The New Party was a disparate bunch. The Conservative MP for West Belfast, William E. Allen, and the Liberal MP for Galloway, Cecil Dudgeon, also agreed to join (although two of the Labour MPs continued as Independents before rejoining Labour). Also among its earliest recruits were William Joyce, later to be known as the infamous 'Lord Haw-Haw', and Peter Dunsmore Howard, then the current captain of the England rugby union team, and later, after his flirtation with Mosley's ideas, a Conservative, a journalist, and playwright. One of the most unlikely recruits was the champion boxer Ted 'Kid' Lewis, a Jew.

At a New Party committee meeting in May 1931, Mosley floated the idea of forming a group of fit young men who would provide security at political meetings and protect New Party members from other political groups. The idea sounded too close to the Sturmabteilung used by the Nazis. It was leaked to the press. A few days later, the *Evening Despatch* reported, 'Sir Oswald Mosley ... today started to organise an army of "storm troops" composed of young men who will, when necessary, use the "good old English fist" in aid of their leader's programme.'

In August 1931, the *Daily Herald* carried a story headlined 'Mosley Fascist Secret – "Iron Core" of Youth'. The newspaper published an extract from a Mosley speech in which he urged that the New Party should build 'an Iron Core ... around which every element for the preservation of England will rally when a crisis of this kind [a challenge from the Communist Party] comes'. The same month, the *Berlin Tageblatt* newspaper reported that Adolf Hitler would soon be visiting England to meet 'Winston Churchill and Sir Oswald Mosley and inform them of the foreign political aims of his party'. That, of course, never happened.

In the October General Election, all but two of Mosley's New Party candidates lost their deposits. Cynthia, now in very poor health and alarmed by her husband's fascist tendencies, did not stand, and Mosley moved from Smethwick to contest her Stoke-on-Trent seat. He finished bottom of the poll with 10,500 votes. Eighteen other New Party candidates polled less than 1,000 votes each. At Stepney, Ted 'Kid' Lewis could manage only 157 votes on behalf of the New Party.

In December 1931, the *Daily Herald* reported that 'the new Nupa Club' in Chelsea's King's Road 'has a treat in store':

> The club, which turns out to be none other than the 'Youth Movement' of the New Party, Sir Oswald Mosley's semi-Fascist organisation, has, among other advantages, talks by famous people every Tuesday. On Tuesday, 19 January, the 'famous' person is the nephew of Herr Hitler, leader of the German Nazis or Fascists. There is a canteen where meals may be obtained, but alcoholic drinks are not served. 'You see,' it was explained, 'this club is for young men.' A sentence in the particulars of the club reads: 'There no obligation on members to join the Party, and politics are not pushed down members' throats.' Facilities are provided for Rugby, cricket, boxing, fencing, billiards, and physical training with first-class sports instructors. There is also debating, speech-making, and political training. The minimum subscription is a shilling month, but those who can pay more are expected to do so.

After the election defeat, Harold Nicolson, who edited the New Party newspaper *Action*, begged Mosley 'not to get muddled up with the Fascist crowd'. Mosley told Nicolson, 'We have been swept away in a hurricane of sentiment ... our time is yet to come.'

Chapter 7

Rowdy Streets

'He mounted to the high platform and gave the salute – a figure so high and so remote in that huge place that he looked like a doll from Marks and Spencer's penny bazaar.'

Colin Brooks of the *Sunday Dispatch*

On 1 October 1932, Oswald Mosley, then aged 35, formally launched the British Union of Fascists. It was not Britain's first fascist organisation – and the earliest, British Fascisti, had taken none of its inspiration from Adolf Hitler. It was a strange organisation that was eventually turned into a limited company. Founded in 1923 by Miss Rotha Lintorn-Orman, an upper-middle-class wartime ambulance driver who was, by her own account, decorated with the Croix de la Charité for her bravery, it came on the scene to combat communism. To that end, it cooperated with the Anti-Socialist and Anti-Communist League, the Economic League, which was a privately funded anti-communist pressure group, and the Tory 1912 Club.

Herself a Tory by inclination, but passionately anti-communist, in 1923 Lintorn-Orman advertised in the Duke of Northumberland's right-wing newspaper *The Patriot* for like-minded people – Oswald Mosley, a former Tory MP who was by then teetering on the brink of joining Labour, appalled her – asking for recruits to help her halt the Red Revolution. It was a good time to launch such a cause, with a Labour government soon to be in power and with the middle and upper-classes fearful for their property and livelihoods (the Zinoviev Letter would stoke those fears still further). Hundreds answered her call, and the result was her British Fascisti, the Italian-sounding name having much to do with her admiration for Mussolini, whose march on Rome had resulted in his National Fascist Party gaining power in Italy.

British Fascisti's platform was a curious mix of ideals, but, broadly, it defended the British crown and parliament. It wanted the UK to enter into close economic ties with its 'colonies including Canada and Australia'. The use of the word 'colonies' to describe those sturdily 'independent' Dominions is enough to know British Fascisti's own mindset. It had a deep mistrust of all aliens, although not especially Jews above all others. When it provided security at several Conservative Party meetings, one Tory MP who thanked them for their services was the Paris-born Jew Sir Philip Sassoon. Another Tory, Sir Charles Burn, the MP for Torquay, alongside his membership of the Conservative Party joined British Fascisti and sat on its nine-person council. At the same time, he retained his position as aide-de-camp to King George V.

As tales of her debauched lifestyle led to her mother, Blanche, withholding funds, Lintorn-Orman's influence on the organisation waned, while its London president, Brigadier-General Robert Blakeney, was unhappy with the way that she had attempted to guide British Fascisti.

Blakeney, who had once commanded a Royal Engineers balloon section and later became the general manager of Egyptian State Railways, anglicised the name to British Fascists, arguing that 'Italian methods pure and simple' could not succeed in the UK because, compared to the Italians, when it came to combating communism, the British were more prone to apathy. Mussolini had already declared that 'fascism is not for export'.

Speaking to a meeting at Portsmouth's Albert Hall in June 1925, Blakeney said that 'Communistic Russia is now being led by German Jews ... The German Jews said that the British Empire had to be destroyed'. He formed the British Fascists into a limited company but when Lintorn-Orman died in March 1935, at the age of 40, in the Canary Islands, it was bankrupt, and almost defunct. Its death knell was sounded when Oswald Mosley founded the British Union of Fascists and many of British Fascists' membership – crucially the active core – jumped ship.

The organisation had already been weakened by its members defecting to other fascist groups, notably when the extremely antisemitic Arnold Leese, a veterinary surgeon who was an expert on camels, broke away to join the short-lived National Fascists before, in the summer of 1928, forming his own Imperial Fascist League (IFL), whose emblem was a swastika in the middle of a Union Flag. In September 1936, Leese's violent antisemitism would earn him a prison sentence when, along with a fellow IFL member, Walter Whitehead, a printer, he was convicted at the Old Bailey over two articles published in the July issue of the IFL newspaper, *The Fascist*. The charges were that they together had published and printed 'divers, scandalous and libellous statements regarding His Majesty's Jewish subjects, which would have a tendency to promote ill-will and hostility between two classes of the King's subjects, so as to create a public mischief'. Leese was sentenced to six months' imprisonment. Whitehead was fined £20.

The Imperial Fascist League, which propounded that democracy was dead and a new 'governing state' which would control all trade and industry must be formed – its slogan was 'Boycott the ballot box' – was never a large organisation, but it was one that bothered Lintorn-Orman. In October 1928, after three former British Fascist members had written to the editor of the *St Pancras Gazette* claiming that the Imperial Fascist League was 'the one organisation consecrated to the service of the British race and Empire in every sphere of national activity', she reminded the editor that

> the British Fascists have been in existence since May 1923 and have always adhered to their original aim, namely to give every service to HM the King and to any loyal Government in power in the event of attempted revolution or general strike ... In view of the possible misunderstanding that may arise from publication of the previous letter, I trust that you will see your way to publishing this.

Which he did.

According to the rival British Fascists, the IFL's membership was in the low hundreds, and its headquarters were two rooms and no telephone over a tailor's shop in Craven Street, Charing Cross. Yet, despite its relatively modest structure, the Imperial Fascist League, which wanted to send all Jews to Madagascar, made a lot of noise. Writing to the *Western Morning News* in June 1930, Leese said, 'The mystery which has surrounded Fascism in Britain had been manufactured artificially, partly by its enemies (the political parties, alien control over "public" opinion etc) and partly by the British Fascists who have never understood their subject.' Leese had also criticised Oswald Mosley for never tackling the 'Jewish question' and regarded him as a 'kosher fascist'.

In November that year, from the altogether grander address of Chandos House at Buckingham Gate, once the home of the Austrian ambassador, Leese wrote to the editor of the *West Sussex Gazette*:

> There is available gold to the tune of £5,000 million in the Dead Sea. It is necessary for the Jew to get control over it, or their gold monopoly (which includes world political power) will go west. There is also the Potash Monopoly of Germany to be protected by preventing the full use of the Dead Sea Salts. Wailing walls did you say? Not a bit of it ... I recommend to you the secret history of the world ... you will then see the connection between the loss of the *Hampshire* with Lord Kitchener on board and the loss of the *R101* with Lord Thomson on board.

The death of the War Minister, Kitchener, who in June 1916 was en route to Russia to attend negotiations with Tsar Nicholas II when he was one of 737 lost after the armoured cruiser HMS *Hampshire* hit a German mine off the mainland of Orkney, and that of the Air Minister Thomson, who perished when the rigid airship crashed in France on its maiden voyage in October 1930, had been the subject of conspiracy theories. In 1937, the German airship *Hindenburg* would suffer a similar fate when trying to dock in New Jersey and more myths would be born.

The editor replied, 'Mr Leese throws his squibs about like a boy on November 5 ... if Mr Leese wants to hit targets, he must learn shooting ... "Secret history" usually camouflages fairy tales, and we know enough good history, and fairy tales here, to help even our Fascist friends to their legitimate ends.'

In November 1931, the *Daily Mirror* reported:

> Wild scenes at a meeting of the Imperial Fascist League last night when a number of unemployed interrupted. The disturbance started when the League secretary, Mr Leese, his black shirt decorated with British war medal ribbons, began to speak. Demonstrators shouted him down and began to sing the 'Red Flag' – chairs were thrown, and Fascists and demonstrators engaged in hand-to-hand fighting. Suddenly police entered the hall and the demonstrators scattered. One man was taken to the police station. Several people were injured.

In February 1932, Robert Forgan, one of Mosley's original supporters when he split from Labour, acting on Mosley's instructions approached

Leese with the proposal that the Imperial Fascist League should throw in its lot with the New Party and accept Oswald Mosley as their leader who would have complete control over the organisation and all policy decisions. Leese, as Mosley probably expected, turned down the idea out of hand, but the British Fascists' Neil Francis-Hawkins, who many saw as a leader preferable to Lintorn-Orman, quite liked the idea. However, when Lintorn-Orman was told that he had agreed, she flew into a rage and the British Fascists' grand council rejected the offer.

The New Party idea had all but expired anyway. In March 1932, Harold Nicolson wrote in his diary that 'the death of the New Party has now been frankly discussed and the ice broken'. Nicolson, whose association with Mosley would soon end now that his friend was fully embracing fascism, saw two problems: the New Party was not new anymore, and it was no longer a party.

The following month, Mosley told a New Party meeting at its headquarters in Great George Street that David Margesson, the Tory government chief whip, had asked him to rejoin the Conservative Party, and that Joseph Kenworthy, a former Liberal MP who had resigned his seat and won a by-election at Central Hull for Labour, had asked him to lead the Labour Party. Mosley was not interested in either proposition. He wanted to coordinate all Britain's fascist groups into one body under his autocratic leadership. He said that he could never re-enter the 'machine' of the old parties; it would place him in a straitjacket. There was nothing left to do but wind up the old New Party and strike out with another new party.

On 1 October, at the former HQ of the New Party, Mosley addressed the first meeting of the British Union of Fascists (BUF). Most of the thirty-two founder members, all wearing black shirts, were there to hear him speak. He told them that those who joined the cause would have to be prepared to 'march with us on a great and hazardous adventure'. Those who did march would have to prepare themselves to face abuse, misunderstanding, bitter animosity, and, quite possibly, danger. In return, the BUF, he said, could offer them the belief that they were fighting so that a great land might live.

That day also saw the launch of Mosley's book, *The Greater Britain*, which offered an alternative to capitalism and communism to end the Great Depression. The following day, in its 'Talk of the Town Outside Mayfair' column, *Reynolds's Illustrated News* commented:

Sir Oswald Mosley is making his bid for dictatorship. I can commend his latest manifesto – 'The Greater Britain', British Union of Fascists, 2s 6d net – as an excellent study of political dialects. Sir Oswald presents an essentially anti-English sentiment in so English a way as to disarm criticism.

One proposal, however, rather lets our own little Il Duce [Mussolini] down. Since the war, physical fitness has been a cult with the youth of Britain; its organisation has been voluntary and spontaneous. Sir Oswald wants to make physical fitness compulsory in his Fascist creed. That idea is too aggressively Italian to catch on here.

The founder members of the BUF included several of those who had followed Mosley from the Labour Party and the Independent Labour Party, and subsequently disaffected members of the Labour movement. In his book *The Fascists in Britain*, Colin Cross describes the typical long-serving Blackshirt as 'a man of lower middle-class, not particularly clever but capable of loyalty and sacrifice ... Without sacrificing his social rank, which was a grade above the manual worker, he could take part in a revolutionary movement'. The man bought his black shirt for five shillings (25p) and paid a shilling (5p) a month subscription if he was in work or fourpence (less than 2p) if he was unemployed.

One of Mosley's most pressing concerns was to organise the Fascist Defence Force. It would be commanded by Eric Hamilton Piercey who had experience with the New Party's band of young security men, the 'Biff Boys' who had wielded the 'good old British fist'. In October 1934, Eric Hamilton Piercey, an inspector in the special constabulary, was found not guilty of damaging a press photographer's camera during a BUF meeting that Mosley was addressing at Plymouth. Several others at the meeting were found guilty of that charge and of committing a breach of the peace, and some of them were sentenced to six weeks' hard labour. It was typical of BUF meetings, where rowdy opponents would turn up to find themselves faced by black-shirted BUF stewards who had travelled in black vans protected by armour-plating and wire, and who were armed with cudgels. When Mosley spoke at Leicester in April 1935, the *Leicester Evening Mail* reported, 'Fifty women who have trained in ju-jitsu and ambulance work will help to steward Sir Oswald Mosley's meeting at the Granby Halls ... they will deal with women interrupters.'

A typical event was the one that attracted more than 1,000 people to an army drill hall in the centre of Derby in May 1934. Mosley told his audience that they would already have noticed that the Blackshirts' way of conducting meetings was different from the methods of the parties of the past. In the same way, the methods of the Blackshirts would be different when they had won power. Blackshirts, he urged, held their creed with the force of a religious conviction. To them, it meant everything in the world. It was a creed which aimed at the revival and restoration of a great country. It had collected and inspired thousands of young men and women to dedicate their lives to the cause, and they were resolved to give their service to the nation. They wanted by their organisation to break down every barrier of class. One of the small barriers of class was difference in dress. Within their own ranks, they had already achieved classless unity, which later they would bring to the nation as whole.

When the Blackshirts spoke in the early days, said Mosley, they met with organised attempts to stop them putting their case to the public. In those early days, fighting at their meetings was common. Such a thing was very rare today, he said. Opposition had come to an end using counterforce against force, and, in organising on those lines, the Blackshirt was of enormous service.

Mosley said that his listeners had heard, no doubt, that Blackshirts were out for violence. The charge was totally untrue, he said. No single case had ever been proved against the movement of breaking up its opponents' meetings. In the early days, on the other hand, until their own methods were effective, there was proof of attempts to break up Blackshirts' meetings. Where Blackshirts were in small detachments, he alleged, they were still subject to attack. The Blackshirt policy, Mosley claimed, was the right that every political movement claimed – to put its case before the country. Blackshirts did not interfere with other people putting their case forward, but they insisted on the same right for themselves. That was the beginning and the end of the charge brought against them that they organised for violence. They had had to organise in order to repress the violence brought against the new movement, and to ensure that their case should be heard, said Mosley.

For all his talk of simply wanting the BUF to have the same freedom as every other political party to put its case, Mosley's own case was that there would be only one political party – the British Union of Fascists. The present system of several parties seeking to form a government was unworkable, he argued.

Such a view was always going to draw protestors to BUF meetings. The following day, under the headline 'Scenes in Streets – Blackshirt Steward Injured at Derby', the *Derby Evening Telegraph* reported:

> Rowdy scenes in the streets around the Drill Hall, Derby, followed the meeting addressed by Sir Oswald Mosley, the leader of the Blackshirt Movement, last night. One man was arrested by the police, and a Blackshirt steward was taken to the Derbyshire Royal Infirmary for treatment to an injury to his eye. While the meeting was in progress, a big crowd collected in Newland Street and Becket Street where a number of men and women paraded with anti-Blackshirt banners and endeavoured to hold counter-meetings. They were kept on the move by a strong detachment of police officers, both mounted and on foot. At the conclusion of the meeting, when the Blackshirts left the hall there was a disturbance in Becket Street, and police promptly intervened.
>
> Most of the stewards at Sir Oswald Mosley's meeting came from Birmingham. Sir Oswald marched at the head of a squad of his stewards into Friary Street, where many of the Blackshirts boarded omnibuses. After walking through the centre of the town, followed by a big crowd, the leader returned to Becket Street and left again in his car.

The Derby newspaper published a letter from Harold Boardman of the National Union of Distributive and Allied Workers, who wrote:

> Some hundreds of people were in the vicinity of the Drill Hall, Derby, yesterday evening, and witnessed the importation of Mosley's black-shirted medley crowd, most of whom wore such bewildered expressions as to make one feel that they were really watching the transportation of sheep, marshalled as they were from their charas [charabanc, an early form of bus] to the hall by two or three pugilistic-looking individuals. Much that took place outside the hall was amusing, but there was also much that cannot be treated flippantly. I witnessed two instances of deliberate provocation by the Blackshirts: to quote only

one is sufficient to arouse the indignation of any decent-minded persons; indeed, many of the onlookers who had gone merely out of curiosity became fired at the sight of such despicable brutality.

A girl of 17 or 18 stood outside the main entrance, unobtrusively holding for sale some political papers, when one of the Blackshirts came along, grabbed at the girl's wrist, and knocked the papers from her hand, tearing one of them into pieces. I spoke to one of the Blackshirts regarding the incident, and his reply is worth publishing: 'Between you and I, we have paid a penny to the girl for the damaged paper; it would be better to keep it quiet and say nothing about it.' His reply was significant – it proved the authenticity of my evidence – but what is more important, it demonstrated how coolly is the Fascist policy of violence accepted by those whose alleged purpose is the welfare of the masses. In asking you to publish this letter, I must state that I am not in any way connected with the Communist Party, being a member of the Labour Party and the secretary of a trades union.

The disturbances at Derby and in other provincial towns and cities was small beer compared to what had taken place four months earlier at London's Olympia, when a crowd numbering close to 15,000 gathered to hear Mosley speak. Two hours before the scheduled start of the meeting, opponents numbering according to some estimates 10,000, and drawn from a wide range of anti-Mosleyites – communists, those on the extreme left of the Labour Party and the Independent Labour Party, trades unionists, and pacifists – arrived with their banners and placards to be greeted not only by Blackshirt stewards but also by police officers on foot and mounted. The event had attracted a wide range of folk, young men and women in evening dress, middle-class families with small children, and workmen still in their working clothes. There were also politicians, big business, and leading journalists, all keen to see how much traction Mosley's influence had gained.

As the meeting got under way, said the *Manchester Guardian*, it was clear that Mosley had 'nothing to learn from the theatricalism of Hitler or Mussolini'. There was a massed band of Blackshirts, the Union Flag and the black and yellow flag of the BUF, arc-lamps with a greyish-blue tinge, and platform draped with 'drugget of tinned-salmon pink'.

Rowdy Streets

For two hours, Mosley's speech was interrupted by protestor after protestor. Each one, including two men who were seen being pursued by several Blackshirts across roof girders high above the audience, were evicted before Mosley could continue. Out of sight of the audience, protestors were assaulted. There were cuts and bruises, teeth knocked out, and noses broken. It was not only one of Britain's biggest indoor political meetings, but it was also one of the bloodiest. An economics student from Sheffield University, 21-year-old Jacob Miller, spent nine days in St Mary Abbot's Hospital in Kensington after suffering head wounds and concussion after being thrown over a balcony on to the floor below. Later, he recounted his expedience:

> I was anxious to hear Sir Oswald's speech and, at first, I was fed up with the interruptions. But later I became indignant and when he said, 'We are not intimidated by these interruptions', I interjected, referring to the audience, 'We haven't been intimidated but we are being fooled.' As soon as I had spoken, six Fascists rushed at me, picked me up and threw me over the balcony into the body of the hall. This was a drop of about ten feet [3 metres] and I became unconscious for a few moments. Some more Fascists, who were waiting below, then got hold of me and took me outside the meeting to a yard. More stewards followed and when they threw me down again, I was surrounded by at least twenty men. I was helpless, and they immediately began to beat me, smashing me about the head and body.

A week later, Clark Hall, the BUF's assistant propaganda officer for Sheffield, warned Jacob Miller's fellow students to be careful if they were considering heckling Mosley when he spoke in Sheffield later that month: 'The hooligans who have broken up every political meeting in the city during the past few years will not be given free play at the City Hall ... I wish them every luck if they attempt to break up our meeting. They'll need it.'

Of the Olympia meeting, the *Manchester Guardian* reported:

> The meeting ended in a mild chaos – not from interrupters but from a general stampede of the audience, who had plainly grown tired of Sir Oswald's two-hour monologue. After

ten o'clock it was plainly a struggle between Sir Oswald and the decision of the licensing justices of the borough of Hammersmith. The licensing justices won, and Sir Oswald was robbed of his triumphant exit.

While both sides accused each other, with tales of razors, knuckledusters, and rubber hoses, there was a full debate in the House of Commons about the Olympia event. One thing was certain: it had earned the British Union of Fascists an indelible reputation for brutality.

From 1934, the BUF stepped up its campaign against the Jews. Antisemitism became a central plank in Mosley's thinking. Yet, in his early days in politics, he had shown no signs of being antisemitic and, indeed, had mixed freely with Jewish people. Early issues of the BUF's *The Blackshirts* newspaper argued that Hitler was not antisemitic, and if Jews were victimised and assaulted, it was not because of their religion but because they were 'internationalists and pacifists'. In May 1935, Hitler sent him a telegram congratulating him on an antisemitic speech. Mosley replied with his own telegram to the German leader:

> Please receive my greatest thanks for your kind telegram in relation to my speech in Leicester, which was received while I was away from London. I esteem greatly your advice in the midst of our hard struggle. The forces of Jewish corruption must be overcome in all great countries before the future of Europe can be made secure in justice and peace. Our struggle to this end is hard, but our victory is certain.

In that speech, at the Granby Halls, Mosley called upon Jews to 'put Britain first or be deported':

> For the first time we openly and publicly challenge the great Jewish interests of this country, commanding politics, commanding the Press, commanding the cinemas, dominating the City of London and killing industry with their sweat shops ... these great interests have not intimidated and never will intimidate the Fascist movement.

In November 1935, Stanley Baldwin, who had taken over from the ailing Ramsay MacDonald a few months earlier, called a General Election that resulted in the UK having another National Government, albeit one with a reduced majority. Along with one-third of his fellow National Labour MPs, MacDonald had lost his seat, although, despite being in poor health, in January 1936 he returned after winning a by-election for the Combined Scottish Universities. In November 1937, MacDonald died while on a sea cruise that was meant to restore his health. Labour was now led by Clement Attlee.

The BUF had not contested any parliamentary seats – its platform was voter abstention and 'Fascism next time'. The Blackshirts were having no impact whatsoever when it came to running the country, although Mosley continued to draw the crowds. At the Albert Hall in March 1936, there were the usual scraps and tussles – and seventeen arrests – and hecklers were thrown out as Mosley told his audience that 'even Hitler was not antisemitic before he saw a Jew'. 'Well-dressed women were among the many people who laughed and applauded at this jibe,' according to the *Birmingham Gazette*.

The BUF now began to increase its antisemitic campaigns in cities with large Jewish populations, such as Leeds and Manchester, but London was always the main target. Of the UK's 350,000 Jewish residents, 230,000 of them lived in the capital, and 150,000 of those had made their homes in the East End. When Mosley announced his intention of marching through the streets of the East End on 4 October 1936, tens of thousands of people signed a petition calling for the march to be banned. The Home Secretary, Sir John Simon, refused to do so, and all leave for police officers in the East End and for Special Branch officers at Scotland Yard was cancelled. When the *Daily Mirror* asked why the march was being allowed to go ahead, Simon's private secretary, Mr A. S. Hutchinson, told the newspaper that there had been no foundation for him to consult other Cabinet ministers because 'that might be interpreted as a restriction of freedom of speech'.

Anti-fascists, adopting the slogan 'They shall not pass', which was used by the Republicans who defended Madrid during the Spanish Civil War that had begun that year, planned their opposition. By 2.00 pm on that Sunday, there were more than 50,000 people waiting to block the entry into the East End of Mosley and his men, who were estimated to number 3,000. The centre of the action was in the west-to-east running Cable Street, where baton-charging police tried to clear a way through the barricades that had been erected there. Thus, 4 October 1936 is indelibly known for the Battle of Cable Street. Fenner Brockway, the secretary of the Independent Labour Party, who had narrowly escaped being trampled by police horses, telephoned the Home Office to urge that the march be stopped, or at least diverted. That was now obvious to everyone.

Mosley, who was wearing the new BUF uniform of black military-cut jacket, grey riding breeches, a black peaked military hat and a red armband, was still at Royal Mint Street when Sir Philip Game, the Metropolitan Police commissioner, told him that he must disperse his men. The march was called off and, by 4.00 pm, BUF members were escorted from the area. The London District committee of the Communist Party of Great Britain issued a statement:

> East London workers, supported by all London in united action, have barred the road to Mosley. Gentile, Jew, Catholic, Protestant, Labour and Communist, men, women and children, determined that Fascism shall not pass here, have given Mosley the most humiliating defeat ever suffered by any figure on English politics.

The *Daily Herald* reported:

> Home Secretary Sir John Simon must ban, once and for all, the provocative marches and counter-marches of Fascists in military uniform. This is the insistent demand of the chiefs of Britain's biggest cities. Manchester is sending a deputation to the Home Secretary and has issued an appeal to all local authorities to join it in protest. Bristol, Birmingham, Leeds, Hull, Swansea and Cardiff are raising the issues with the Watch Committees...

The Battle of Cable Street led to the 1936 Public Order Act that gave the Home Secretary the power to ban marches in the London area, while chief constables could apply to them to ban marches in their local areas. The Act also made it an offence to wear political uniforms and to use threatening and abusive words during political gatherings.

Like Hitler after the failed Munich beer hall putsch of 1923, Mosley now decided to use democratic means to gain a foothold. But in the London municipal elections of 1937, a campaign that saw Mosley attack Labour for doing nothing to solve London's housing problem, and BUF supporters attack Jewish financiers, shopkeepers, landlords, and rival politicians, won over very few people. The BUF took only 18 per cent of the vote.

By now, Oswald Mosley had remarried. Cynthia Mosley had died in London in May 1933, aged 34, from peritonitis following acute appendicitis. Mosley, a notorious womaniser, had been having an affair with the wildly ambitious Diana Mitford, the daughter of one of his wealthiest supporters. Diana and her sister, Unity, were regular visitors to Germany where they met Adolf Hitler – who thought that Unity was 'a perfect specimen of Aryan womanhood' – and other high-ranking Nazis. On 6 October 1936, Hitler was one of only six guests when Oswald and Diana (who was divorced from an heir to the Guinness brewing family) were married in secret in the drawing room of the home of the Nazi Propaganda Minister Joseph Goebbels.

For the remainder of the 1930s, Mosley and the BUF continued to be active but did not achieve any electoral success, although his 'Britain First' rally at Earls Court exhibition hall in July 1939, only two months before the outbreak of war, attracted a reported 30,000 attendees to make it the biggest indoor political rally in British history.

When war was declared in September 1939, Mosley's British Union of Fascists would be considered more a nuisance than a threat. The German blitzkrieg into France and the Low Countries in the spring of 1940 would change all that. On 23 May, a large number of uniformed and plain-clothes officers from Scotland Yard raided the BUF's headquarters in Great Smith Street, Westminster. Mosley was not there, but that afternoon, five police officers were waiting for him when he returned to his flat in Grosvenor Street, SW1. His home, Savoy Farm at Denham in Buckinghamshire, was also searched. Mosley and many others were arrested under new powers to Defence Regulation 18B conferred on the Home Secretary, Sir John Anderson. Several of his followers were eventually moved to the camps on the Isle of Man where they were segregated from those interned as enemy aliens. Mosley, though, was kept in Brixton prison where he remained until December 1941 when he was reunited with Lady Diana, who was being held in Holloway prison. There they lived in 'married quarters' – a small house with a garden inside the prison walls – until November 1943 and their release on grounds of Sir Oswald's health. The Mosleys were placed under house arrest for the remainder of the war.

Chapter 8

One of the World's Most Evil Places

'In Nazi Germany, it has become a crime to believe that all men are equal in the sight of God.'

Paul Massing

At just after 9.00 pm on Monday, 27 February 1933, pedestrians near the Reichstag heard the sound of breaking glass. Then they saw flames erupting from Germany's parliament building. Soon the glare could be seen all over Berlin. Police on horseback and on foot kept at bay the ever-growing number of spectators, while firefighters, aided by floodlights, poured water on the flames. By the time the blaze was under control, the debating chamber and the gilded cupola of the building where Germany's laws had been made were in ruins. The next day, British newspapers reported:

> The hall presented a scene of desolate wreckage, with all the deputies' seats, diplomats', public and press galleries destroyed, and the iron pillars supporting the golden dome twisted out of shape ... although the police assert that Communists are responsible, some people think that the fire may have been started by the Nazis with the object of provoking trouble.

Ninety years later, historians are still divided on the matter.

At the scene, police arrested a 24-year-old Dutchman, Marinus van der Lubbe, a heavy drinker who was well known in the Netherlands as a communist agitator. Almost blind after an industrial accident, van der Lubbe had once claimed sole responsibility for a strike at a factory in Leiden, and had appeared keen to be punished. He now claimed that he alone had set fire to the Reichstag. A police officer said that, when van der Lubbe was taken into the ruins of the building, 'We neither indicated the direction nor influenced him in any way. He was almost delighted to show us the path he had taken. He said he had an excellent sense of direction because of his poor eyesight.'

On 10 January 1934, van der Lubbe was executed – beheaded – in a prison yard in Leipzig. The cases against Ernst Torgler, the German communist leader, and three Bulgarian communists, all charged with complicity, were found to be not proved. German newspapers buried the verdicts on them, without comment, on inside pages. Seventy-five years later, under a law passed in 1998 that allowed pardons for people convicted of crimes under the Nazis, based on the concept that Nazi law 'went against the basic ideas of justice', the German government posthumously pardoned van der Lubbe (in 1967, a West German court had, bizarrely, changed his sentence to an eight-year prison term).

Whatever the truth – whether van der Lubbe had help (either from communists or Nazis), or was acting alone – one day after the fire, Hitler seized upon it to have von Hindenburg declare a national emergency, 'For the Protection of the People and the State', that made permanent the Decree for the Protection of the German people that had been introduced as a temporary measure on 4 February 1933, and which gave the Nazis far-reaching powers by placing constraints on the press and authorising the police to ban political meetings and marches. At a stroke, it eliminated all political opposition.

Thousands of communists and Social Democrats were arrested, and their meetings and publications outlawed. Yet the Nazi Party was still unable to capture an absolute majority in the Reichstag elections of 5 March 1933, the ninth and last German federal election of the Weimar Republic. It was also the last free election to be held in Germany until after the Second World War.

On 18 February 1933, the chairman of the Reichstag Nationalist Deputies had told a meeting in Cologne that 'the election results and figures do not interest the Cabinet'. That may have been so, but although the Nazis polled a far greater share of the vote – 43.9 per cent – Hitler was initially forced to maintain his coalition with the Nationalist DNVP. He needed a two-thirds majority to pass the Law to Remedy the Distress of the People and the Reich – also known as the Enabling Act – which would allow him to make laws without consulting the Reichstag. The KPD, the largest Communist Party outside the Soviet Union, was already banned, and when the Catholic Centre Party voted with the Nazis, the Act was passed on 23 March. Hitler also outlawed the Social Democratic Party, itself rooted in the workers' movement. Germany was now firmly established as a dictatorship. The Third Reich – Hitler viewed the Holy Roman Empire (800 to 1806) as the First Reich or empire, and the 1871 German Empire founded by Otto von Bismarck as the Second Reich – was born.

On 10 March 1933, Victor Klemperer, a Jewish professor at Dresden Technical University, wrote in his diary:

> Hitler Chancellor. What up to election Sunday on 5 March I called terror was a mild prelude. Now the business of 1918 is being exactly repeated, only under a different sign, the swastika ... On Saturday, the 4th, I heard part of Hitler's speech from Konigsberg ... the unctuous bawling, truly bawling of a priest...

Members of the SDP and the KPD faced a bleak future. The first concentration camp was already open, not yet for the victims of a mass-extermination programme, but for 'enemies of the State'. The camp, at Dachau, near Munich, held political prisoners together with others who had been condemned in a court of law. Gradually they would be joined by Jews, gypsies, Jehovah's Witnesses, dissenting clergy, homosexuals, and just about anyone brave – and unwise – enough to publicly criticise the Nazis. People were held under *Schutzhaft*, the power to imprison, on the theory of 'protective custody', without judicial proceedings. It was based on that law of 28 February 1933 – the day after the German parliament building had been burned down – which suspended clauses of the Weimar constitution guaranteeing civil liberties to the German people.

Initially set up by local SA on an ad hoc basis, camps soon existed throughout Germany. One of the most infamous was Columbia-Haus, a former military prison near Tempelhof airport in Berlin. By mid-1933, the Gestapo was using Columbia-Haus to hold prisoners undergoing interrogation and torture. In late 1935, the Gestapo increased the size of the cells at its headquarters. Around the same time, the SS closed the SA concentration camps it had used to persecute its enemies during the first few years of Nazi power and in their place began building larger camps. Of the original camps, only Dachau survived. Columbia-Haus was shut down on 5 November 1935. A few miles away, work was under way to put the final touches to the Olympic Stadium.

No matter who had been unfortunate enough to be dragged through the gates in the early days of the concentration camps, Hitler's main target would always be the Jews. It seems he felt that their destruction was the very reason for his existence. In his position of dictator, Hitler could at last attend to the menace, and, as April 1933 dawned, he began with a boycott of Jewish businesses.

Although this itself was a failure, it marked the beginning of a tragic downward spiral for the Jews, for Hitler had no shortage of supporters for his overall aims. Following its successes in the March election, the Nazi Party had been flooded with applications for membership from people cynically dubbed by the old hierarchy as 'March Violets', latecomers who now jumped on the Nazi train as it gathered steam. The Nazi *Gleichschaltung* – the process by which all existing organisations and associations were nazified or suppressed – was fully under way. Under the absolute leadership of Adolf Hitler, the State, not the individual, was supreme. From the moment of birth, one existed only to serve the State and obey the Führer.

Millions readily agreed. Bureaucrats, industrialists, even intellectual and literary figures, were attracted by Hitler's crude pageantry. Some of those who disagreed, many of whom had Jewish blood, wisely departed. More than 2,000 of Germany's finest minds, including scientists, engineers, architects, writers, artists, and filmmakers, fled the country. They included the psychologist Sigmund Freud, the Nobel Prize-winning writer Thomas Mann, film director Fritz Lang, actress Marlene Dietrich, composer Kurt Weill, conductor Otto Klemperer, the great tenor Richard Tauber, and the eminent architect Walter Gropius. Ernst Jokl, founding president of the World Physical Exercise Council, also fled. Albert Einstein, widely regarded as the greatest scientist of the twentieth century, was visiting California when Hitler came to power; he never returned to Germany.

For those who remained, there was now the heady cocktail of fear and optimism, fuelled by a never-ending stream of Nazi parades and rallies. And everywhere there were the flags, thousands upon thousands of them, red, white, and black swastika flags and banners. They flew from every flagpole, hung from almost every window, lined every main street.

The boycott of Jewish businesses began at 10.00 am on Saturday, 1 April 1933. Stormtroopers stood at the doorways to Jewish stores, shops, and offices, holding posters proclaiming: 'Germans, defend yourselves against the Jewish atrocity propaganda, buy only at German shops' and 'The Jews are our misfortune'. Most Germans were interested only in a bargain, or in getting their weekend shopping done as quickly as possible, so they ignored the SA and their posters. Saturday was also the Jewish Sabbath and so most of the smaller neighbourhood shops owned by observant Jews were already closed; the brown-shirted stormtroopers found themselves picketing shops that were not even open. There was some violence, however, and in Kiel, a Jewish lawyer was killed.

The boycott lasted one day, but it was immediately followed by a series of laws which were much more effective in robbing Jewish people of their rights:

On the same day as the boycott of Jewish businesses, a law was introduced which banned Jews from teaching in state schools.

On 7 April, the Law for the Restoration of a Professional Civil Service was introduced, Article 3 of which specified that 'Civil servants who are not of Aryan descent are to be retired; if they are honorary officials, they are to be dismissed from their official status.'

On 11 April came the first legal definition since the passing of the Enabling Act had given Hitler absolute power, of who was a Jew: 'A person is to be considered non-Aryan if he is descended from non-Aryan, and especially from Jewish parents or grandparents. It is sufficient if one parent or grandparent is non-Aryan. This is to be assumed in particular where one parent or grandparent was of the Jewish religion.'

On 22 April, Jews were prohibited from serving as patent lawyers and from serving as doctors in state-run insurance institutions.

On 25 April, a law against the overcrowding of German schools restricted the proportion of Jews admitted to public education institutions to their proportion in the population.

On 6 May, the Civil Service law was amended to close loopholes in order to keep out honorary university professors, lecturers, and notaries.

On 2 June, a law was introduced that prohibited Jewish dentists and dental technicians from working with state-run insurance institutions.

On 14 July, the Nazi Party was declared the only party in Germany, while a law was introduced which allowed for past naturalisation to be revoked and German citizenship cancelled. It was primarily aimed at Jews naturalised since 1918 from the formerly eastern German territories.

On 22 September, the Nazis established the Reich Chamber of Culture; a week later, Jews were excluded from all cultural and entertainment activities including literature, art, film, and theatre.

On 28 September, all non-Aryans and their spouses were prohibited from government employment.

On 4 October, a law was introduced to restrain the free expression of opinion unacceptable or in opposition to the Nazi Party. Jews were prohibited from working as journalists, and all newspapers were effectively placed under Nazi control. In addition, anti-Jewish signs were posted throughout Germany, 'Jews not welcome' being one of the milder ones.

On 10 May 1933, there occurred something as sinister as any of the above. Students from universities hitherto regarded as among the finest in the world gathered in Berlin and other German cities to burn books with 'un-German' ideas. The works of Freud, Einstein, and Mann, among many others, went up in flames as students gave the Nazi salute. In Berlin, the Propaganda Minister, Joseph Goebbels, told the book burners: 'The era of extreme Jewish intellectualism is now at an end.'

Within a few months of the Nazis taking control of Germany, millions of its citizens had been condemned to a life of terror. By the end of 1933, it has been estimated that a total of 150,000 people languished in concentration camps. Late that year, at Aschaffenburg camp in Bavaria, a group of SS guards killed several Jewish inmates. The guards were arrested, but SS officers insisted that their men were not subject to civilian authority and Heinrich Himmler, Reichsführer of the SS, demanded that no charges be brought against them. It was a decision that set a precedent for mass murder in concentration camps across the Third Reich.

That the rest of the world was ignorant of the Nazi terror is impossible to imagine, for there was plenty of reference material available for those who chose to read it. After escaping from Germany, Gerhart Segar, a former Social Democrat member of the Reichstag and secretary-general of the German Peace Society, wrote graphically of his imprisonment in the Oranienburg camp, situated in an abandoned brewery 35 kilometres north of Berlin's city centre. Seger's book, *A Nation Terrorized*, was the first published eyewitness account of Hitler's concentration camps. It was first published in Europe in 1934, and in the USA the following year, and it sold half a million copies. In the book's foreword, Heinrich Mann, elder brother of the exiled Thomas Mann, wrote: 'You have escaped from one of the most evil places in the world.'

If further evidence was needed, it came in *Fatherland*, also published in the USA in 1935. Paul Massing, arrested for being a member of the Communist Party, provided a graphic testimony to the cruelty of the

Nazi regime when he wrote his book under the nom de plume of Karl Billinger. In Columbia-Haus, Massing suffered terrible beatings at the hands of the SS:

> The two Blackshirts standing behind me seized me and rushed me downstairs to the cellar, where the 'preparatory squad' was already on hand. From a tin pan they lifted wet horsewhips, which cut sharper after being soaked in water.
>
> 'Pants down!'
>
> I stood motionless. In a moment I lay, stripped from the waist down, across a table. Four men held me; three others flogged me. At the first lash I thought I should leap to the ceiling. My whole body contracted convulsively. Against my will I let out a shrill cry. The second stroke, the third, the fourth – not quickly but at measured intervals, spaced so as to keep me from losing consciousness, to make certain that my nerves would register each blow in all its agonising pain. I was aware of but one racking desire – to be dead, to be dead, to be dead, and have this over, finished, done. My body did not seem to belong to me anymore. After ten or twelve lashes I felt the blows only as dull detonations in my head. I no longer had the strength to cry out. The twenty-fifth stroke was followed by a brief pause, during which the men changed places. One of them poured a pitcher of cold water over my head to render me fit for further treatment. Then they started afresh. When it was over, they dragged me back to my cell. Closing the door, they said they would be back shortly to return me to the investigation court.

The Nazis' obsession with racial purity had not stopped at purging Germany of Jewish blood. In April 1933, the Prussian Minister of the Interior, Hermann Göring, ordered local authorities to produce statistics concerning the 'Rhineland Bastards', the offspring of German women and colonial soldiers who served in the French occupation force in Germany in the 1920s. The remit also covered children of German colonialists who married African women and returned with them to Germany after the Great War. It was agreed that the best way to end this 'black curse' was by sterilising people of mixed race. The gypsy Roma and Sinti people were also targeted for sterilisation.

In June that year, the Committee of Experts for Population and Racial Policy was established by the Interior Minister, Wilhelm Frick. Its main aim was to draft a law for 'the prevention of hereditarily diseased progeny', which effectively meant the sterilisation of anyone considered to be 'hereditarily ill'. So-called Hereditary Health Courts were set up to rule on individual cases. Where to draw the line, though? Nazi ideas of racial flaws included schizophrenia and manic depression, as well as Huntingdon's chorea, hereditary blindness, hereditary deafness, hereditary epilepsy, and chronic alcoholism. In the next ten years, around 400,000 Germans were to be sterilised under this law.

By the end of the year, the Nazis had turned their attention to criminals and other members of what could be regarded as the general lower order; here again there was a hereditary twist to their thinking with claims that habitual criminals had inherited this trait from their forebears. The term 'vagrant' was an extremely vague label and seemed to encompass almost anyone who roused Nazi suspicions but who did not readily fall into one of the more clearly defined categories. Although many of those arrested were soon released, many others, seen as 'disorderly vagrants', were imprisoned or forced to join labour schemes. The Law against Dangerous Habitual Criminals already allowed for the imprisonment of anyone with two criminal convictions for an unlimited period in protective custody – that term again – and now it was extended to cover 'beggars, vagabonds, pimps, prostitutes and the workshy'.

It was inevitable that the homosexual community would eventually be targeted and in June 1935, the criminal code was amended to include any form of 'criminal indecency' between men, and behaviour likely to offend 'public morality'. Homosexual men now faced up to ten years in prison. The same month, the Nazis took further steps to, in their view, cleanse the nation with an amendment to the Law for the Prevention of Hereditarily Diseased Progeny: compulsory abortions could now be carried out on 'hereditarily ill women or women who become pregnant by a hereditarily ill partner' up to six months into their pregnancy. The Law for the Protection of German Blood and German Honour – one of the so-called Nuremburg Laws passed in September 1935 – already prohibited marriages and extra-marital relations between Aryans and non-Aryans; in November 1935, the Ministry of the Interior introduced rules requiring couples to provide 'testimonials of fitness to marry'.

The second Nuremburg Law, the Reich Citizenship Law, stripped Jews of their German citizenship and introduced a new distinction between 'Reich citizens' and 'nationals' intended to prevent 'progeny deleterious to German blood'.

Finally, the Nazis turned upon religion. Jehovah's Witnesses would not undertake military service, and since they also believed in the imminent return of a Messiah who, in their eyes, was obviously not Adolf Hitler, they too were marched into the camps. Roman Catholics might have felt themselves safe after Hitler signed a concordat with the Vatican guaranteeing the freedom of the Catholic Church to conduct its own affairs without interference from the State. That the concordat was negotiated by the former German Chancellor, and now Vice Chancellor, Franz von Papen, the son of a wealthy Catholic family, should have been of additional comfort. But Church leaders who opposed Nazism were not safe; within days of the concordat being signed in July 1934, throughout Germany Catholic priests and nuns were being arrested on trumped-up charges.

Then, in the Olympic Year of 1936, Pastor Martin Niemöller of the Confessional Church published a major document opposing the Nazis' religious policies. Niemöller had been an early supporter of Hitler, and in 1933 had described the Nazi programme as a 'renewal movement based on a Christian moral foundation'. The following year, he published his autobiography *From U-Boat to Pulpit*, a right-wing nationalist view of the war and its aftermath which was popular with Nazi Party members and sold 90,000 copies in its first few weeks. He seemed to agree with Hitler's views on race and nationhood, but not with his approach to religion. Now the publication of Niemöller's views triggered a purge of the Protestant Church too.

Yet, despite all this, the average German citizen – provided they were of Aryan stock, heterosexual, and hardworking – did not seem to mind trading other people's personal freedoms for the economic miracle that was apparently taking place in their country. When Hitler came to power early in 1933, German unemployment stood at just over six million. By the time the world descended on Berlin for the Olympic Games three years later, that had fallen to two million. But was it an economic miracle?

There were a number of factors responsible for the drop in numbers, not all of them the sign of a burgeoning economy. Jews had lost their citizenship and were therefore not included in the unemployment figures, even though they had also lost their jobs under the Nazis. Women were removed from the statistics. And the threat of a concentration camp place for the 'workshy' presumably encouraged people to take whatever job was going. In March 1935, Hitler announced that he would introduce military conscription; thousands of young men would soon be removed from the unemployment figures when they were drafted into the army. And an army needs weapons, so the need for munitions workers further reduced the figure.

There were many tangible benefits, however. The Nazis had introduced a public works scheme and thousands more men were made to join the *Reichsarbeitsdienst* (National Labour Service) to build new autobahns, dig irrigation ditches, and plant new forests. The autobahn programme, announced in February 1933, was huge. Hitler himself turned over the first spadeful of earth outside Frankfurt in September that year, and under the direction of chief engineer Fritz Todt, the fourteen-mile motorway between Frankfurt and Darmstadt was opened on 19 May 1935. The autobahn programme provided immediate work for 100,000 workers and eventually assured wages for some half a million. It certainly impressed Olympic visitors. Hitler also encouraged the mass production of wireless sets, not least as a means of supplying a steady stream of Nazi propaganda to the German people. Youth unemployment was dealt with by the Voluntary Labour Service and the Voluntary Youth Service, whose members also planted forests, repaired riverbanks, and helped reclaim wasteland. The German Labour Front, meanwhile, looked after the workers' interests – trades unions had been banned – although in return for not being sacked on the spot, workers could leave their job only with permission from the government, which alone arranged new jobs.

Writing in the *Daily Herald* in April 1933, Hannen Swaffer had picked up on the story of Walther Rathenau, the industrialist and liberal politician who in 1922 had become the Weimar Republic's Foreign Minister – and so was the first Jew to hold a Cabinet post in Germany – and was murdered six months later: 'he was assassinated by a group of fanatics, officers and students, who believed that he was a traitor – and only because he was a Jew ... Now he is to be killed a second time – squares and streets called after Walther Rathenau in various towns will now bear Adolf Hitler's name.' In the same newspaper, Madame Tussaud's exhibition in Baker Street advertised its 'new model – Herr Adolf Hitler'.

Anyone who stood in Hitler's way would be eliminated, even men who had once been his staunchest allies. Ernst Röhm, who had taken the German Workers' Party and turned it into the National Socialist German Workers' Party that, under Hitler, became the Nazi Party, was one such man. Hitler and Röhm had been close friends for more than a decade, but Röhm was unhappy with the way that the Nazi revolution was slowing down, and only his paramilitary SA stormtroopers could speed it up again with a second revolution. When Röhm wanted the SA integrated into the new Wehrmacht that was being prepared to replace the Reichswehr, the regular German armed forces since 1919, the old generals would not hear of it, and Hitler wasn't keen either. He knew that he could maintain power only if the Reichswehr was with him. After failing to talk Röhm round, he accused his former friend of plotting a putsch, and on the night of 30 June 1934, Röhm and other leaders of the SA were murdered by members of Heinrich Himmler's SS. The 'Night of the Long Knives' or the 'Blood Purge', as it became known, accounted for hundreds of other troublesome figures, including Kurt von Schleicher, the last Chancellor of the Weimar Republic, and Gustav von Kahr who, eleven years earlier, in the aftermath of Hitler's failed Munich beer hall putsch, had declared the Nazi Party a banned organisation.

Opposition at home silenced, Adolf Hitler could now fully focus on his plans to continue Germany's long-held goal of 'Lebensraum'.

Chapter 9

Hitler's Games

'Hitler, we who covered the Games had to concede, turned the Olympics into a dazzling propaganda success for his barbarian regime.'

William L. Shirer

On 5 August 1936, the recently knighted British Conservative MP Henry 'Chips' Channon arrived in Berlin. The American-born Channon had inherited enough money for him never to have to work again; he and his wife, Honor, a Guinness heiress, ran one of the most hospitable houses in London. Now, the Channons were in the German capital to be themselves entertained by the old aristocracy and the new regime. On the afternoon of their arrival on a flight from Gatwick – the home of the Surrey Aero Club had recently been licensed as a public aerodrome – they went for a walk. In his diary, Channon wrote, 'Berlin was crowded with foreigners and the streets beflagged. Honor and I went for a walk down the Unter den Linden, an avenue of banners blowing in the breeze, and everywhere we heard the radio booming "Achtung", and then giving the latest Olympic result.'

When the International Olympic Committee met in Barcelona in April 1931 and recommended Berlin as the stage for the 1936 Olympic Games, they awarded them to what was still a democracy. By the time those Games got under way five years later, Germany was in the grasp of a fascist dictatorship and the Olympics had been delivered into the hands of one of the most evil regimes the world has ever seen.

The Nazis had persuaded the International Olympic Committee and several governments – albeit fairly apathetic ones – that they could stage a fair and free Olympics. And, having been allowed to keep the Games, they indulged in a few cosmetic measures – removing anti-Jewish posters for a couple of weeks; ordering their followers to be pleasant to foreigners – even if they looked like Jews – all of which sent most people away with a fairly relaxed view of life in the Third Reich. Visitors went home blissfully unaware that a few miles from the Olympic Stadium, a new concentration camp had just been opened. While spectators enjoyed the great athletic spectacle, just a short train ride away, Jews, gypsies, communists, and other enemies of the Nazi State languished with no hope and no future.

Yet a full two years before the Berlin Olympics, some British sportsmen were already seeing for themselves the changes that had overtaken Germany, and how sport and politics were inexorably intertwined in the Third Reich. In May 1934, Derby County, then a leading team in English football, made a four-match visit to Germany. By train to Dover and then a cross-Channel steamer to Ostend, the Derby party eventually reached the German border to find a country swathed in the swastika emblem; the Nazi State was firmly established. Dave Holford was then a 19-year-old outside-left from Scarborough, excited to be included in the tour party despite his lack of experience. He was also staggered by what he saw in Germany:

> Everywhere we went, the swastika was flying. If you said: 'Good morning,' they'd reply with 'Heil Hitler'. If you went into a cafe and said, 'Good evening,' they would respond with 'Heil Hitler.' It was a country where everything had a military overtone. Even then, it occurred to us that this was a nation preparing for war.

Derby played in Cologne, Dusseldorf, Frankfurt, and Dortmund. All agreed that if the football had been hard work, overall, the tour had been an enjoyable one. Good hotels and plenty of time to relax and enjoy the scenery were just the ticket after a strenuous English season. There was, though, one overriding blot on the collective memory. Just as the England team would be obliged to do in Berlin, four years later, the Derby players of 1934 were ordered to give the Nazi salute before each game. George Collin, a full-back from County Durham, remembered their dilemma:

> We told the manager, George Jobey, that we didn't want to do it. He spoke with the directors, but they said that the British ambassador insisted we must. He said that the Foreign Office were afraid of causing an international incident if we refused. It would be a snub to Hitler. So, we

did as we were told. All except our goalkeeper, Jack Kirby, that is. Jack was adamant that he wouldn't give the salute. When the time came, he just kept his arm down and almost turned his back on the dignitaries. If anyone noticed, they didn't say anything.

Thereafter, every British team which visited Germany had a similar story to tell, although when Manchester City went there in May 1937, at the end of a season in which they had won the Football League championship, they decided on a collective response to Hitler's regime. Despite having just won the title, City, like Derby before them, found it hard going and won only one of their five matches. Peter Doherty, their Irish international inside-forward, brought back vivid memories of the trip:

Most of their players seemed to be in the German army already and were sent away to special camps to prepare for the games. It was a shock. We'd just had a long, hard season and went there for a holiday. One of the games was against a German representative team in the Olympic Stadium in Berlin. The entire stadium was swarming with armed guards, all wearing swastikas. We knew we'd be expected to give the Nazi salute before the kick-off, but when the time came we just stood to attention. Afterwards we were treated with enormous kindness, though, and the Germans just seemed to want to send us away with a favourable impression of their country. But you couldn't fail to see the military preparations everywhere. The whole country seemed to be one huge armed camp.

In 1938, England would give the full-flung version of the Nazi salute after Sir Neville Henderson, the pro-appeasement British ambassador to Berlin, persuaded the FA secretary, Stanley Rous, and a committee man, Charles Wreford Brown, that there would be an international incident if they did not; and, anyway, he pointed out, it was simply a courtesy to their hosts, not an endorsement of Hitler's regime. Perhaps most importantly, it would 'get the crowd in a good mood'. The England captain, Eddie Hapgood, wrote later: 'The worst moment in my life, and one I would not willingly go through again, was giving the Nazi salute in Berlin.'

Frank Broome of Aston Villa would have the unusual experience of being required to give the Nazi salute twice in as many days in May 1938.

> The Germans had invaded Austria the previous March and now there wasn't a separate Austrian international team – which had been one of the strongest on the Continent – just one for 'Greater Germany'. England were due to play in Berlin, but the FA told the Germans that they couldn't include any Austrian internationals. They agreed on the proviso that Villa would play a German eleven the following day, and that could include Austrians. What struck me, though, was how the military was everywhere. You couldn't possibly have visited Germany and not realised that they were gearing up for war.

The FA's hope that Germany would not benefit from the Anschluss was realised. England won 6–3 in the Olympic Stadium, although one of the German goals was still scored by an Austrian, Hans Presser from Rapid Vienna. The following day, Aston Villa beat a German Select XI 3–2 before 110,000 spectators who sweltered in 90-degree heat at the Reichssportfield. This German team contained no less than nine Austrian internationals. Broome scored in both games, only twenty-four hours apart.

Whether being required to give the Nazi salute had any bearing on the varied reactions of British sport to the regime is a judgement now difficult to make, but while the disgruntled footballers were all working-class professionals – Jack Kirby himself had grown up in the South Derbyshire coalfield – the people charged with Britain's Olympic dreams were all solidly amateur, and aristocratic at that. Viscount Portal, the president of the British Olympic Association (BOA), was a good shot, an excellent fly-fisherman, maintained a stud and yachted. The BOA's chairman, Lord Burghley, was one of Britain's most famous athletes who had won gold in the 400m hurdles at the 1928 Amsterdam Games and silver as a member of the 4 x 400m relay team in Los Angeles. Burghley, educated at Magdalene College, Cambridge, and a Conservative MP, was one of Britain's three representatives on the IOC, along with Lord Aberdare, a fine tennis player in his days at Winchester and Oxford, and Tonbridge-educated Sir Noel Curtis-Bennett, a distinguished civil servant whose brother was a famous criminal lawyer. In January 1936, while addressing a lunch given by the British Ice Hockey Association for the American ice hockey team, which was on its way to the Winter Games at Garmisch-Partenkirchen, Curtis-Bennett complained: 'There are a lot of well-meaning busybodies who are trying to mix sport with politics.' One can assume that he was not referring to the Nazi government of Germany.

The debate in Britain rumbled on. The Oxford University undergraduate magazine *Isis* claimed that the 1936 Olympics would take place in a 'hate-poisoned, crazy atmosphere'. Lord Aberdare responded through the *Oxford Magazine*, long regarded as the official commentator on university affairs:

> These Games are entirely in the hands of the International Olympic Committee ... seriously alarmed at the time of the ill-treatment of the Jews ... they got guarantees from the German authorities that German Jews of all nations will be welcome ... Germany will be represented by more Jews than has ever been the case before.

Aberdare's point of view was not shared by another Oxford man, Dr William Temple, a former Balliol student and president of the Union, and now Archbishop of York. Temple, a fierce critic of the Nazi regime throughout the 1930s, attempted to get a letter to Hitler, pleading with him to remember the true Olympic spirit and 'show yourself no less generous than the Greeks ... Issue a general act of amnesty for the benefit of all those who are suffering imprisonment for religious or racial reasons.' The BOA immediately distanced itself from Temple's missive, which was sent through the German Organising Committee and is highly unlikely ever to have been passed on to the Führer.

Besides liberal churchmen like Temple, other voices were now raised against Britain having anything to do with the Berlin Olympics. Newspapers such as the liberal *Manchester Guardian* and the Labour-supporting *Daily Herald* were joined by the Trades Union Congress, whose general secretary, Sir Walter Citrine, became involved in a controversial sporting fixture between England and Germany. Unlike the debate raging in America, the issue of whether to take part in the Olympic Games had been slow to take off in Britain, but at the end of 1935 there came an event which triggered a huge reaction. In December that year, England were due to play Germany in an international football match at White Hart Lane, the home of Tottenham Hotspur, a club which, by an unfortunate coincidence, numbered many Jewish people among its supporters. In mid-October, there were reports in British and American newspapers of a young Jewish footballer who had been beaten to death after a game in Upper Silesia. Accounts varied: Edumund Baumgartner was a member of the crowd and had been killed by Nazi supporters at the end of the game; or he had been murdered on the pitch after putting his team, Rybnik, in front against Ratibor. The German chargé d'affaires in London, Prince Bismarck, was summoned to the Foreign Office to explain but instead claimed that the whole thing had been invented by the American press. In late October, an anti-Nazi rally attended by 18,000 people in Hyde Park heard Clement Attlee, the new leader of the Labour Party, warn that what was happening in Germany 'would lead the world to war and destruction'. Again, there were demands for the football international to be called off.

The most alarming feature of the game was that over 10,000 German fans would be travelling to London to see their team in action, and they planned to march to White Hart Lane through predominantly Jewish neighbourhoods. The *Manchester Guardian* reported that anti-Nazi supporters were planning to distribute leaflets outside all London's major football grounds, highlighting the Baumgartner business and calling for the England–Germany game to be cancelled. When the newspaper asked the Tottenham secretary for his opinion, he said that it was really none of the club's business. The game was an international fixture arranged by the Football Association, whose attention they had drawn to protest letters received by the club. The Anti-Nazi Council wrote to the FA, pointing out that the Nazis would simply use the game as a propaganda opportunity, while the TUC asked to meet with the Home Secretary.

On 1 December 1935, the *Observer* reported:

> Sir John Simon, the Home Secretary, yesterday made arrangements to receive tomorrow a deputation representing the General Council of the Trades Union Congress who had appealed to him to prohibit the match, on the grounds that it was possible the German supporters would pass in procession through London streets on the day of the match. Sir John Simon, in reply to the protest, said he was ready to receive a deputation, but he did not think that interference

on the part of the Government was called for, and he stated that the introduction of political feeling into what should surely be a purely sporting contest was most undesirable. Sir Walter Citrine, secretary of the General Council of the TUC, in a further letter to Sir John Simon, said that 'such a large and carefully organised Nazi contingent coming to London might confirm the impression among people in this country that the event is being regarded as of some political importance by the visitors.' Dr Von Hoesch, the German ambassador, called at the Foreign Office in connection with the matter. He discussed it with an official, the upshot of the conversation being that both governments are of the same mind – that the match should be regarded purely as a sporting event.

The British government obviously already agreed. One month earlier, a Foreign Office official called Ralph Wigram had told the Home Office that 'the match should help to promote friendly relations between our two countries'. This opinion was from the man who was providing Winston Churchill with intelligence about German rearmament. Just over twelve months later, Wigram died in mysterious circumstances, officially from a pulmonary haemorrhage, although there were also suggestions that he had committed suicide because he was deeply depressed by the international situation. Nevertheless, it seems that the Foreign Office wanted the game to go ahead; the Home Office would rather it did not – but did not see how they could prevent it. Their dilemma became even greater when it was announced that the Nazis' Reich Sports Minister, Hans von Tschammer und Osten, together with two senior officials charged with delivering the Berlin Olympics, Dr Theodor Lewald and Carl Diem, would visit London in early December, their main intention being to attend the international.

On 1 December, the *Observer* told its readers:

> It is possible that a representative of the German Embassy will be present to meet the German football team when they arrive by air at Croydon tomorrow for their match against England at Tottenham on Wednesday. The German players intend to stay four days, leaving the day after the match. A motor-tour of London has been planned for them, and it

is also possible that they will watch the King drive in State along the Mall on his way to open Parliament on Tuesday. No recent sporting event has been treated with such high seriousness in Germany as this match. Cheap trips to London and back – 60 marks (£3 at par) – have made it possible for 10,000 Germans to travel to England to see the match. Between 1,600 and 1,800 passengers will disembark from the *Columbus* at Southampton early on Wednesday morning. Three special trains will convey them to Waterloo. After a trip round London and lunch, they will proceed to the football ground. Between 7,500 and 8,000 Germans will travel via Dover, and special trains will bring them to London. A description will be broadcast throughout Germany. Sir Percy Vincent, the Lord Mayor, will attend the match with the sheriffs.

The Foreign Office was sending two representatives to the match itself, but not to the official dinner at the Victoria Hotel, given in the Germans' honour by the FA. There would be no royal presence either. The Prince of Wales had told the German ambassador that he would attend, but in the event, he was not among the crowd of 54,000 who saw England win a good-natured, sporting game by three goals to nil as the Union Flag and the swastika fluttered side by side over White Hart Lane's main stand. Before the game, there had been fourteen arrests for insulting behaviour outside the ground, all of them people demonstrating against Nazism. The 10,000-strong German contingent were impeccably behaved.

At the post-match banquet, Sir Charles Clegg, the FA chairman, clearly irritated, chose to criticise the TUC. The following day, Sir Walter Citrine lashed back: 'So far as the remarks about perverting football into politics are concerned, the trouble is that Sir Charles Clegg does not bother to inform himself of the nature of sport in Germany. If he did, he would realise that football there is part of the Nazi regime.' Citrine also issued a pamphlet, pointing out that Felix Linnemann, head of the German FA, held his job only at the whim of the Reich Sports Leader. The FA secretary, Stanley Rous, wrote later: 'If the Government of the day does not stop a match, how can sporting bodies grade the character and politics of another country?'

Olympic year dawning, and the political furore surrounding the football international over, those hoping for a smoother passage towards

Above: The horrors of the Great War. Blinded Allied troops lying in the open at a first-aid post. *Authors' collection*

Right: Children use worthless currency as building blocks. By November 1923, 4 trillion German marks would buy just one US dollar, while bank interest rates stood at 900 per cent. *Illustrated London News*

Workers employed in building the autobahns greet Hitler as he arrives to open another section of Germany's new road network. *Authors' collection*

Inmates under SA guard at the Oranienburg camp near Berlin, pictured shortly after Hitler came to power in 1933. *USHMM, courtesy of National Archives and Records Administration, College Park*

Above: April 1933, Nazi stormtroopers block the entrance to a Jewish-owned store in Berlin. *USHMM, courtesy of National Archives and Records Administration, College Park*

Right: Adolf Hitler in a suitably dynamic pose for the man who saw himself as Germany's saviour. Millions of Germans agreed with him. *Illustrated London News*

Derby County goalkeeper Jack Kirby is the only player refusing to give the Nazi salute when the club played in Berlin in 1934. *Authors' collection*

Oswald Mosley is saluted by members of his British Union of Fascists. *Alamy*

Jimmy Thomas MP, the man at the centre of one of the biggest political scandals of the 1930s. *Authors' collection*

Crowds queuing to attend the murder trial of socialite Elvira Barney at the Old Bailey in 1932. *Alamy*

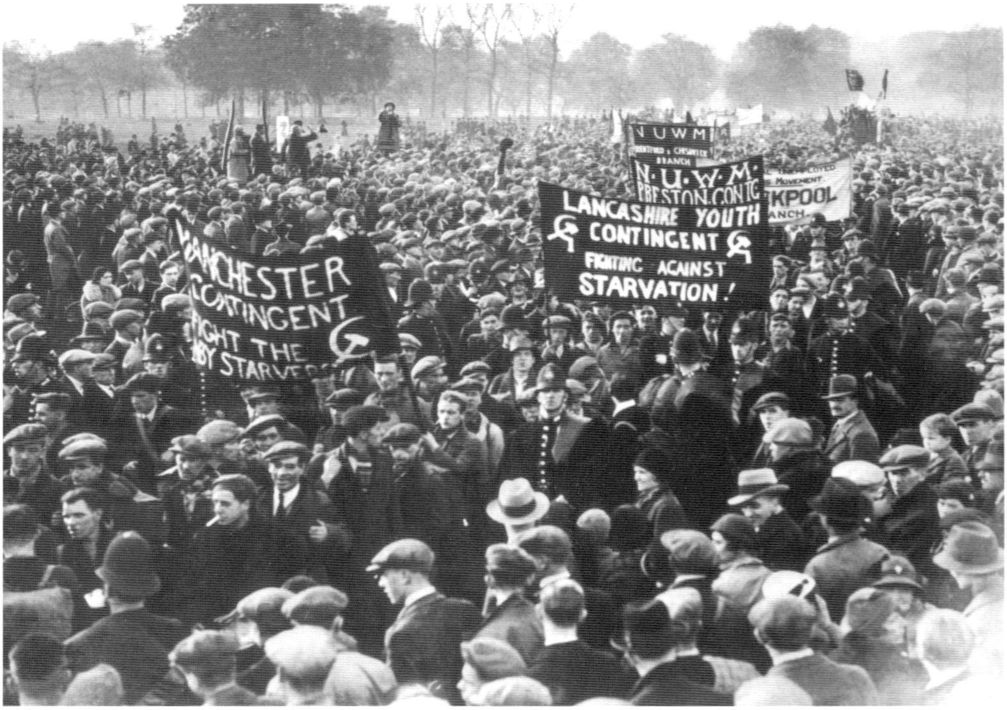

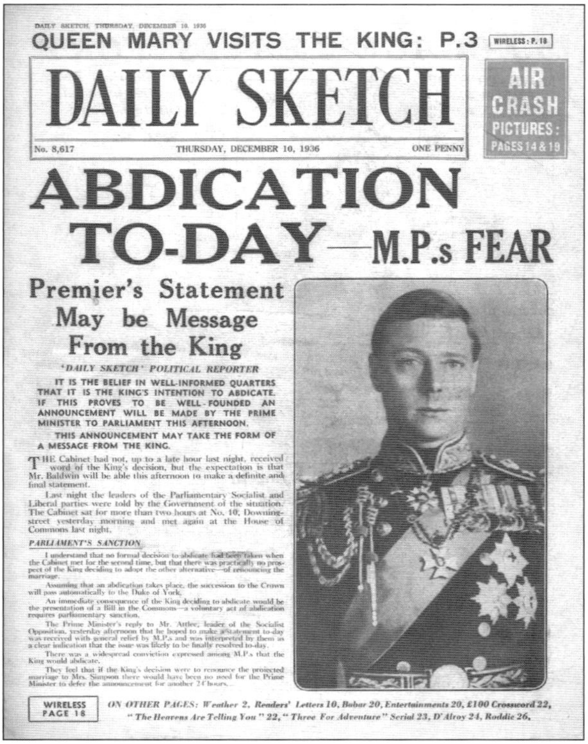

DAILY SKETCH, THURSDAY, DECEMBER 10, 1936

QUEEN MARY VISITS THE KING: P.3

WIRELESS: P. 18

DAILY SKETCH

AIR CRASH PICTURES: PAGES 14 & 19

No. 8,617 THURSDAY, DECEMBER 10, 1936 ONE PENNY

ABDICATION TO-DAY—M.P.s FEAR

Premier's Statement May be Message From the King

'DAILY SKETCH' POLITICAL REPORTER

IT IS THE BELIEF IN WELL-INFORMED QUARTERS THAT IT IS THE KING'S INTENTION TO ABDICATE. IF THIS PROVES TO BE WELL-FOUNDED AN ANNOUNCEMENT WILL BE MADE BY THE PRIME MINISTER TO PARLIAMENT THIS AFTERNOON.

THIS ANNOUNCEMENT MAY TAKE THE FORM OF A MESSAGE FROM THE KING.

THE Cabinet had not, up to a late hour last night, received word of the King's decision, but the expectation is that Mr. Baldwin will be able this afternoon to make a definite and final statement.

Last night the leaders of the Parliamentary Socialist and Liberal parties were told by the Government of the situation. The Cabinet sat for more than two hours at No. 10, Downing-street yesterday morning and met again at the House of Commons last night.

PARLIAMENT'S SANCTION

I understand that no formal decision to abdicate had been taken when the Cabinet met for the second time, but that there was practically no prospect of the King deciding to adopt the other alternative—of renouncing the marriage.

Assuming that an abdication takes place, the succession to the Crown will pass automatically to the Duke of York.

An immediate consequence of the King deciding to abdicate would be the presentation of a Bill in the Commons—a voluntary act of abdication requires parliamentary sanction.

The Prime Minister's reply to Mr. Attlee, leader of the Socialist Opposition, yesterday afternoon that he hoped to make a statement to-day was received with general relief by M.P.s and was interpreted by them as a clear indication that the issue was likely to be finally resolved to-day.

There was a widespread conviction expressed among M.P.s that the King would abdicate.

They feel that if the King's decision were to renounce the projected marriage to Mrs. Simpson there would have been no need for the Prime Minister to defer the announcement for another 24 hours.

WIRELESS PAGE 18

ON OTHER PAGES: Weather 2, Readers' Letters 10, Bubar 20, Entertainments 20, £100 Crossword 22, "The Heavens Are Telling You" 22, "Three For Adventure" Serial 23, D'Alroy 24, Roddie 26,

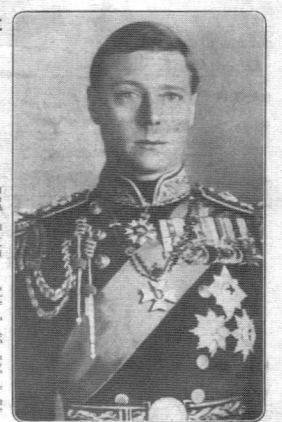

Above: 'Hunger marchers' descend on Hyde Park in 1932. *Alamy*

Left: Now Britain knows. The *Daily Sketch* reports on the impending abdication of Edward VIII in 1936. *Alamy*

Right: Clement Attlee, the leader of the Labour Party. *Eon Images: www.eonimages.com*

Below: Prime Minister Stanley Baldwin (left) and Winston Churchill. *Alamy*

Above: Peace in our time? On his return from Munich, Prime Minister Neville Chamberlain waves that infamous piece of paper. *Alamy*

Left: Police officers at Welshpool explain about gas masks. The van in the background was used as a testing chamber for the masks. *National Library of Wales/Geoff Charles*

Britain sending a team to the Berlin Games were soon to receive a rude awakening. On 7 March 1936, one month after he had officially opened the Winter Games at Garmisch-Partenkirchen, Adolf Hitler violated the Treaty of Versailles and the Locarno Pact by sending German military forces into the Rhineland and occupying the hitherto demilitarised buffer zone between Germany and France. It was Hitler's most blatantly provocative act so far, one daring the international community to react. So far as the Summer Games were concerned, there was inevitable concern in France. How could a nation which had already suffered dreadfully at the hands of Germany in one devastating war take part in the world's greatest sporting festival in Berlin when German soldiers were again poised on her borders?

The crisis can be measured by the words of Britain's Foreign Secretary, Anthony Eden, who, the following day, wrote:

> We must discourage any military action by France against Germany. A possible course which might have its advocates would be for the Locarno signatories to call upon Germany to evacuate the Rhineland. It is difficult now to suppose that Herr Hitler could agree to such a demand, and it certainly should not be made unless the Powers who made it were prepared to enforce it by military action.

Paris-Soir suggested that a boycott of the Berlin Games would not only serve to embarrass Germany, it would also cost the Nazis several million pounds in foreign currency. In the corridors of the League of Nations, the idea of a boycott was again floated, while several British newspapers suggested that the Games could not now go ahead. The *Daily Telegraph* went so far as to claim that the Summer Olympiad was about to be cancelled, but the British Olympic Committee countered swiftly with a rebuttal.

Indeed, ten days after Hitler's march into the Rhineland, the BOC made a public appeal in *The Times*, asking for funds to send its athletes to Berlin. Over the signatures of the Lords Portal, Aberdare, and Burghley, and Sir Noel Curtis-Bennett, it read:

> The British Olympic Council are convinced that in sending a team to Berlin they are acting in the best interests of sport. The Olympic Games have always stood for the ideal of

harmony and reconciliation between nations, and it would be nothing short of a calamity if, at this very critical stage in world affairs, this country, to whom the world so often looks for a lead, were not fully represented.

Other members of the BOC simply just did not like the way the Nazis had 'professionalised' Olympic sport. Sir Arnold Lunn, whose family owned the Lunn travel agency which became Lunn Poly, was the 'father of alpine ski racing'; not least, he was the man who invented the slalom. Lunn led the British team to the Winter Games. The British were amateurs, in contrast to the German team, which was sponsored by the State. This angered Lunn. 'There are still some people who ski just for fun,' he told the German media.

In 1936, all British Olympic sport was 100 per cent amateur. Even top-flight track and field athletics, which for many years had been opened to the working class, remained staunchly amateur. Although there were plenty of prizes such as canteens of cutlery and clocks for the winners of meetings all over the country, its ranks remained officially unpaid. Two weeks after the German reoccupation of the Rhineland, the Amateur Athletic Association held its annual meeting in London. One of the AAA's affiliate members was the National Workers' Sports Association (later, the British Workers' Sports Association), which had been founded at a meeting at Transport House, headquarters of the Labour Party, on 26 July 1930. The NWSA tabled a motion calling for Britain to withdraw from the Berlin Games. This time, the mood was different, almost certainly due to the situation in the Rhineland; Hitler's trampling over international agreements had brought his regime into sharper focus still. Now there was hardly a speaker at the AAA meeting who did not harshly criticise Germany.

Yet the question of whether Britain should boycott Berlin was still one that agonised most delegates. Britain had just been to Germany to participate in the Winter Games, so not to take part in the Summer Games would be inconsistent, and probably pointless. The *Manchester Guardian* reported the feeling that isolating Germany at this time would surely be a dangerous move; tact was needed, not an increase 'in the bitterness which she at present feels for her neighbours'. One proponent of Britain's continued involvement was the Jewish sprinter, Harold Abrahams, who had won gold at Paris in 1924. The former Cambridge University student felt that Britain's presence at the Games could have only a positive effect on the delicate international situation. The NWSA agreed to defer a vote on their motion; when it was finally taken, at an extraordinary general meeting in May, it was defeated by 200 votes to eight.

The position of the AAA, the British Olympic Committee, and the British government was that, while obviously it would have been much better if the Games had not been awarded to Berlin in the first place, it was now far too late to do anything about it. In any event, if they themselves boycotted Berlin simply because they did not agree with the politics of the host nation, then how could the British position be that sport and politics must not be mixed? Of course, this might be seen as a convenient get-out clause: surely, when that same host nation's politics included banning athletes simply on the grounds of their religion or colour, did not morality have to be considered?

There was also an irony in that, had Berlin not been awarded the 1936 Games, then they would have gone to Barcelona. After the effects that Nazism was having on Germany became clear, several 'counter Olympics' were planned by those favouring a boycott of Berlin. In Spain, an *Olimpiada Popular* (People's Olympic Games) was planned for Barcelona. The idea was supported by the left-wing coalition, the Popular Front, after its success in the Spanish elections of early 1936. No Spanish athletes would be sent to Berlin. Instead, they would compete in their own Games, the cost of which would be shared by the Spanish government, the regional government of Catalonia, and the city of Barcelona. Foreign teams would be accommodated in hotels constructed for the Barcelona World's Fair in 1929. The Barcelona Games were scheduled for 19–26 July.

A few days before these Games were due to begin, almost 6,000 athletes had been registered from twenty different nations. Spain had registered more than 4,000 competitors, France had sent a large team, and other participating nations included the USA, Great Britain, Holland, Belgium, Czechoslovakia, Denmark, Norway, Sweden, Palestine, and Russia. Teams were effectively representatives of workers' sports associations. In the American team was Bernard N. Danchik, a gymnast and a clerk with the Bookkeepers', Stenographers' and Accountants' Union in New York City. He was also a member of Rabbi Wise's Committee for Fair Play in Sports. Danchik sailed to Spain with a team of eight other American athletes, most sponsored by their trades unions. On 19 July, four days after their arrival, they were awakened by the sound of gunshots outside their Barcelona hotel. Rather than competing in the alternative Olympic Games, they had become eyewitnesses to the outbreak of the Spanish Civil War. On the third day of fighting, the athletes marched through the streets, demonstrating their support for the people's militia that had revolted against the army led by the fascist General Francisco Franco. When a French athlete was killed, the Spanish government ordered the evacuation of all foreign teams.

In June, the SS's own newspaper, *Der Schwarze Korps*, had commented on the white German heavyweight boxer Max Schmeling's unexpected victory over Joe Louis, an African American, in a non-title fight at Yankee Stadium: 'The sporting spirit of the great masses of population felt instinctively that our comrade saved the reputation of the white race...' In the House of Commons on 22 July 1936, less than two weeks before British athletes were due to parade at the opening ceremony in Berlin, Sir Geoffrey Mander, the Liberal spokesman on foreign policy, insisted that Anthony Eden demanded from the German government an assurance that the Olympic Games would not be used for propaganda purposes. A fellow Conservative, the Ayr MP, Lieutenant-Colonel Thomas Moore, jumped to the Foreign Secretary's aid, asking: 'Does the Right Honourable Gentleman not view with disfavour these impertinent pin-pricks to a friendly nation?' Moore was greeted with cries of 'Hear! Hear!' from the government benches.

Six days earlier, the Jewish track and field athlete Gretel Bergmann – who had just equalled the German and European high-jump record of 1.60 metres – had been told that her recent performances had not been good enough to win her a place in the German team after all. At 4.00 am on the day that Bergmann realised she had been used as a pawn in the sick game of Nazi propaganda, police surrounded all Roma encampments in Greater Berlin and transported the inhabitants and their wagons to Marzahn, an open field located near a cemetery and sewage dump in the east of the city, well away from the Olympic complex. Sanitary conditions were poor and contagious diseases soon began to flourish.

Meanwhile, as the youth of the world prepared to converge upon the Third Reich, on 16 July 1936, Victor Klemperer, who the previous year had been dismissed as a professor at Dresden Technical University, under the Law for the Restoration of a Professional Civil Service which excluded Jews and other political opponents of the Nazis from all civil service positions, had written in his diary, 'And where will we be in two months' time, once the Olympics is over and it is open season on the Jews?'

On 6 February 1936, in Garmisch-Partenkirchen, about 96 kilometres south of Munich, on the border between Bavaria and Austria, before the start of the Winter Olympics, 65,000 spectators had gathered to greet the 756 winter sportsmen and women of twenty-eight nations who lined up to march past the saluting base where Hitler, bareheaded despite a snowstorm, had already received a rapturous welcome. Like most teams, the British (who were wearing black armbands as a mark of respect to the late King George V, who had died at Sandringham on 20 January) raised their arms in the Olympic salute. This went down well in the stadium, being greeted by roars of approval from the thousands who assumed this was the Nazi salute. On 1 August 1936, at the opening ceremony for the Summer Games in Berlin, the British team instead favoured a smart eyes-right, a gesture that drew only polite applause from most of the 78,000 paying ticket holders in a crowd of 91,000.

The star of the Berlin Games was the black American athlete Jesse Owens, winner of five gold medals, who, so the story goes, was snubbed by Hitler, who refused to shake his hand. Owens himself was always happy to acknowledge that he had received a warm reception from German spectators at least, who even went so far as to chant his name: 'Yess-say... Oh-vens... Yess-say... Oh-vens...' And for a long time, he was also ready to point out that he, personally, had never been snubbed by Hitler. Eventually, however, constant denial became too much trouble and Owens just went along with the story. Later, he would say that he was so upset by Hitler's theories of a 'master race' that he fouled on the long jump take-off board. Today, one of the main thoroughfares leading to the Olympic Stadium in Berlin is named Jesse Owens Allee.

Whatever the truth behind Hitler's 'snub' to black athletes, the issue at least served to underline the true nature of the Olympic hosts. In the wrestling hall, Germany's Werner Seelenbinder, a staunch communist, had finished fourth in the Greco-Roman light-heavyweight division and was thus denied the opportunity to mount the winners' podium and defy Hitler by not giving the Nazi salute. After war was declared in September 1939, Seelenbinder joined the German resistance movement and was arrested in 1942. After two years of torture, he was beheaded in Brandenburg prison.

The Berlin Games ended on 16 August. Germany topped the table with eighty-nine medals, thirty-three of which were gold. Great Britain finished in tenth place with fourteen medals, including four gold. Five weeks earlier, half an hour's drive to the north of the Olympic

Stadium, a new concentration camp had been opened. The first inmates of Sachsenhausen had been convicted of no crimes. Now the Berlin Olympics were over, would the world begin to take notice?

In July, Victor Klemperer had wondered if, once the Games were over, it would be open season on Jews again. Now he had the answer. In late August, Klemperer was to write: 'I often very much doubt whether we shall actually survive the Third Reich.'

In the two months that followed the Games, Nazi persecution of the Jews resumed with further laws aimed at them. The Berlin Labour Court ruled that German employees who married Jews or other non-Aryans could be dismissed from their jobs, while Jewish-owned employment agencies were closed, as was the Association of Independent Artisans of the Jewish Faith, a German Jewish mutual aid society. Hans Frank, Reich Minister Without Portfolio, explained the need to exclude Jews from the legal profession: 'We National Socialists have started with anti-Semitism in our fight to free the German people, to re-establish a German Reich ... It took all the self-confidence of German manhood to withstand and to triumph in this fight to substitute the German spirit for Jewish corruption.' Jewish teachers were forbidden to tutor Aryan children. Jews who converted to Christianity and were baptised were still declared Jewish. And the Reich Chamber of Culture ordered all Jewish art dealers in Berlin to close their galleries by the end of the year.

Chapter 10

Pharaohs and a Führer

'Hitler ... took upon himself the responsibility of deciding who, in matters of culture, thought and acted like a Jew.'
Henry Grosshans

In 1934, Adolf Hitler told the world, 'I am in love with Nefertiti.' Coming from the promoter of the mythical Aryan race, it was an extraordinary statement. Of course, it was his way of telling everyone who cared that no amount of pleading on behalf of the Egyptian government was going to achieve the return to its homeland of the ancient bust of the Egyptian queen that had, for more than a decade, been the prize exhibit in Berlin's Agyptisches (Egyptian) Museum.

The bust was just one of thousands of ancient exotic artefacts that graced display cases in countless museums across Europe and North America. The first three decades of the twentieth century had been a golden era for archaeologists. Discoveries, or more accurately rediscoveries, had been made of several civilisations – of the Minoans at Knossos, the Hittites in Hattusas in modern Turkey, and at the supposed 'Lost City of the Incas' at Machu Picchu in Peru.

Along with other parts of Europe, and the USA, Germany had long held a fascination for all things ancient and Egyptian. The country had become a respected centre of Egyptology. Its government had financed an archaeological institute in Cairo. German researchers, like Adolf Erman and Heinrich Schafer, had helped decipher Egyptian grammar and art, and several American Egyptologists had chosen to train in Germany.

By the early 1910s, Egypt was awash with archaeological excavations financed by Europeans. Britain had been occupying the country since 1882 and its archaeologists had been running several excavation sites, most notably in the Valley of the Kings. Some 402 kilometres away to the north, in Amarna, archaeologist Ludwig Borchardt, leading a team from the German Oriental Company, uncovered the remains of the workshop of the sculptor Thutmose. Here, in 1912, amongst much unfinished work, Borchardt found a painted stucco-coated limestone bust. An object of remarkable quality and great beauty, it was determined to depict Queen Nefertiti, the principal wife of Pharoah Akhentaten.

The expedition was funded by James Simon, a wealthy German cotton manufacturer and social philanthropist, who, between 1897 and 1918, donated half a million gold marks to fund excavations in the Near East, more than even the Kaiser had given. Simon arranged for the bust to be taken to Berlin and, in 1920, he donated it, along with many other remarkable finds in his collection, to the Berlin museum in which it now rested. It quickly became one of the most copied works of ancient Egyptian art and is still considered an icon of feminine beauty.

In 1923, several British newspapers published what it claimed were the first photographs of the bust on display. The *Illustrated London News* described the queen as 'Tutankhamun's charming mother-in-law'. Britons were just as fascinated as their German cousins, but the connection to 'King Tut' made them especially so because they were also gripped by the news coming from the Valley of the Kings where a British-funded expedition, led by Howard Carter, was making its own remarkable discoveries – the tomb of Tutankhamun himself.

The valley was just across the Nile from the ancient city of Thebes, modern Luxor. Carter had initially travelled to Egypt to work as an artist recording finds and had worked on countless digs across the country, including at Amarna. In 1907, he took a job with Lord Carnarvon, the wealthy aristocrat and amateur Egyptologist. In 1914, when Carnarvon received a licence to search for the tomb of Tutankhamun, Carter had taken control.

In December 1922, *The Times* published a report by its Egypt correspondent, Arthur Merton, in which he revealed a 'remarkable archaeological discovery in Egypt':

> On Wednesday afternoon, Lord Carnarvon and Mr Howard Carter revealed to a large company what promises to be the most sensational Egyptological discovery of the century. The find consists of, among other objects, the funeral paraphernalia of the Egyptian King Tutankhamun.

The find had been much anticipated; the pair had been searching for the tomb of Tutankhamun for the best part of a decade, although the Great War had interrupted work for four years, and so little had been achieved that Carnarvon had given Carter just one more season of digging. As Carter would later say, 'We had almost made up our minds that we were beaten and were preparing to leave The Valley and try our luck elsewhere.'

But then, in November 1922, 'hardly had we set hoe to ground, in our last despairing effort, than we made a discovery that far exceeded our wildest dreams'. Supposedly, Carter was called to look at a spot where a young water fetcher had been digging with a stick. He had uncovered a stone step. Slow and careful work revealed an entire flight of them, leading down to a sealed door. Initially, thinking they might have discovered a cache of treasure, Carter had the site covered over while Carnarvon travelled from Britain. Three weeks later, Carter and Carnarvon broke open the door to reveal another chamber, itself containing sixteen steps down to another door. It was just the first of what proved to be several chambers.

In his book of 1923, *The Discovery of the Tomb of Tutankhamun*, Carter described what he saw when that door was prised open: 'At first I could see nothing, the hot air escaping from the chamber causing the candle flame to flicker, but presently, as my eyes grew accustomed to the light, details of the room within emerged slowly from the mist, strange animals, statues, and gold – everywhere the glint of gold.'

Carter and Carnarvon entered the chamber and stood surrounded by an amazing array of objects. According to Merton's words, distributed to newspapers across the land by the Press Association, they found 'magnificent coaches ... unnumerable [sic] boxes of exquisite workmanship ... inlaid with ebony and ivory'. Another box contained what were believed to be royal robes and golden sandals painted with hunting scenes.

> There was a stool of ebony, inlaid with ivory, with the most delicately carved ducks' feet; also a child's stool of fine workmanship. Beneath one of the coaches was the State throne of King Tutankhamun, probably one of the most beautiful objects of all ever discovered ... There were also four chariots, the sides of which were encrusted with semi-precious stones and rich gold decoration.

In the ancient Egyptian tradition, the burial had included 'trussed duck, haunches of venison' as 'provisions for the dead'. There were also 'some remarkable wreaths still looking evergreen, and one of the boxes contained rolls of papyri which are expected to render a mass of information'.

Indeed, it did. And much inspiration, too, for art and design, fashion and architecture. If Egyptology had been popular throughout the century, the latest discovery took it to fever pitch. Egyptian images and iconography appeared everywhere, even before the bulk of the treasures were removed. Due to what the *Illustrated London News* called 'hereditary tomb-robbers who lived in the area', great care was taken to ensure the security of the site and the finds. 'Guards are always on duty, and the whole valley closely patrolled by the Camel Corps.' It took two years of careful work before the mummified remains of the king himself, protected by its case and within its coffin, were found. Carnarvon had died in Cairo in April 1923 from blood poisoning after a severe mosquito bite became badly infected by a razor cut. Rumours of a supposed 'mummy's curse' found written on the wall of the tomb were, it is believed, the work of a newspaper reporter not given first access to the site. Members of the team who entered the tomb did not die at a greater rate than the rest of the population, and their deaths were not more mysterious. Carter, who continued working on the tomb, dismissed such talk as 'tommy-rot'.

Unlike those from Amarna, most of the finds remained on home soil, being exhibited at Cairo's Egyptian Museum. Although the British Museum contains many Egyptian artefacts, Tutankhamun's mummy is the only one in the Valley of the Kings that remains in its original tomb. What the British Museum did have, as early as November 1924, was its own copy of the bust of Nefertiti. Even the replica drew crowds to the museum's Egyptian Gallery to see what *The Sphere* called 'the most beautiful woman of old Egypt'. Over the next few years, thousands of copies were made and sold. Busts of an Egyptian queen graced homes around the world.

In 1929, the Egyptian government made concerted attempts to have Nefertiti returned home, claiming that the bust had been smuggled out of the country. The German government insisted that the object had been given to Borchardt as part of his share of the finds. Germany was very proud of its Egyptian collection, but Egyptology itself was about to face an existential crisis. With the rise of Nazism came a debate, in which many noted German academics became entangled, about just how appropriate the collecting of exotic cultural objects could be. Without much evidence, Leipzig University's Walther Wolf, a distinguished archaeologist and Egyptologist, sought to align his profession with his Nazi sympathies by suggesting that ancient Egyptian culture owed much to a sort of racial collective and suggested its pharaohs were führers. Others, including some of Wolf's own colleagues, argued that Egyptology concerned study of 'a foreign race, of a nature alien to us' and that it should be discouraged.

Then there were the people behind the discoveries. For three decades, James Simon was heralded as one of the greatest patrons in German museum history. But he, and his archaeologist Ludwig Borchardt, were both Jewish. Simon died in 1932, and Borchardt in Paris in 1938, having sought refuge there after the Nazis rose to power. The prejudices of anti-Jewish sentiment would see their contributions ignored for decades. From 1933, all objects donated by Jewish patrons or discovered by Jewish archaeologists were relabelled as 'gifts' with no mention of the name of their benefactors. In the UK, there were no such concerns. All things modern and exotic became more and more celebrated. Carter, who died in his flat close to the Royal Albert Hall in 1939, became the most famous archaeologist in Britain.

In Germany, it was not just historians and archaeologists who found their work in peril from Nazi ideology. Artists, designers, and architects, too, fell foul of the new regime. The Bauhaus School had been founded in Weimar in 1919 by architect Walter Gropius. It had moved to Dessau and eventually to Berlin. It promoted a radical re-imagining of design which balanced form and function, avoided ornamentation, and focused on creating buildings, objects, and art suited to a modern lifestyle. Its students studied materials and colour theory before taking classes in disciplines that included metalworking, weaving, pottery, cabinetmaking, wall-painting, and typography.

To take account of changes in manufacturing, from 1923 it began to concentrate on designing for mass production. Bauhaus's policy of accepting students from diverse social and educational backgrounds did not sit well with the growing antisemitism that swept across Germany. Neither did the school's employment of two masters of Jewish descent, or education of seventeen Jewish students. Gropius assured the authorities that all the students were genuine German 'Aryans' and that most of those of Jewish origin had been baptised into Christianity and were not receiving financial aid.

Bauhaus style – and the associated International style – were decreed as 'un-German'. Nazi writers had publicly criticised elements of design such as flat roofs, which they considered unsuitable to northern weather and so 'cosmopolitan modernism', 'foreign', and probably Jewish in origin. It was considered 'degenerate' and was accused of being a front for communists and social liberals. Under pressure from the Gestapo, who had entered it and interrogated its students and staff, the Berlin school closed in 1933. Many of its masters and students joined others and fled the country. Those who settled in the British Mandate of Palestine city of Tel Aviv built the world's largest collection of more than 4,000 Bauhaus-style buildings. Those who arrived in Britain joined an already-flourishing community of modernists. German emigres were not, it must be noted, universally welcomed in Britain. Anti-German sentiments dated back to the Great War, and there were pockets of antisemitism in Britain too. The newcomers were encouraged to avoid speaking German in public and to study British etiquette in order to blend in.

German Jew Erich Mendelsohn was a pioneer of modernism. In his homeland, his assets were seized by the Nazis, and he was struck from the list of the German Architects' Union and excluded from the Prussian Academy of Arts. He fled to England, where he was able to continue his work; perhaps his most famous building was the De La Warr Pavilion at Bexhill-on-Sea, which he co-designed. Sleek, sweeping, clean lines of Art Moderne, known more often as Art Deco after the Exposition Internationale des Arts Decoratifs et Industriels Moderne held in Paris in 1925, became hugely popular across the UK in the design of modern mansions and of many public and commercial buildings. In London, the Hoover Building and Broadcasting House reflected the ultra-modern design and construction. The Savoy, Dorchester, and Mayfair Hotels embraced Art Deco's elegant decadence. Further afield, buildings like the new Philharmonic Hall in Liverpool and the Midland Hotel in Morecambe, from a municipal complex in the centre of Derby complete with magistrates' court and open bus station, to homes in places as far flung as Bristol and Ilkley, Milford Haven, and the Isle of Wight, were all constructed in Art Deco style. Hundreds of cinemas across the land used Art Deco styles and motifs drawing inspiration from the treasures found in Egypt and 'the Orient', Africa, and the Far East. From architecture, this modernism translated itself into interior design and to fashion.

Adolf Hitler, meanwhile, was now much more concerned about finding more living space for the Aryan race.

Chapter 11

Flags Flying, Bands Playing...

'The stage seems set in Europe today for strife. Adolf Hitler, a little intoxicated with power and consumed with overwhelming ambition, is rattling his sword.'

E. F. Iddon, *Sunday Mercury*

Lebensraum – living space – had been the goal of Imperial Germany since the late nineteenth century. A German geographer and ethnographer called Friedrich Ratzel coined the term. Influenced by the work of Charles Darwin, Ratzel's theory was that species migration was a crucial factor in social adaptation and cultural change, but the growth of German industrialisation after the Franco-Prussian War of 1870 saw Lebensraum thought more of in economic terms – settling colonies that were rich in raw materials would help Germany become self-sufficient; the British and French colonies were classic examples – rather than the intellectual Ratzel's vague spiritual and nationalistic ideals.

Lebensraum became a key element for Germany's territorial ambitions during the Great War, but, long before that, many Germans had looked not only overseas but also to the east, to a region that they believed was wasted on 'racially inferior' people, for more living space – other people's living space.

During the war, when the British naval blockade meant material shortages at home, Germany had managed to extend her influence as far east as Minsk before defeat left her without any colonies at all, including the eastern military administration of 'Ober Ost', which it had just gained.

For Adolf Hitler, the sense of loss was immense. In *Mein Kampf*, he wrote, in typically turgid style:

> For it is not in colonial acquisitions that we must see the solution of this problem, but exclusively in the acquisition of a territory for settlement, which will enhance the area of the mother country, and hence not only keep the new

settlers in the most intimate community with the land of their origin, but secure for the total area those advantages which lie in its unified magnitude.

Lebensraum became the core of his foreign policy, a key component of his imperial and racist vision. But first he had to regain those parts of Germany that had been 'stolen' by the Treaty of Versailles, and after that bring all the German-speaking nations of Europe into Germany. Then he would deal with settling Germans in western Russia, and deporting Russians to Siberia. Within weeks of the Night of the Long Knives, violence, pure and simple, was the answer of Austrian Nazis when they tried to take over the government in Vienna. On 25 July 1934, they murdered the Austrian Chancellor, Englebert Dollfuss, in his chancellery. Hitler had already made clear his intention to take Austria into a union – Anschluss – with Germany, despite this being in direct contravention of the Treaty of Versailles. But then so much of what he was about to do would contravene that treaty.

Mussolini, quick to blame Hitler for Dollfuss's assassination, mobilised Italian troops on his country's border with Austria. Another attempted putsch had failed. Hitler backed off, replaced the German ambassador in Vienna with Franz von Papen, and prevented the conspirators in Dollfuss's death from entering Germany.

Then, in January 1935, a referendum was held to determine the status of the Territory of the Saar Basin, a region of Germany that since 1920 had been governed by Britain and France (with France given control of the coalmines there) under a League of Nations mandate. The Nazis' opponents within Germany had campaigned for a continuation of the mandate, and even Hitler was surprised when more than 90 per cent voted in favour of the Saar being returned to Germany. On 1 March 1935, the *Northern Daily Mail* reported:

> The almost frenzied rejoicings accompanying the handing over of the Saar to Germany today reached their peak when Herr Hitler made a surprise triumphal entry into Saarbrucken about noon ... thousands of Saarlanders and visitors from all parts of Germany stood in the streets and cheered tumultuously as the Führer's sleek black car glided through ... Shouts of 'Heil Hitler!', cheers, laughter and loud greetings rang from the open windows of the cafes which were crowded with rejoicing visitors.

The same month, after France announced that it was extending compulsory military service from one to two years, the German Cabinet passed a law introducing universal military conscription and fixing the strength of the Reichswehr at thirty-six divisions, some 360,000 men. Hitler, who had hurried back to Berlin from Bavaria, where he had been convalescing, issued a proclamation. Joseph Goebbels called foreign correspondents to the Propaganda Ministry, where he read to them Hitler's words:

> There is a cry for war today as if there had never been a world war or a Treaty of Versailles ... we recall Mr Baldwin's observation that any nation which fails to develop its defences will never find itself a powerful nation ... Germany was prepared to adopt the MacDonald plan. Germany took it as the groundwork of disarmament, but it was shattered on the opposition of other powers. Since disarmament has not come, Germany could no longer take part in such conferences.

The following day, the London *Sunday Dispatch* reported, 'According to opinion in Government circles, Germany has torn up the Treaty of Versailles defiantly before the rest of Europe.'

There was no cause for concern, however, at least according to the German Foreign Minister, Baron von Neurath, who told Reuters, 'Now that Germany has assumed what she considers necessary for equality, and Herr Hitler has announced that this force will never be used for the purposes of aggression, a general feeling of security should be more easily brought about.' All very well, but another war was now never far from anyone's mind. As far back as February 1933, Lord Londonderry, Britain's Air Minister, had warned the Air Commission of the Disarmament Conference in Geneva that 'the abolition of naval and military aircraft without effective control of civil aviation would only be to enhance indiscriminate bombardment from the air of the great centres of civilian population'. 'Even if military and naval aircraft were abolished, large airliners and other civil and commercial machines could speedily be modified for attacking purposes and used for bombing cities and towns,' he said.

In June 1935, Germany negotiated the Anglo-German Naval Agreement that regulated the size of the Kriegsmarine and the Royal

Navy. It was controversial because it allowed Germany to enlarge her navy beyond what had been set out in the Versailles Treaty, and the British had signed off on it without consulting the French and Italian governments. Nine months later, on 7 March 1936, German military forces re-entered the Rhineland. The Treaty of Versailles forbade German forces from all lands west of the Rhine and within 50km east of it. The Locarno Pact of 1925 had reaffirmed the national boundaries between Germany and France and between Germany and Belgium as set out at Versailles, and led, in 1926, to Germany joining the League of Nations. No longer was she an outcast. But, as Harold Nicolson wrote later, 'The Heavenly alchemy of the Locarno spirit, the triumphant splendour of those autumn days, did not prove of long endurance.'

Since 1930, the Rhineland had been a demilitarised zone after Allied forces withdrew from the territories they had occupied since 1919. The Rhineland was a major industrial region that produced coal, iron, and steel resources. It also presented a formidable natural barrier to neighbouring France. Hitler, who had withdrawn Germany from the League of Nations when he came to power in 1933, had had his eye on the Rhineland ever since, and now he marched 22,000 troops into it. The *Daily Mirror* reported:

> France, in January, warned Britain that if Germany attempted to militarise the Rhineland, 'France would be obliged to take military measures of the utmost importance.' These moves by Hitler may not indicate that he will launch an ultimatum or confront Europe with the accomplished fact of the remilitarisation of the Rhineland. His main purpose is probably to re-establish the sovereign rights of Germany over her own territory.

Hitler had attacked the 1935 Franco-Soviet Treaty of Mutual Assistance, the aim of which, so far as France was concerned, was to find herself a new ally and counteract the increasing strength of Germany, but Berlin reported that, in a note handed to foreign ambassadors that morning, he had offered to sign a twenty-five-year non-aggression pact in the west, if Britain and Italy agreed to be guarantors. He had also agreed to return to the League of Nations and withdraw his troops from the Rhineland – if France and Belgium also demilitarised their borders with Germany.

The League of Nations appeared to be quite happy with that. From Geneva, it issued a statement: 'The German memorandum is one of the most statesmanlike proposals that has ever emerged from any European chancellery, and the offer to return to the League disarms the French Government, which has always made this a preliminary consideration of any rapprochement with Germany.'

The *Sunday Pictorial* described the scene: 'Germany marched troops with flags flying and bands playing through the Rhineland ... and last night they were encamped on the French frontier at Saarbrucken and Strasbourg ... the German and French armies are separated only by the span of a bridge instead of a trip of thirty-one miles [49.8 kilometres].'

Neither France nor Britain – where public opinion was firmly against any action – was prepared for a military response, though. As Baron von Neurath had said a year earlier, 'I am sure that another war would end Europe.'

Chapter 12

A Most Inconvenient Dilemma

'All those who waited for vengeance for their crumbled temples may reassure themselves because we shall not go back.'

Benito Mussolini

On Wednesday, 2 October 1935, a German refugee, Dr E. Conze, gave a lecture at the start of a two-day conference arranged by the education committee of the Sheerness and District Economical Co-operative Society, at the Unity Hall in the Kent town.

Dr Conze, a member of the National Council of Labour Colleges, told his audience that, despite the title of his talk, 'Germany Yesterday and Today', there was no great difference between the Germany of yesterday and today. Germany's foreign policy had not been altered by Hitler coming to power: he was only continuing what others had been doing from 1918 to 1933. Germany had been preparing for a new war ever since the last one ended. Everyone in Germany was being impressed that they were a superior race and, as such, had a right to rule the world. After a few years of such teaching, they could imagine the whole nation willing to go to war. Initially there had been opposition from people who declared that whatever war may come, they would oppose it and shoot their officers at the first opportunity. Their mouths had to be closed, and so their leaders were sent to concentration camps. Free speech was suppressed. For three years before Hitler came to power, there was rule by emergency decree. Therefore, it had been difficult to say, 'Let us fight for democracy against the Nazis,' because there was no democracy for which to fight. The Germany of today was only the Germany of yesterday coming to maturity. The main purpose of Nazi and fascist movements was to prepare for a new war.

Dr Conze said that Germany and Italy were trying to do the same as Britain had done. One of the fundamental differences of the world today was that, while Britain had built her empire at a time when colonies could be got very cheaply, hungry countries like Germany, Italy, and Japan soon saw that the most prosperous countries were those with colonies. That is why they had turned to fascism. It was the only way 'that they can get a modern war'. Benito Mussolini, said Conze, had been drilling the entire Italian nation for twelve years. This was the purpose of fascism, he said: to gain an empire by war.

The day after Dr Conze delivered his lecture – Thursday, 3 October 1935 – the *Daily Herald*'s front-page headline broke the news: '50,000 ITALIANS INVADE ABYSSINIA – "WAR ABOUT TO BEGIN," MUSSOLINI'S CRY TO NATION.' It reported, 'Fifty thousand Italian troops with aeroplanes, tanks and artillery have advanced eighteen miles [30 kilometres] into territory claimed by Abyssinia ... In Rome last night it was admitted that troops had moved to "new and better positions".'

The *Manchester Guardian* reported that the long-expected invasion had begun at dawn as 'thousands of young Italian infantrymen cheering as they crossed the border from Eritrea, began the heavy slog up the valleys'. The newspaper said that Italian bombers had struck first at the border town of Adowa, the scene of Italy's humiliating defeat at the hands of the Abyssinians in 1896. Two of the bombers were reported to be piloted by Mussolini's sons, 19-year-old Vittorio and 18-year-old Bruno. His son-in-law, Count Galeazzo Ciano, piloted another.

The *News Chronicle* said that there were 'frenzied scenes in Rome where the British Legation was so strongly guarded as to resemble a fortress'. In the Italian capital, 'streets suddenly blazed with flags, loudspeakers in all public squares broadcast the National Anthem, marching songs and war hymns, children raised their voices, chanting the Fascist hymn'.

That day, according to Mussolini, some 20 million black-shirted fascists had dashed to their party headquarters in every city, town, and village in Italy, to gather around wireless sets and listen to his speech. Il Duce (The Leader) told the Italian nation:

> A solemn hour is approaching in the history of our country ... It is the most gigantic demonstration that the history of the human race records. Twenty million men with one heart, one will and one determination. This demonstration signifies that the identity between Italy and Fascism is complete, absolute and unalterable ... For many months the wheel of

destiny under the impulse of our calm determination moves towards a goal. In this last hour the rhythm has become faster and cannot now be stopped.

It is not only an army which now marches towards its goal, but 44 million Italians who are marching in unison with this army ... When, in 1915, Italy united her forces with those Allies, what promises there were ... For twenty years we waited patiently while there was drawn round us a circle which would have suffocated our rising vitality.

With Ethiopia [the modern name was now being used as well as 'Abyssinia'] we have been patient for forty years, but now it is enough. At the League of Nations, instead of recognising Italy's just claims, they dare to speak of sanctions ... We must not pretend not to know the possibilities of tomorrow. To sanctions of an economic character, we shall reply with discipline, with sobriety and with sacrifice. To measures of a military order, we shall reply with measures of a military order. To acts of war, we shall reply with acts of war.

Let no one think he can bend us. But let it be said once more ... we shall do all in our power to ensure that a colonial war shall not assume the character and range of a European conflict...

The following day, the *Daily Herald* carried an editorial:

War has begun. Under the cynical pretext of 'taking the necessary measures of defence,' Signor Mussolini's armies have invaded Abyssinia. The League [of Nations] is thus relieved of all responsibility of deciding who is the aggressor. Italian war preparations have been so long and so open, Italy's intention to attack so soon as weather permitted has been so boastfully avowed, Italy's ambition to conquer and enslave her neighbour has been so frankly admitted, that her guilt is beyond question. The time for discussion has passed. The time for action has arrived. Every effort to negotiate a peaceful settlement and to prevent the outbreak of war has failed. It is now the duty of the League to stop the war which conciliation has not succeeded in averting ... the duty of the League now is not to consider Signor Mussolini's feelings. It is, we repeat once again, to stop the war. And to that supreme task all its efforts and all its resources must be devoted.

The propaganda war was also soon in full swing. On New Year's Eve 1935, a message from Addis Ababa claimed that twenty-three Italian officers had been killed in a battle on the northern front, while that day's communique from Rome said that 'there is nothing of importance to report on the Eritrean and Somali fronts'.

News reports by British journalists from the war zone soon brought waves of indignation. On 31 December, the Press Association reported that a Swedish Red Cross hospital 32 kilometres from the border town of Dolo had been destroyed by an Italian airstrike. Up to thirty people were killed, most of them Abyssinians. It was claimed that attack was a reprisal for the execution of an Italian pilot, 26-year-old Tito Minniti, who bailed out when his aircraft was shot down. He was castrated and beheaded: by Abyssinian troops, according to Italy; by local civilians, according to Abyssinia. Whoever was responsible, the atrocity was used to justify the Italians' use of mustard gas, which violated the 1925 Geneva Protocol that Italy had signed.

The attack on the Red Cross hospital was described by the Swedish consul as 'the most dastardly crime … it could have been committed only by barbarians … soldiers are able to take cover during air-raids, but Red Cross workers must stand to their posts, ready to attend to the wounded'. It also raised concerns for the welfare of Andre Melly, a Liverpool-born 37-year-old British surgeon who had won the Military Cross while serving with the Royal Field Artillery during the Great War. Melly was leading the British Red Cross unit in Abyssinia. He had escaped the bombing but, five months later, was killed by a revolver shot from the leader of a mob of drunken looters after he stopped his car to pick up a wounded Abyssinian.

As the *Daily Herald* editorial said, Mussolini's intentions had indeed been obvious for some time. In June 1935, the UK's Foreign Secretary, Sir Samuel Hoare, had warned the Cabinet that while it was Germany and Japan that posed the most serious threat to British interests, there was a 'most inconvenient dilemma' developing in East Africa where Benito Mussolini was threatening an invasion of Abyssinia in order to unite the Italian colonies of Eritrea and Italian Somaliland.

The crisis had its roots in the so-called Wal Wal Incident. In 1930, Italy had expanded her area of influence in the region by building a fort at the Wal Wal oasis in the Abyssinian territory of the Ogaden tribe, on its border with Italian Somaliland. On 22 November 1934, an Ethiopian force of about 1,000 men surrounded the fort and demanded that it be handed over to them. Their demand was refused and when an Anglo-Abyssinian border commission arrived the following day, the risk of an armed conflict appeared to have eased, but only temporarily. The British members of the commission withdrew but the Abyssinians remained. More Italian soldiers arrived, and on 5 December 1934, a skirmish broke out. Its origins were unclear but, during two days of fighting, according to some reports 107 Abyssinians were killed, and fifty Italians and Somalis (who were serving under the Italians) also lost their lives. In January, five Italian soldiers died in an ambush there.

Writing in the *Daily Herald*, journalist Norman Ewer pondered on what 'Mussolini is really up to'. Ewer felt that there were three possibilities: that he was deliberately picking a quarrel with Abyssinia to create an opportunity to achieve Italy's old ambition of annexing Africa's last independent kingdom; he was aiming for a spectacular victory over a weak opponent which would gratify his Fascisti 'and make them feel fine'; or he was blustering because he knew that, legally, he was hopelessly in the wrong. Ewer wrote, 'If the first, then there is trouble. If the second or third, then things may go off quietly.'

Whatever Mussolini's motive, each side blamed the other. Abyssinia protested to the League of Nations; Italy demanded an apology. The League's findings were inconclusive and the seeds for Italy's invasion were sown.

The British Cabinet now reconsidered its strategy. An all-out war between Italy and Abyssinia could possibly have threatened British Sudan, but ministers believed that it was not worth actively resisting the Italian advance. It was acknowledged that conflict would be a 'calamity', not least because the government wanted to avoid Italy re-establishing relations with Germany. In June 1935, Britain sent her Minister for League of Nations Affairs, Anthony Eden, to Rome to attempt to broker a deal that would prevent war, but Mussolini was resolute. The Permanent Under-Secretary at the Foreign Office, Sir Robert Vansittart, gained French support to put precautionary measures (possibly sanctions) before the Council of the League of Nations. Reaction in Britain was mixed. In July, in a letter to the *Daily Telegraph*, the anti-appeasement campaigner Frank Lucas wrote:

> Europe has at its disposal sanctions that Italy could not defy, provided we have the courage to use them. But instead of that the English Press, with a few honourable exceptions, has been taken up with nauseating discussion of our own interests. Later on, one gathers, we shall be very firm with Italy about the water of Lake Tana. Meanwhile, Ethiopian blood is a cheaper commodity.

The same month, the American-born 'Chips' Channon, who would be elected as the Conservative MP for Southend in the November General Election, wrote in his diary, 'I am bored by the Italian–Abyssinian dispute, and really I fail to see why we should interfere … Why should England fight Italy over Abyssinia, when most of our far-flung Empire has been won by conquest?'

With French support, in September 1935, Sir Samuel Hoare made a speech to the League in favour of sanctions, but Mussolini was again undeterred. 'Chips' Channon asked, 'Is it war? All now depends on the Megalomaniac Mussolini. But how can he hope to fight all Europe unless Hitler backs him up?'

Cabinet members now feared that sanctions might provoke war, and Il Duce sensed that. In his speech upon the invasion of Abyssinia, he said, 'Until it is proved to me to the contrary, I refuse to believe that the people of Great Britain wish to shed their blood and to drive Europe towards catastrophe to defend a barbarous and indelibly branded African country unworthy of ranking among civilised people.'

By December, Britain was the only League member not to have imposed oil sanctions, before reluctantly joining in because of the need for collective security. The USA continued to supply oil. Sir Samuel Hoare and the French Prime Minister, Pierre Laval, came up with a plan to end the Italy–Abyssinia War and at the same time maintain the Stresa Pact – of which Mussolini was a signatory – that was designed to prevent any further changes by Germany to the Treaty of Versailles, especially regarding Austria's independence. In the hope that it would satisfy Mussolini's military ambitions in East Africa, the Hoare–Laval Plan, which was initially kept secret, offered Italy yet more of Abyssinia's unconquered territory. The document was leaked, however, and harsh criticism in Britain and France saw both Hoare, who had been ordered by his doctor to rest, and Laval, resign. Mussolini never responded to the Hoare–Laval Plan.

On 19 December 1935, Stanley Baldwin, disavowing his Foreign Secretary, announced that the plan was 'absolutely and completely dead'. Two days later, the Press Association reported:

> No Italian reply to the peace plan will be sent either to the French or British Foreign Offices. The official spokesman added that the plan would probably have been accepted basis for discussion. 'On Wednesday,' he said, 'the Fascist General Council was engaged in examining the proposals very attentively and would probably have made a reply not definitely rejecting them but including our own reservation. Now, however, that the British Foreign Secretary, one of the joint authors of the proposal, has resigned, there no point our replying to them, particularly as the British Government, in the words of Mr Baldwin, has stated already that the proposals are dead once and for all. If any further proposals are made, whether by the League of Nations or by England and France, Italy will give serious attention, but in the meantime, we are proceeding in own way. We will now go straight ahead with our programme. Our position is clearly defined in the communique issued after the Grand Council last night. There is considerable confusion abroad, but we are certain of what we want, and we see our way clearly before us. Mussolini in his speech at Pontinia on Wednesday, said that he would not send settlers to a remote and barbarous land unless he was quite sure that they would be safe, and we will proceed to make certain that they will safe.'

Thus, for fear of driving Mussolini into Hitler's arms, no action was taken against Italy. Although fighting persisted until February 1937, by May 1936, Abyssinia – a member of the League of Nations but offered no protection by it – left to an unhappy fate, had already become part of the Italian Empire. Seven months earlier, at the Unity Hall on the Isle of Sheppey, Dr Conze had warned that Europe was 'rapidly stumbling into war'.

Chapter 13

The Man Who Leaked the Budget

'His voice was full of determination. But his eyes were dimmed with tears ... The strain of the afternoon had been great.'

Daily Mirror

On Thursday, 9 April 1936, the Chancellor of the Exchequer, Neville Chamberlain, had some depressing news for the Cabinet. The international situation meant that Britain faced the largest programme of defence spending ever undertaken by the country in peacetime. The previous December, Britain's failed attempt to deal with Mussolini over his obvious intention to invade Abyssinia had resulted in the resignation of the Foreign Secretary, Sir Samuel Hoare, whose joint pact with the French had sought to cede most of Abyssinia to Italy. In March, Hoare's successor, Anthony Eden, was faced with a situation of even greater magnitude when Adolf Hitler marched German troops back across the Rhine in direct defiance of the Treaty of Versailles. This Italian and German provocation, explained Chamberlain, meant that he would have to increase the basic rate of income tax by threepence (1.25p), and, as a further measure to raise additional revenue for defence, he was also going to add twopence (less than 1p) to the duty on tea. There were still twelve days to go before he was due to make his Budget speech to Parliament, but this unprecedented notice of a Chancellor's intentions – the longest of any in history – was to avoid interrupting Parliament's Easter break.

After the Cabinet meeting broke up, Jimmy Thomas, the Secretary of State for the Colonies, went off to his newly acquired Milbury House in Florida Road at Ferring-on-Sea, some 5 kilometres west of Worthing in Sussex. The five-bedroomed detached home that had been built for the Canadian actor Raymond Massey in 1927 was a huge leap from Thomas's poverty-stricken boyhood as an illegitimate child brought up in Newport by his widowed washerwoman grandmother. He had enjoyed a rapid rise through the trades union movement, during which he had merged three separate railway unions into the all-powerful NUR, and in 1910, he was elected Labour MP for the railway town of Derby. The man who had begun working life as a 12-year-old, 6s-a-week (30p) railway engine cleaner was now a pillar of the establishment, photographed almost daily in a grey topper at Ascot, or in a morning coat at Buckingham Palace.

The next day, Good Friday, one of Jimmy's friends and business associates, Alfred 'Cosher' Bates, met Thomas on the golf course at Goodwood. The two had known each other for twenty years, ever since Bates was living in Dulwich and trying to establish himself in business. In that endeavour he had succeeded spectacularly and now owned two racing newspapers, *The Leader* and *The Jockey*, and also ran an advertising agency whose main clients were bookmakers and football pools companies. Physically, Bates was an unattractive figure, a stout man with a pasty face, hair that was permanently greased down, and eyes that blinked and shifted constantly from behind his spectacles. On Easter Saturday, he drove Thomas to Kempton Park Races. The following day, they played golf at Worthing. On Easter Monday, they motored to Brighton, where Thomas stood Bates lunch at the Royal Albion Hotel, an elegant early nineteenth-century building on the seafront, unusual in that its grand Ionian and Corinthian columns faced inwards from the sea. The Royal was an establishment much patronised by authors, artists, actors, and well-known sportsmen of the day – indeed, its owner, Harry Preston, had entertained the Prince of Wales there – and Thomas and Bates would have felt completely at home in such salubrious surroundings.

The next day, Bates returned to London, but Thomas remained in Sussex until the end of the following week. Back in his office on the morning of Tuesday, 21 April, he received a visit from Sir Alfred Butt, the Conservative MP for Balham and Tooting, a theatre impresario, racehorse owner and breeder, and an inveterate gambler. That afternoon, Neville Chamberlain laid his Budget before the Commons, and before the House rose, Thomas made a speech on the former German colonies that had been mandated to Britain after the First World War. He refuted Opposition claims that the UK government was thwarting Germany's legitimate desire to expand. The Secretary of State for the Colonies warned of the impression that would be created in other countries by the ignorance displayed by some Opposition speakers. What was said in the British Parliament today could be proclaimed in Germany tomorrow as facts when, in reality, it was an absolute travesty of the facts. 'Rule out this talk about Germany looking upon the Colonies as merely an expansion for her people,' he told the House. 'Prior to the war, experience proved that Germany did not look on them in that light.' It was a short but effective speech, greeted with ministerial cheers, and as he sat down, Thomas could feel pleased with himself.

Two days later, he would feel anything but. On 23 April, the *Daily Express*, in a banner headline, asked the question: 'DID THE BUDGET SECRETS LEAK OUT?' The newspaper reported that Lloyd's underwriters had reported losses of between £40,000 and £50,000 on an insurance scheme against a rise in income tax. In the Commons, the Conservative MP for Lewisham East, Lieutenant-Colonel Sir Assherton Pownall, called attention to a form of city gambling, which he said had resulted 'from a leakage of Budget secrets'. Investors could insure against a possible increase in income tax, and the previous week Lloyd's was quoting a rate of between five guineas (£5.25) and ten guineas (£10.50) per cent. Owing to the rush of business, quotations soon went up to fifteen guineas (£15.75) and on the morning of the day that the Budget would be announced in the afternoon, there was such a rush from brokers who had been instructed to pay any amount of money to cover the risk that the rate was increased to forty-five guineas (£47.25) per cent.

'Anyone who would be prepared to pay forty-five guineas would do so only if he had the certain knowledge that he was backing a horse after the race had been won,' said Sir Assherton, who was himself a member of Lloyd's. It was, he said, the first time in his experience that the Budget secrets had leaked – for that must be the case – and he urged the Chancellor to get in touch with the committee of Lloyd's, which was making its own inquiry into why, compared to other years, there had been this sudden and disproportionately large amount of insurance taken out against a rise in specific taxes.

Newspapers throughout the country seized upon the story. In the *Western Mail*, 'Our Own Correspondent' asked if there had been a leak or if it was simply a coincidence that a heavy insurance had been carried in the City against the risks of an increase in income tax and the tax on tea. The newspaper said that Whitehall had repudiated the suggestion that there could have been any irregular disclosure and had declared that it would have been impossible for official information to have leaked in any way: 'Only a handful of highly paid officials have Budget details in their possession. The Chancellor does not even consult the Cabinet except on some major issues involving policy. This year Mr Neville Chamberlain did not even submit his proposals to the Cabinet as a whole but saw only the Prime Minister about them.' This did not tally with the fact that Chamberlain had briefed his colleagues almost two weeks before he stood up in the House and made his Budget public.

The rumour mill was soon in overdrive. On Saturday, 25 April, the *Daily Herald* reported that 'wild rumours are flying about Westminster as to the source of the special information which led to these operations' that had 'resulted in certain people profiting most improperly through insurance operations'. The paper said that brokers who had been 'bitten' by the demands for insurance might be ordered to disclose the names of clients for whom they had acted. One member of Lloyd's told the *Herald*, 'The brokers who accepted heavy insurances against the risk of an increased income tax and tea duty did so in perfectly good faith.'

The issue of just how key elements of the Budget had apparently come to the knowledge of those who could gain most was now occupying more column inches than the Budget itself. Still kept off the pages of the nation's newspapers but now the subject of intense Westminster gossip was the name of Jimmy Thomas. Here were the 'facts': Alfred Bates had first seen the Colonial Secretary and then correctly forecast a major Budget change; Alfred Butt had done the same, apparently going straight off to take out insurance as soon as he had finished speaking with Thomas on that morning of Budget Day; Thomas liked a gamble, whether it was on the horses or the stock market, and was likely to need a cash injection. The imputation was easy enough for anyone to make, and the rumour was that Thomas and his stockbroker son, Leslie (who later became a Conservative MP), had cooked up a plot to benefit from prior knowledge of the Budget. When it reached Thomas's ears, he was reported to be desperate to contact Leslie. And, when he did, he was horrified to learn that Leslie had indeed taken out insurances against a rise on income tax and tea duty. Jimmy was even more shocked to learn that the beneficiary of this was none other than his old friend Alfred 'Cosher' Bates, the man in whose company he had been throughout the Easter weekend, immediately following Chamberlain's explanation of why he was having to increase those rates.

Leslie was apparently indignant that his name had been dragged into the furore. What was he supposed to do? He had simply followed his client's instructions. Jimmy was at least relieved to learn that Leslie himself had not made one penny out of the transaction. Jimmy Thomas demanded from Prime Minister Stanley Baldwin a full investigation into the charges and counter charges that were swirling around him. Baldwin referred Thomas back to Chamberlain, and then the matter went before the Cabinet along with the report of Lloyd's own inquiry into the affair. It was decided that, under an Act of 1921, Parliament should be asked to approve a judicial tribunal to investigate the allegations.

In the Commons, Chamberlain said that it was common knowledge that business was often done at Lloyd's in what might be described as speculation upon the outcome of the Budget, and it was not surprising that in the circumstances of the present year, some business of that kind should have been undertaken:

> Though it was not generally anticipated that there was likely to be any increase of taxation, the public had not been without warning on the subject, and, in particular, the *Manchester Guardian* had prophesied increased taxation, and the bulletins of the Press Association which were issued to the newspapers, had more than once indicated that further taxation might be expected.

'But in the course of the week,' Chamberlain continued,

> I received a communication from the chairman of Lloyd's [Neville Dixey, a Liberal Party politician and a specialist in the marine insurance market], intimating that, in his view, there were some circumstances about the transactions that had taken place this year which indicated the possibility of a leakage of some kind ... From what he told me I was convinced that this was a matter that could not be allowed to rest, and which must be pushed down to the very bottom.

The Leader of the Opposition, Clement Attlee, said that it was a fortnight since the occurrence, a fortnight that had been full of rumours, and it was a pity that the Chancellor had not resolved to make the inquiry at once. On 5 May, both Houses passed the motion without division. It would be a unique event, and in view of its unprecedented nature, no rules of procedure or lists of witnesses had been prepared. The Labour Party took exception to the nature of the tribunal, arguing that the Director of Public Prosecutions should have been called into action, and that the proper vehicle of inquiry was a Select Committee of the House of Commons, since the matter at issue affected the honour of Parliament. Attlee declared, 'The essential thing with which the House has to deal is that there has been a leakage and one which must have come from a narrow circle of very highly placed persons.'

Chamberlain announced that the tribunal would be chaired by Mr Justice Porter. Educated at Cambridge University, where he took a Third in Classics and a Second in Law, Porter's legal career had been interrupted by the First World War, in which he was an army captain and was appointed MBE for his service. His fellow members would be Gavin Simonds KC and Roland Oliver KC. When Thomas learned who would be chairing the tribunal, he told a friend: 'They've gone and picked the toughest rascal they could find.'

Bates admitted paying Thomas £15,000, his claim that it was an advance for a forthcoming autobiography, the details of which had not been previously discussed, sounding implausible. Butt had made money after talking with Thomas on Budget Day itself. The outcome was a foregone conclusion. The Budget Secrets Tribunal found that Thomas had indeed made unauthorised disclosure of information to both men. A Fleet Street correspondent for several regional newspapers summed up: 'The finding is patently and entirely based on inference, but those inferences, when marshalled in their chronological order, become so overwhelming in their meaning as to leave no one in any doubt that the tribunal has come to a just conclusion.' When the House debated the findings, Prime Minister Baldwin told it: 'Let us hope with all our hearts that we may never again take part on so painful a scene in this House.' The *Morning Post* summed up the mood: 'A very painful duty was decently and unflinchingly performed.'

Both Thomas and Butt had no option but to resign their seats. In a diary entry for 11 June 1936, Henry 'Chips' Channon wrote:

> At 3.30, J.H. Thomas entered, sad and aged, but sunburnt still. He sat immediately below the gangway on an aisle seat. Very soon took place one of the most poignant scenes the House has ever witnessed, when the Speaker quietly said, 'Mr Thomas', and the poor man rose. He read a written statement which was simple and rather heartrending. He accepted the findings of the tribunal but declared that

he had never consciously betrayed a budget or any other secret. He was leaving the 'Ouse' after twenty-seven years in its midst. He had now only his wife who still trusted him and loved him. He hoped no other member would ever be in a situation as cruel, as terrible as the one he today found himself in. Then he sat down for only a second, and there was a loud murmur of pity and suppressed admiration through the House. There was scarcely a dry eye. Mr Baldwin sat with his head in his hands, as he often does, Winston Churchill wiped away his tears. Thomas then rose again and slowly made his way out, not forgetting to turn and bow, for the last time, to the Speaker.

That night, Clement Attlee made a statement in the Commons:

> I think a word should be said as to where there is a heavy share of blame for the downfall of Mr Thomas, and that is the corrupting influence of wealth and the corrupting influence that emanates from gamblers in the City who have led astray the right honourable gentleman from the path of public service upon which he was set at the start of his career.

Was the former engine cleaner who still dropped his aitches indeed guilty, or instead the victim of snobbery? All attempts by Jimmy Thomas to rehabilitate his reputation were frustrated by the relentless coldness in which the British establishment then – unlike today – treated those who had breached its code. Jimmy Thomas was to end his days shunned by former political colleagues and old workmates alike. Before he died in 1949, the man who had once walked with kings looked back on his early days: 'The most enjoyable meal I ever had was to open my wife's basket on a snappy winter morning, on the footplate of my engine, and find a juicy pound of steak which I fried for myself on the shovel. You come to a meal like that with an appetite that no public banquet can command.'

Chapter 14

An Affront to the National Conscience

'We all looked so utterly shabby and weary in our wet clothes that we presented London with the picture of a walking distressed area.'

Ellen Wilkinson MP

On the evening of Wednesday, 30 September 1936, some 200 men filed into the Ellison Street Church of England School in Jarrow to be examined by the local medical officer, Dr P. A. Dormer. He was assessing the men's fitness to undertake a near-300-mile (483km) march to London. About 180 were selected that night – 'Good stout fellows and quite capable of undertaking the journey,' according to Dr Dormer. Those chosen were handed kitbags, socks, and boot soles. Those who failed the medical protested that they were as able as the men who had been passed fit, but it was to no avail.

The marchers would begin at 10.00 am the following Monday, when they would be led to the borough boundary by a mouth organ band, and accompanied by the mayor, Alderman J. W. Thompson, wearing his robes and chain of office, and by the town clerk. It was planned that the first day would see the men, their number made up to 200 by then, march around 18 kilometres as far as Chester-le-Street. The Leeds Conservative Club and the Leeds Co-operative Society had promised to provide hot meals when they arrived in that city, and many places en route had also offered comfort and support. They would arrive in London on 31 October, to present a petition to the government requesting that their Durham town see the re-establishment of industry there.

Two years earlier, Jarrow's main employer, Palmer's Shipbuilding & Iron Company, had posted a loss of more than £88,000 (the equivalent of £7 million in 2022). The yard was sold to the government-run National Shipbuilders Securities, which, under a restrictive covenant that had excluded the use of the yard for shipbuilding for several years, closed it down, sending local employment spiralling to 68 per cent. For eighteen months, a small part of the yard was used as a steel foundry, but plans to build a steelworks on the site came to nothing after the British Iron and Steel Federation, which had its own plans for the industry, objected.

The unemployed marching on London was nothing new. The so-called 'hunger marches' had been a sad feature of British life since the 1920s. They came not just from the North but from Wales, too. In 1927, a full two years before the Wall Street Crash sent the world economy into free-fall, there were calls in the Rhondda Valley for a march on London to highlight the poverty in the Rhondda. That protest never took place, but in October 1932, when some 3,000 marchers from all over Britain set out for London, many of them came from the Rhondda Valley. That march, the biggest of all, was named 'Great National Hunger March against the Means Test'. The Means Test had been introduced in 1931. Officials visited families to assess whether they needed dole money, and, if so, how much. It created huge tension as the unemployed had to sell treasured heirlooms and use what savings they had managed to scrape together, before they received dole, which was cut by 10 per cent that year anyway.

The marches were mostly organised by the communist-led National Unemployed Workers' Movement (NUWM) and were generally unsupported by the Labour Party and the TUC, both bodies fearing any association with communism at a time when rumours of the 'Red Peril' infiltrating the Labour movement were rife. The Jarrow marchers had been organised by the local borough council and had absolutely no connection to the NUWM – the *Newcastle Journal* reported, 'Arrangements for the Jarrow march have been carried on up to the last minute, and in order that no political element shall be construed, neutral colours have been chosen for the banners to be carried by the marchers' – and Labour and the trades unions again officially remained aloof.

Local opinion was not always supportive, either. Before the men set off, the columnist 'St Bede', writing in *The Shields Gazette*, was worried about 'perturbing vagueness' of the enterprise:

> It is time now, I think, that the general public, on whom Jarrow must rely for support and sympathy, should be given a full and detailed description of the arrangements made for the marchers ... I am very sorry to say that from the very beginning there has been a 'hush-hush' policy ... I have no desire at all to place obstacles in the way of the venture, but I would appeal to those in command to put their

> house in order and to do it publicly so that people may be reassured ... On Tuesday we heard for the first time about how much money has been subscribed ... I am willing to gamble that if the public had known their difficulties, the leaders in this business would have obtained much more than the £757 they have got.

On the day after the marchers set off, the *Newcastle Journal* commented, 'One of the best things we can hope for them is that the fine weather which has so far attended their journey will continue. We have no liking for this effort ... it would probably have been cheaper to send the deputation by train, and, from the point of view of practical results, just as effective.'

While many on the route provided comfort for the marchers, this was by no means universal. The *Derbyshire Times* reported:

> Chesterfield Town Council decided not to provide accommodation at the Markham Hostel for the blind marchers who are expected at Chesterfield in the course of their march to London, and not to entertain unemployed men from Jarrow who propose to march to London to draw attention to the industrial situation in Jarrow.

The *Nottingham Evening Post* commented that the Jarrow march would 'be regarded as an imitation of those which have been organised by the Communists in former years, and as a means of calling attention to a problem which is already painfully in the public mind, it is wholly unnecessary'. The Jarrow effort was doomed to failure, said the newspaper:

> Many who sympathise with the hard lot of Jarrow and other towns stricken by industrial depression regret that the men should be asked to waste their time and energy in a march on London in order to present a petition to Parliament. That ancient right has, for good or ill, shrunk to a formality, and it serves no purpose. The member presenting the petition merely announces its purpose and the number of signatories. It is then dropped into a receptacle behind the Speaker's chair, and, except for a report by a committee months afterwards that the petition was or was not in order, the House hears no more of it.

How right the newspaper was about the outcome, at least. On Wednesday, 4 November 1936, a red-haired firebrand, Ellen Wilkinson, Jarrow's MP, presented the petition – contained in a black leather-bound book with gold lettering on the front, and signed by more than 11,000 people – to the House of Commons. It asked that 'His Majesty's Government and this honourable House should realise the urgent need that work should be provided for the town without further delay'.

During the last five years, said Miss Wilkinson, Jarrow had passed through a period of industrial depression without parallel in the town's history, with its shipyards closed, and its steelworks denied the right to open. Whereas formerly 8,000 skilled workers were employed, now only 100 were at work, and that on temporary schemes. The town could not be left derelict.

Sir Nicholas Gratton-Doyle, the Conservative MP for Newcastle upon Tyne North, presented a further petition, signed by 68,500 people of Tyneside and adjacent areas, on behalf of Jarrow. The Prime Minister, replying to Miss Wilkinson, said that between July and the opening of Parliament he had received similar resolutions and signed letters from public bodies about Jarrow, and one telegram, five postcards, and eight letters (one of which was signed by eight persons) from individuals throughout the country. These included communications on the proposed steelworks at Jarrow. Walter Runciman, the President of the Board of Trade, told the House that the latest information was that there were 1,185 shipbuilders, skilled and unskilled, resident in Jarrow. In addition, 818 general labourers were unemployed in that town. Some of them were probably unskilled shipyard workers. He referred to a recent reply in which the Prime Minister said the present unemployment position at Jarrow, while still far from satisfactory, had improved during recent months. There was every reason to hope that the industrial improvement now taking place in the Tyneside area would continue, with consequent demand for shipyard workers.

James Chuter Ede, the Labour MP for South Shields, the neighbouring constituency to Jarrow, was appalled: 'The Government's complacency is regarded throughout the country as an affront to the national conscience.'

And that was that. The petition was never debated, and the marchers, who had returned home by train, were told that their dole had been reduced because they had made themselves unavailable for work for the whole of October.

The UK had begun to emerge from the Great Depression late in 1932, a recovery due largely to growth in the construction industry and consumer goods sector, while there was also a modest improvement in exports. Yet high levels of unemployment in places like Jarrow lasted throughout the 1930s, and the final three years of the decade would see another recession. On 5 November 1936, the *News Chronicle* commented, 'It is now commonly accepted among the experts that we are now in a period of prosperity ... it must seem incredible that anybody can use the word "prosperity" ... while there are marches from stricken towns like Jarrow, while there are millions of people underfed.'

Others more fortunate offered help. Later that month, the Birmingham *Sunday Mercury* reported:

> Selby's shipyards, oil mills and flour mills are busy, and the residents are taking a novel course to offer thanks for their own prosperity by helping the less fortunate people of Jarrow ... hundreds of Selby residents are to 'exchange' dinners with hundreds of people in Jarrow. For a meal of pea soup and a cup of water or tea, 300 Selby people will pay 1s 3d [6p], and in Jarrow 500 unemployed will have a free dinner of roast beef, vegetables, Christmas pudding, fruit, and tea, coffee or cocoa.

Not everyone had given up hope. Mrs Clare Silva-White, of St Peter's Vicarage in Sunderland, wrote to the *Newcastle Journal*, 'Let no-one say that the Jarrow march has been a failure ... Thousands who, seeing them set forth, wished them "good luck in the name of the Lord" may rest assured that in a hundred ways unrecorded by *Hansard* that prayer will have been answered.'

The Jarrow march was a defining event in 1930s Britain. There was a subsequent and bigger hunger march that began the same month (October 1936), but, like all the others, it achieved little or nothing, and it was to be the last. The 1936 Public Order Act that had come about as a result of the Battle of Cable Street and was passed to control extreme political movements like Oswald Mosley's British Union of Fascists also had a direct effect on hunger marches because it not only gave the Home Secretary the power to ban marches in the London area, but it also gave chief constables the right to apply to ban marches in their local areas.

In November 1936, in a debate on a clause which dealt with the regulation of processions, fears were raised by several MPs that it could be used to prohibit, or at least hamper, hunger marches. Ellen Wilkinson argued that the present law was sufficient, perhaps more than sufficient. She cited the experience of the marchers at York, where, she said, the chief constable had refused to allow them through the city, with the result that they had to take roundabout routes to a poor law institution and a supper of bread and margarine, instead of the place where a hot meal had been prepared for them.

The *Yorkshire Post* reported that the observation of Edward Turnour, an Irish peer who was thus not disqualified from sitting in the House of Commons – which he did for forty-seven years – that probably the chief constable was doing something that he had no right to do 'brought Miss Wilkinson to the amazed realisation that she was, for once, in complete agreement with the most conservative of Conservatives'. Wilkinson thought the clause would merely regularise the methods of bullying chief constables, and foresaw, in any future hunger march, legal conflicts at every county boundary. Despite what the *Yorkshire Post* called 'a dusty debate', the opposition was very small, for the clause was approved 247 votes to thirteen.

H. Weaver, a letter writer to the *Motherwell Times*, replying to a previous letter from 'Fascist Admirer', said:

> 'Fascist Admirer' should have read my previous letter in a proper manner. I stated that the workers' propaganda was not to destroy the company for whom they worked but to destroy the rotten system under which those worse off than themselves were forced to exist ... He says that if Hitler was to rule in this country, then he would have swept the hunger marchers into the army. Well, all I can say in that case is, 'God help the army that would have been,' for the majority of them were physical 'misfits' due to the rotten system mentioned before.

And just in case anyone had forgotten the Austrian with the Charlie Chaplin moustache, the *Blyth News* reported that Ashington Rotary Club member Mr F. S. Houghton had just returned from a visit to Berlin, 'where he found the workers to be in solid support of Adolf Hitler'.

Chapter 15

The Empty Hell of War

> 'Guernica ... has been reduced to a blazing mass of ruins after the most appalling air-raid in the history of modern warfare. Hundreds of civilians were killed in three and a half hours of continuous bombing by German aeroplanes.'
> Christopher Holme of the Press Association

On Sunday, 19 July 1936, *The Observer* newspaper reported, 'Late last night it was learned that the revolt among Spanish troops in Spanish Morocco had spread to Seville ... Trouble has apparently broken out in other parts of Spain, and also in the Canary Islands.' The Spanish Civil War had begun. Britain was going to do her best to keep out of it. Germany would use it as a rehearsal for a bigger war.

The potential for conflict in Spain had been bubbling for years, ever since 16-year-old Alfonso XIII was crowned king in May 1902. He had been the monarch since his birth – his father, Alfonso II, had died six months before – but his mother had assumed the powers of regent until he was considered old enough. His accession heralded a long period of political instability that saw thirty-three separate Spanish governments formed in the next twenty-one years as the monarch regularly interfered in parliamentary affairs.

In September 1923, with Alfonso's support, General Miguel Primo de Rivera overthrew the democratically elected government and established a nationalistic dictatorship around the notion of 'Country, Region, Monarchy'. It lasted for seven years before, in January 1930, with Spain's economy – which had always been ailing, with precious little industry and an inefficient agricultural system – worsening still further as a result of the global depression, Alfonso forced Primo de Rivera's resignation. But the king had become too closely associated with the dictator, and, in August that year, an alliance of Republicans, Catalans, and former liberal monarchists agreed to depose Alfonso.

Republican and Socialist successes in the following year's municipal elections led to demands for his abdication. The military withdrew its support for the monarchy, and Alfonso left Spain. When the boat train on which he had travelled arrived at Victoria railway station on 23 April 1931, 'a great cry of welcome went up from the huge crowd'. Fifteen hundred people welcomed his arrival at Claridge's Hotel, where he was greeted by ex-King Manuel II of Portugal, whose own reign had ended with the fall of the monarchy there in 1910. Manuel had spent the rest of his life in Twickenham. Alfonso maintained his claim to the throne in exile until his death in Rome in 1941.

In October 1933, Primo de Rivera's son, José Antonio, formed a far-right nationalist group, Falange Española ('Spanish Phalanx'), whose aim, initially bankrolled by Mussolini, was to overthrow Spain's Republican government. When, in February 1936, the left-wing coalition Popular Front won a majority in the Spanish parliament, it triggered a wave of industrial strikes and saw arson attacks on scores of churches, clubs, and newspaper offices. In one incident, a woman was stabbed to death by a butcher in the village of El Hoyo de Pinares while she was walking in a procession celebrating the left-wing victory. The butcher's action was in retaliation after his son was 'boxed around the ears' after refusing to salute the red flag carried at the head of the procession.

Right-wing military leaders began to plot the overthrow of the government, and in July, after the assassination of the right-wing leader José Calvo Sotelo by government security forces, the army mutiny began in Spanish Morocco as 43-year-old General Francisco Franco broadcast from the Canary Islands to announce that the rebellion against the Second Spanish Republic had begun. Although several provincial capitals soon fell, Franco was unable to secure Madrid – and a civil war ensued.

In Britain, Stanley Baldwin's predominantly Tory National Government, fearing the spread of communism in the Soviet Union to other parts of Europe, decided on a policy of non-intervention. On 29 October 1936, Baldwin told the House of Commons that there had been breaches of the Non-Intervention Pact – which the previous month had been signed by twenty-seven countries including Britain, Germany, the Soviet Union, France, and Italy – on both sides, but he refused to lift the ban on sending arms to the Spanish government. For Labour, Clement Attlee and Arthur Greenwood, Minister of Health in the short-lived Labour government of 1924, demanded that the embargo should end. Greenwood said that the Labour Party regarded the situation in Spain as a grave tragedy. It was not the spontaneous uprising of an oppressed people, but the carefully engineered conspiracy that had originated outside Spain and was 'aided and abetted by other powers'. 'What happens in Spain may well happen elsewhere,' declared Greenwood. 'There is the new aggression, and aggression is never satisfied. If there is a rebel victory it will be repeated in other countries.'

Labour's Philip Noel-Baker, who had just won a by-election for the Derby seat after Jimmy Thomas had resigned in disgrace following the Budget leak, called the agreement 'a hypocritical sham'. Noel-Baker was correct. Soviet planes had been en route to Spain earlier that month to aid the Madrid government, and in November, Mussolini signed a secret agreement with the Spanish Nationalists that, in return for military aid for the Nationalists, allowed Italy to establish bases in Spain in case of war with France. Over the next three months, Mussolini supplied Franco's forces with 130 aircraft, 2,500 tonnes of bombs, 500 cannons, 700 mortars, 12,000 machine-guns, fifty tanks, and 3,800 motor vehicles.

Inevitably, Hitler also sent aid to Franco, although he attempted to avoid detection by delivering men, aircraft, and tanks through Portugal. The German Condor Legion was also formed. Set up for special duty with Franco's forces, it consisted of military personnel, bombers, fighters, reconnaissance aircraft, and even a seaplane squadron. It was seen by the Luftwaffe as an opportunity to try out aircraft, logistics, and tactics that would be essential in the event of a major war in Europe, tactics that now included the bombing of civilians. On 26 April 1937, the Condor Legion carried out one of the most infamous military operations in the history of warfare. The *News Chronicle*'s front-page headline summed up the horror: 'FRANCO WIPES OUT TOWN ... FUGITIVES FALL UNDER BULLETS OF SWOOPING REBEL PLANES.' The Birmingham *Evening Despatch* told a similar story: 'MEN, WOMEN AND CHILDREN PERISH IN FLAMES'. The Press Association's special correspondent, Christopher Holme, painted a horrific picture of Guernica, 32 kilometres from Bilbao and the ancient capital of the autonomous Basque Country:

> Starting late yesterday afternoon German bombers came over in uncounted numbers – seven at a time – accompanied by equally numerous fighters. From the first planes the crews leaned out, dropping hand grenades while the frightened

populace rush to a few bomb shelters. Hundreds raced desperately for the fields where they were systematically followed and machine-gunned by swooping fighters ... relays of bombers dropped high-explosive bombs. More than 1,000 are estimated to have hit the town. Incendiary bombs followed. When the planes finally finished their work of destruction the whole town, including architecturally precious churches were ablaze. Casualties cannot be counted but literally hundreds of men, women and children must have been roasted alive, torn to pieces by explosives, and drilled with machine-gun bullets ... the only military objective in Guernica is the barracks which suffered only one casualty.

The death toll in Guernica has long been disputed. At the time, the Basque authorities claimed that 1,650 of the town's inhabitants had been killed, and 889 were wounded. Later estimates suggested that between 200 and 250 people lost their lives that day. Whatever the figure, condemnation was worldwide. The *New York Times* reported 'wholesale arson and mass murder, committed by rebel airplanes of German type'. Immediately prior to the Condor Legion raid, aircraft from the Aviazione Legionaria, a force set up by Mussolini in 1936 to support the Nationalist coup, had attacked the Renteria bridge on the outskirts of Guernica. The Aviazione Legionaria had already been involved in several bombing raids over Spanish cities, including the bombing of Madrid, all intended to terrify the civilian population, and on the same page as news of the Guernica air-raid, the *News Chronicle* reported, 'In a new wave of rebel aggression, Madrid has been shelled four times in twenty-four hours', while 'two warships crept under the cover of fog to within three miles [4.8 kilometres] of Valencia and dropped sixty-five shells on the city'.

The suffering of the ordinary people of Spain caught the public imagination. On 25 June 1937, the *Daily Herald* reported that, at a mass meeting at London's Albert Hall, within four minutes £500 was collected in aid of the 4,000 Basque refugee children now in England. Cheques, pound notes, dollar notes, and silver poured in so quickly that stewards were hard put to pass them to the platform. 'Five pounds came from an Italian without the permission of Mussolini ... in [a] matchbox was 10s 1d [50p] and a scribbled note, "All I have got".'

The Duchess of Atholl, who presided, explained that the 'Spanish painter, Pablo Picasso' was unable to attend 'due to his working on a picture of the destruction of Guernica in the Spanish pavilion at the Paris Exhibition'. Picasso's large oil painting – 3.49m (11ft 5in) tall and 7.76m (25ft 6 in) wide – entitled *Guernica*, with its composition that includes a gored horse, a bull, a screaming women, a dead baby, a dismembered soldier, and flames, saw it hailed as the most powerful anti-war painting of all time.

The Spanish Civil War had already stirred into action young men from well beyond the borders of that country, and if many governments had fought shy of providing military hardware to the combatants, individuals had no such reservations, and the so-called International Brigade was soon growing in numbers in support of the Republicans. Again, though, the British government stepped in, attempting to prevent volunteers from fighting in Spain. On 9 January 1937, it announced that it intended to invoke the 1870 Foreign Enlistment Act. The *Daily Herald* explained how the ban would work:

> The offence of enlistment in the service of a foreign state is complete as a British subject 'without the licence of His Majesty' accepts or agrees to accept any commission or engagement in the military or naval service of a 'foreign State' ... therefore, British subjects who agree to fight for the rebel government, as well as those who agree to fight for the Spanish government, are equally guilty of an offence...

Many Britons had already joined the cause, however. In November 1936, the *Belfast Telegraph* reported that 18-year-old Esmond Romilly, a nephew of Winston Churchill's wife, Clementine, was fighting with a British machine-gun section of the International Brigade defending Madrid. When a reporter told his family, his mother 'almost collapsed'. She said, 'We have been living in agony, wondering what had become of him ... he went away in one of his silly, youthful, angry moods.' Two years earlier, Esmond Romilly had run away from Wellington College after *Out of Bounds*, a magazine of 'advanced views' (there was a long article on masturbation) that he edited, had been banned. His father, Colonel Bertram Romilly, said at the time that it was clear that his son 'had been influenced by Communists to leave the college'. He eventually joined the Royal Canadian Air Force, and in November

1941, Pilot Officer Esmond Romilly, aged 23, would lose his life when his aircraft failed to return from a bombing raid over Germany. His name is recorded on the Runnymede Memorial.

Altogether it was estimated that more than 40,000 foreigners fought with the Republican army, including 2,000 Britons. Many from the UK were members of the Communist Party, some were unemployed miners. There were also notable literary figures including George Orwell, W. H. Auden, and Stephen Spender. In his 1938 poem 'The Volunteer', Cecil Day-Lewis wrote, 'It was not fraud or foolishness, Glory, revenge or pay; We came because our open eyes could see no other way.'

The International Brigades were disbanded in October 1938, in the hope that, if foreign fighters were withdrawn from the Republican side, then German and Italian military personnel would be withdrawn from the Nationalist side. The announcement was made to the League of Nations by Prime Minister Juan Negrin on 28 September. In December, 309 members of the British Battalion of the International Brigades were met at Victoria railway station by a crowd of supporters that included Clement Attlee and Sir Stafford Cripps. As they alighted from their train from Newhaven, they were greeted by thousands of people waving banners and singing the 'Red Flag'. Attlee told them, 'We are proud of the great work you have done. You have worthily on many a front upheld the traditions of British democracy. We, unfortunately, are ruled by a Government which desires not to help but to hinder the Spanish people.' Bob Cooney, the battalion's political commissar, said, 'Five hundred British and Irish comrades will sleep forever in Spain. They need not have died. They have been killed by the policy of non-intervention.'

Despite the disbandment of the International Brigades, the Axis powers continued to aid the Nationalists right up until the end of the conflict in March 1939, when, after Barcelona had fallen, the Republicans finally surrendered Madrid. Franco refused to negotiate a peace and would now rule Spain until his death in 1975. After his victory, some 500,000 Republicans fled to France. Many of them found themselves in internment camps, and after Germany occupied France in 1940, thousands would die in concentration camps. One always had to keep an eye on Adolf Hitler.

On 5 November 1937, at the Old German Reich Chancellery in Berlin, Hitler had attended a four-hour meeting that had been called, ostensibly, to discuss complaints by Admiral Erich Raeder that the German navy was short of steel and other raw materials, and that the

Kriegsmarine's building programme was in danger of collapse. Also present were Herman Göring, the head of the Luftwaffe, and Werner von Fritsch, head of the army. Neither were willing to reduce their own steel allocations. Hitler, though, soon broadened the discussion into his expansionist plans for a Greater Germany. His military aide, Colonel Friedrich Hossbach, took the minutes and the document became known as the Hossbach Memorandum. It records that Hitler felt that the only way to halt Germany's still falling living standards was to brook no further delay in seizing Austria and Czechoslovakia. Germany was falling behind Britain and France in the arms race. Aggression now was needed to secure Lebensraum. The Hossbach Memorandum, if genuine, and most historians now agree that is, appears to be a blueprint for war, and a war that needed to start within the next two years. It would be used at the Nuremberg War Crimes Trials to prove that certain senior Nazis were planning war. In his memoir, Raeder recalled, 'Just before the conference, Göring had told me that the real object of the speech Hitler was going to make was to spur the army to greater speed in rearming, and after the speech I was convinced that this was so.'

If the meeting had been secret, and Hitler's immediate plans still known by only a few high-ranking Nazis, the British public were not all fooled. Writing to the Birmingham *Daily Gazette* in September 1936, someone signing themselves 'A.C.B.' had warned:

> I think it fair comment on Hitler's speeches that, far from being a contribution peace, they are as dangerous looking as live shells, and act directly as sharp spurs pressing the nations to war. The language of peace is ever lovely and encouraging. Hitler confesses to being in love with the world's best idea, but his words convey nothing but hopelessness and intense hatred. If Hitler is sincere in his belief in peace, he certainly doesn't know much about the art of talking it. When he does, his messages to Germany and to the world will reflect a vision of human friendliness and co-operative effort, and not the empty hell of war.

Chapter 16

God Save the King!

'Of course, I do have a slight advantage over the rest of you. It helps in a pinch to be able to remind your bride that you gave up a throne for her.'

The Duke of Windsor

On the morning of Saturday, 18 January 1936, Britons opened their newspapers to worrying news from Sandringham. George V, their monarch who had led the country through the Great War, was seriously ill. In general, royal courtiers were not given to alerting the King's subjects to every cough and sneeze suffered by His Majesty. So, when an official announcement on the King's condition was made at just after 11.00 pm on a Friday night, it caused great concern. Up to that point, the British people had been told that the King was confined to his room with a cold, and that his condition was nothing to worry about. But now, there had been a development.

'The bronchial catarrh from which His Majesty the King is suffering is not severe, but there have appeared signs of cardiac weakness which must be regarded with some disquiet.' The communique was signed by the King's three doctors – Sir Frederic Willans, Lord Dawson of Penn, and Sir Stanley Hewett.

Some may have questioned the need to worry – seven years earlier, the newspapers had described the King as 'gravely ill' with pleurisy, but he had recovered. And he had recently been seen walking and riding about the Sandringham estate.

Two days earlier, though, Queen Mary had alerted her son David, the Prince of Wales, to his father's condition, and he was now, like much of the family, in Norfolk while a worried Empire waited. The doctors had remained with the King overnight. The village postmistress and her assistants had been on constant duty to relay important telephone calls. A heart specialist – Sir Maurice Cassidy – had examined the King but had now returned to London. A further bulletin noted a slight worsening in the King's condition. The Prince of Wales and the Duke of York returned to London, the Prince to meet with the Prime Minister, the Duke with his wife, Elizabeth, who was herself ill. Both were expected back at Sandringham that evening. Another son, the Duke of Kent, was making his way to Sandringham. As was the Archbishop of Canterbury, Cosmo Gordon Lang, not in a professional capacity, but as 'an old and very dear personal friend of the King'.

British newspapers began to prepare their readers for what was to come. On Sunday, 19 January, Coventry newspaper the *Midland Daily Telegraph* reported that the children of the Duke and Duchess of York – Princesses Elizabeth and Margaret Rose – had been taken back to London by 'their two nurses and a valet'. This was, it warned, 'a further indication of the serious nature of the King's illness'.

A special edition of the *Sunday Dispatch* reported that only that morning the two princesses, accompanied by a police officer, had played in the deep snow, apparently unaware of the drama unfolding around them. It also reported that good wishes for the King's health had been sent from the governments of France, the United States, Italy, Australia, and Denmark. One message came from Germany, a telegram stating: 'I have just learned of Your Majesty's serious illness. I wish on this occasion to express my most sincere and heartiest wishes for a speedy convalescence and complete recovery – Adolf Hitler.'

All the good will in the world – no matter where it came from – could not save the King. On 20 January, after a reassuring early bulletin recording 'no substantial change', had come one noting 'diminishing strength'. At 9.25 pm came the following statement: 'The King's life is moving peacefully towards its close.' That closure came at just before midnight. A final bulletin noted: 'Death came peacefully to the King at 11.55 pm tonight in the presence of the Queen, the Prince of Wales, the Duke of York, the Princess Royal and the Duke and Duchess of Kent.'

Two days later, the new sovereign, to be known as Edward VIII, spoke before the Privy Councillors at the Accession Council, as he was proclaimed monarch. He promised to follow in his father's steps and to 'work, as he did throughout his life, for the happiness and welfare of all classes of my subjects'.

The *Illustrated Sporting and Dramatic News* had called George V 'a wise and good ruler' and noted, 'The man-in-the-street has lost a King who, by the medium of wireless, became to him the symbol of a Friend.'

God Save the King!

In public, as Prince of Wales, Edward's concern for the poor and disadvantaged, and for the lot of the working man and woman, had done much to cement his reputation. Britons knew him to be modern and progressive, and warmed to his boyish good looks and natural charm.

They were not yet aware that the new King's private life had long been the subject of gossip in high society. His own father was reputed to have complained, 'After I am dead, the boy will ruin himself in twelve months.' It would take only ten.

Since 1930, when his father had given him the lease to Fort Belvedere on the Windsor estate, Edward had created his own private realm, complete with swimming pool, tennis court, and steam room. There he entertained friends and several married girlfriends. It was all kept from the pages of British newspapers, due only to their editors' collective reluctance to upset the much-respected monarch.

Foreign newspaper editors, however, did not feel so obligated. Publications across Europe regularly featured details of the Prince's off-duty life. Photographs of the heir to the throne and his latest lady friend – the glamorous American Mrs Wallis Simpson – embracing and wearing bathing costumes were already selling Continental newspapers. The pair had met in 1931, at a house party held by the Prince's then girlfriend, Thelma Furness, wife of Viscount Furness, where Wallis and her second husband, Ernest, had been invited as last-minute replacements. Several months later, Wallis and Ernest invited the Prince to dinner. In turn, he invited them to Fort Belvedere, where other guests began to notice an attraction between Wallis and the Prince. Wallis's appearances at the Buckingham Palace Jubilee Ball and Royal Ascot seemed to confirm a relationship. By the time George V died, the pair had fallen deeply in love. They had holidayed together, without Ernest, on the yacht *Nahlin*. Other guests included the Mountbattens. More privately, the pair had spent weekends at Fort Belvedere, where Wallis played hostess.

In the United States, excitement at the possibility of an American queen knew no bounds. Some newspapers printed reports about the extraordinary lengths being taken to avoid the British public learning the truth; actions like taking US newspapers off the shelves and ripping pages from magazines.

If British royal watchers had known what to look for, they would have seen clues. The Court Circular mentioned Wallis being at several dinner events with the King, both with and without Ernest. On one occasion, Prime Minister Baldwin and his wife were in attendance.

On 1 October 1936, the *Aberdeen Press and Journal* reported that 'Mrs Ernest Simpson' was among guests at Balmoral.

Three weeks later, a small news item appeared. At Ipswich, Wallis Simpson had been granted a 'speedy divorce' decree nisi. It appeared entirely run-of-the-mill and featured the familiar euphemisms of the time. Ernest took the blame – not contesting Wallis's claim that he had first become 'indifferent to her' and later had 'committed misconduct at the Hotel de Paris in Bray-on-Thames'. Two witnesses, both waiters, confirmed this. None of the reports mentioned that Mrs Simpson was a friend of the King. And certainly not that the King might wish to marry her. In mid-November, Edward invited Baldwin to Buckingham Palace to tell him he planned to marry Wallis. The Prime Minister advised him that the marriage would damage the reputation of the King, the monarchy, and Britain.

There were indeed enormous obstacles to marriage. The King was Supreme Governor of the Church of England, which permitted remarriage only after the death of the ex-spouse. Wallis had two living exes. A civil marriage would put Edward at odds with his church. Baldwin warned that the British people would not accept his choice. Edward proposed making an address in which he could put his case to his subjects. Baldwin refused. Edward said that, should it prove necessary, he would abdicate, but instead proposed Wallis's preferred option of a 'morganatic' marriage. This would mean that she would never be queen in name. The succession would move straight to Edward's brother, the Duke of York, bypassing any children that Edward and Wallis might have. But it would require a change in the laws of succession and would have to be put to Parliament and to the parliaments of all the Dominions of the Empire. In a book written in 1958, but not published until after his death, Lord Beaverbrook wrote that he had tried to persuade Edward to put ideas of marriage on hold until after the Coronation in May. He reasoned that it would give the King time to persuade people to his cause. But Edward would not wait. It seemed that he had calculated Wallis's divorce might be finalised in time for the couple to marry before the Coronation.

Thus, Baldwin presented the Dominions with three options: the King and Wallis to marry, with Wallis becoming queen; the King and Wallis to marry but she not become queen and their children not succeed; the King should abdicate.

While all this played out in private, public preparations for the Coronation continued. The ceremony was to be filmed for cinema newsreels, and some parts of the procession would even be televised, despite the Dean and Chapter of Westminster Abbey's initial concern that such a thing might be a fire risk to the ancient building. Businesses were gearing up for the occasion. In Birmingham, tens of millions of medals bearing lifelike images of Edward VIII, and millions of Union Flags, were being produced for sale to the public.

Baldwin had more pressing matters. His biggest fear was that Edward, who already had the personal support of Winston Churchill, might seek support elsewhere in Parliament, perhaps even forming his own 'King's Party'. Unlikely as it seemed, that would turn the next General Election into a referendum on Mrs Simpson. Or even turn the public against the monarchy

In early December, the crisis came to the attention of the British public with what Lord Beaverbrook would call 'the speech that touched off the publicity gunpowder barrel'. The speech was made by Bishop Blunt of Bradford to his diocesan conference on 1 December 1936. Ostensibly it was about the Church's role in the Coronation ceremony. But it seemed to question Edward's dedication, and the need for him to set a moral example. Beaverbrook would later suggest that the Archbishop of Canterbury himself believed that Edward VIII was more interested in attending nightclubs than church services.

Blunt said that the King would 'abundantly need' God's grace to do his duty faithfully. 'We hope he is aware of his need. Some of us wish he gave more positive signs of such awareness.' To those who were fully aware of the King's relationship with Wallis Simpson, it seemed a fairly obvious swipe at them. To the overwhelming majority of the King's subjects who knew nothing of this moral quandary, it must have been puzzling.

They were about to find out. On 2 December, the *Yorkshire Post* published a story about a 'great deal of rumour regarding the King' which had appeared in some American newspapers. 'Dr Blunt must have had a good reason for so pointed a remark,' the newspaper remarked. The following day, *The Times* ran an extract. While it did not go into detail as to the nature of the rumours, the report warned that 'certain statements' about the King ought not to be treated with 'indifference'. The next day, more detail was revealed about Wallis's ongoing divorce and the involvement of the government in the issue. Most of the national papers – like *The Times*, the *Morning Post*, and the *Daily Telegraph* – supported the government; Beaverbrook's *Daily Express* and the *Daily*

Mail favoured the King. The public, too, initially felt empathy towards their monarch, but as more information came to light, began to support the more practical government position. The *Dundee Courier* wrote of the 'American Society Lady', a woman of 'beauty, charm and a keen wit' with 'a reputation for a knowledge of how to dress to advantage'. Readers were informed about where and when she had first met the King, her English ancestors dating back to the Norman Conquest, as well as her hobbies – gardening and cooking.

'King's Unaltered View. No Question of Compromise. Abdication Possibility', declared the *Belfast Telegraph*. All the comings and goings between palaces and Downing Street were noted: the King with the Prime Minister, the King and Queen Mary, Queen Mary and the Duke and Duchess of York, the Duke of York's private secretary and Number 10 officials, and so on. Wallis was now in hiding with friends in the Home Counties while the royal family cancelled all engagements. The King returned to Fort Belvedere. And everyone waited.

When word from the Dominions came, it offered little support to Edward: if the King refused to give up Wallis, then he must give up the throne.

Britain's constitutional issues were now international tittle-tattle. In France, *Paris-Soir* reported 'the indignation of the English people' over the 'King's wish to marry an American woman'. In Italy, newspapers compared the crisis with that of Henry VIII's first divorce. Austrian newspapers reported that what should be a 'purely private matter' had been elevated to a constitutional issue by the objections of the Anglican Church. Curiously, the only newspaper covering events in Nazi Germany was the *Muenchener Zeitung*, which was confiscated by police before it could be widely distributed. No Berlin newspapers were permitted to make any reference to events. However, even Hitler could not ensure that British matters had no impact on Germany: business on the Berlin Bourse was very slow, due to London and other stock exchanges reacting to the breaking news.

Everything was coming to a head. At the last minute, Wallis offered to withdraw her petition for divorce. But it was too late. The King had made up his mind. He would abdicate. Events now began to move quickly. The King's subjects tuned in their wireless sets to the hourly news bulletins, or hovered around newspaper sellers for the delivery van to drop off the latest issue. The *Derby Evening Telegraph*'s late final edition headline said, 'The King Confers With His Brothers – Meeting At Fort Belvedere on Momentous Day For The Empire.' It reported, 'All the brothers looked pale and tired.' The comings and goings of the day at Fort Belvedere, Buckingham Palace, Piccadilly, and Downing Street were recounted in detail: a military dispatch rider left the Fort for London, bearing official documents; two of the King's advisors were seen arriving at Buckingham Palace. Shortly afterward, a motorcycle dispatch rider left the Palace for Downing Street, followed, a short while later, by the advisors. A crowd of around 200 onlookers gathered opposite Number 10, before being gently shepherded out on to Whitehall by four policemen.

The people would soon learn that much of this traffic had been to do with the delivery of a decisive message from the King.

Late on 10 December, Baldwin took the news to the Commons and announced, 'A message from His Majesty the King, sir, signed by His Majesty's own hand,' and handed the message to the Speaker, who read it out:

> I, Edward VIII, of Great Britain, Ireland, and the British Dominions beyond the Seas, King, Emperor of India, do hereby declare My irrevocable determination to renounce the Throne for Myself and for My descendants, and My desire that effect should be given to this Instrument of Abdication immediately...
>
> (Signed) EDWARD R. I.

It was witnessed by the King's three brothers.

Said Baldwin, 'No more grave message has ever been received by Parliament and no more difficult, I may almost say repugnant, task has ever been imposed upon a Prime Minister.'

The news broke just in time to make the nation's late evening editions. Although the British people had known about the crisis for some days, the abdication still came as a shock.

According to the *North Herald and County Down Independent*, 'The news of abdication ... was received with stunned bewilderment by a nation who had considered such an extreme step possible, but to whom the realisation of His Majesty's renunciation of the Throne has come as a bombshell.'

Many had assumed that Edward would back down, would put his duty to the country ahead of his love for Wallis. By the time the *Derby*

Evening Telegraph published the following day's late final edition, the deed was done. The Abdication Bill passed through both Houses of Parliament in a matter of hours. And, at 1.52 pm on 11 December, Edward VIII gave Royal Assent to the 'His Majesty's Declaration of Abdication Act, 1936', thus bringing his own eleven-month reign to an end. In Whitehall, feelings were far from calm. A crowd of around 2,000, many of them uniformed Blackshirts, gathered, having been prevented from entering Downing Street by a police cordon. Singing of the National Anthem was followed by organised shouting of Blackshirt slogans, which turned to vocal support for Edward. 'We want the workers' king!' 'Put it to the vote!' 'We want Edward!' 'Down with Baldwin!' and, worryingly, 'One, two, three, four, five – we want Baldwin dead or alive!' before police reinforcements managed to disperse them.

The following evening, Edward made his last official broadcast to the nation, a speech that had been polished by no less than Winston Churchill himself. Introduced by the BBC's Sir John Reith as 'His Royal Highness, Prince Edward', he spoke in a clear, calm voice, only occasionally hesitating:

> At long last I am able to say a few words of my own. I have never wanted to withhold anything, but until now it has not been constitutionally possible for me to speak. A few hours ago, I discharged my last duty as King and Emperor, and now that I have been succeeded by my brother, the Duke of York, my first words must be to declare my allegiance to him. This I do with all my heart.
>
> You all know the reasons which have impelled me to renounce the throne. But I want you to understand that in making up my mind I did not forget the country or the empire, which, as Prince of Wales, and lately as King, I have for twenty-five years tried to serve. But you must believe me when I tell you that I have found it impossible to carry the heavy burden of responsibility and to discharge my duties as King as I would wish to do without the help and support of the woman I love.

He then asserted that the decision – 'the best solution for all' – was his alone. And praised his brother's 'long training' and 'fine qualities'.

'And now, we all have a new King. I wish him and you, his people, happiness and prosperity with all my heart. God bless you all. God save the King!' Shortly thereafter, Edward left for Austria, where he had arranged to stay indefinitely as a guest of Baron Eugene von Rothschild near Vienna.

The new King chose George VI as his regnal name, in tribute to his father. Throughout the crisis, he and his family had behaved with grace and dignity. Their collective charm was an important factor in his immediate popularity. The *New York Times* explained:

> He has never made a slip in his private or public life. Above all, he has been what the home-loving British people call a happy 'family man.' He has been modest in his personal life, careful in the choice of his friends, devoted to his British-born wife and a perfect father of two little princesses, one of whom may rule one day as another Queen Elizabeth.

Newspapers north of the border wrote of the King's deep association with Scotland. Others about his 'liking for books and study', of being 'a practical man' and having a great 'understanding of industry'. And that Princess Elizabeth was 'now the most important little girl in the world'. And so Britain, if still reeling a little from the shock of abdication, began to look forward. To a new year. And a new King. And to a much-anticipated Coronation that would take place on its original date, if not for its original monarch.

As the Coronation approached, business began to recognise a marketing opportunity. At the start of May, all manner of products were being associated with the big event. Sharnbrook Nurseries, of Welling in Kent, advertised 'a Coronation garden of Red, White & Blue Flowers to bloom all summer'. Another, unnamed, business asked, 'Why not buy a Coronation tray made by a war-blinded man of St Dunstan's? Then you can be sure your memento is British.'

Perhaps the most unlikely Coronation tie-in came from Carnation Corn Caps, who warned readers, 'Crown your corns before the Coronation! You can't be comfortable in Coronation crowds if you have painful corns.'

An article in the *Daily Mirror* caused residents of one London street great embarrassment. In a feature about street decorations across the capital, the newspaper featured photographs of Emmen's Building,

Chapel Market in Pentonville. The street was adorned with bright decorations, so much so that residents had also put up humorous signs declaring, 'Dear Landlord, Ask no questions, or explanations, rent spent on decorations,' and 'Our Landlord is a good old sort, we have spent his rent to decorate our court.'

All well and good, but by contrast the newspaper had also published a photograph of Links Road in Ealing, where not one decoration had been used. Teasing the residents of Links Road, the *Mirror* declared it 'a nice cosy neighbourhood. But not a flag!' and suggested that the two roads ought both be decorated. By 8 May, friends and family of the Links Road residents had brought in 'Coronation shields, flags and bunting'. One resident, Mrs Grender, explained that 'a uniform scheme of decoration at a cost of five shillings [25p] for each household had been proposed – many had thought the price too high.'

According to the same paper, bunting was, literally, out of reach for the 'hill-folk' of the new Queen's native Scottish Highlands. Unable to obtain flags or bunting in such rural areas, they would

> sleep in sheetless beds tonight, extracting dyes from heathers and wildflowers, they transformed their bedclothes into decorations ... in the great cities and among eternal snows on mountain summits flutter flags ... beside dark tarns in remote rocky fastnesses gipsy tribes have hoisted coloured cloth ... Shipyards and factories will close, their workers recompensed by gifts to make up for the day's wages lost.

Far away in Helston, in Cornwall, the annual Floral Dance took on a decidedly Coronation theme. Instead of wearing garlands of flowers, young ladies were seen sporting patriotic ribbons of red, white, and blue in their hair and 'the customary display of greenery in the streets was belittled by the festooned royal portraits and the Union Jack'.

The *Daily Mirror* reported that 'girls from Black Areas Will Watch'. This referred to around 100 14-to-20-year-old daughters of unemployed miners from 'distressed areas of Durham, Tyneside and South Wales'. They had been brought to London with funds provided by King George V's Jubilee Trust to see the Coronation procession. They were staying at Chigwell Row as guests of the London Association of Girls' Clubs and were living 'under canvas and cooking for themselves'.

God Save the King!

On the morning of 12 May 1937, Londoners awoke to find parts of the city already at work. Those tasked with preparing Westminster Abbey for the ceremony had begun their work well before dawn. Guests began arriving at 6.00 am, with some bringing sandwiches with them – a wise decision because it was going to be a very long day.

According to the *Derby Evening Telegraph*, 'The King and Queen rose just before seven o'clock, and the Princesses half an hour later … Their Majesties breakfasted together in the Chinese Room.' From an upstairs window, the princesses peeked at crowds, who had been gathering for hours. Thousands lined the entire procession route. Among them was 85-year-old Mrs Annie Gough for whom this was a third coronation. She had, according to the *Daily Mirror*, 'trudged all the way to Whitehall' from her home in Perham Road, West Kensington, more than 6 kilometres away. The tiny, 4ft 10in (1.47 metres) tall lady had taken up a position on the steps of the Home Office, but a sympathetic police officer had found her a seat.

While most Britons' Coronation experience was limited to wireless coverage, newspaper reports, and cinema newsreels, those who chose to travel to London were treated to seven separate processions of the military and various types of VIPs. One had representatives in motorcars, another prime ministers of the Empire nations in carriages. The immediate royal family, also travelling in carriages, were greeted with loud cheers and flags waved with great enthusiasm. Princesses Elizabeth and Margaret Rose travelled with the Princess Royal, followed by the Duchesses of Gloucester and Kent. Then, as described on *Pathe News*: 'With a dignified slowness that makes it all seem like it was some sort of gigantic dream, the great golden State Coach moves forward … It's almost unbelievably grand – the sort of superb show that takes your breath away.'

Inside Westminster Abbey, 8,000 guests had waited for more than two hours. Now waiting with them were the little princesses, who wore matching gowns of shimmering cream satin embroidered with gold. Newspapers reported the young Elizabeth as carrying herself with 'regal bearing', while newsreel footage showed both of them swinging their legs impatiently before taking up their elevated viewing spots in the Royal Gallery beside their grandmother, Queen Mary.

Finally, it was time. As the choir sang Sir Hubert Parry's version of 'I Was Glad', so began the long, and ritualistic ceremony. First the Queen, then the King processed up the aisle.

As the King was greeted by the Archbishop of Canterbury, the congregation shouted, 'God Save the King!' They listened as he took his oath in a soft, but steady, voice. And watched as he signed his name, before self-consciously wiping the ink from his fingertips.

Now came the sacred part of the service. Attendants removed the cloak from the King, now seated in the Coronation Chair. As the choir sang Handel's 'Zadok the Priest', four Knights of the Garter held a canopy of cloth of gold above him, to screen him from view, before the Archbishop anointed his head, hands, and breast with holy oil. Now the King was dressed in robes of cloth of gold and the canopy was removed so that all could see what was about to happen. The Lord Chamberlain touched the King's heels with the 'golden spurs of knighthood', and he was presented with the Sword of State, the Orb, the Ring, the Glove, and finally the Sceptre and the Rod. Then the Dean of Westminster brought St Edward's Crown to the King. And, after turning it several times in an attempt to find its front, the Archbishop of Canterbury raised it and solemnly placed it on the King's head. Trumpets sounded a fanfare and the peers shouted, 'God Save the King!' over and over.

King George VI, now laden down with several layers of heavy cloth of gold, wearing a weighty crown and holding his regalia, moved, carefully and rather slowly, from the plain Coronation Chair to the golden throne, shuffling his feet to adjust the footrest as he settled himself. Then, as *Pathe* audiences would learn, 'all the great officers of state, grouped in dazzling array around the sovereign ... In their majestic sweeping robes peers of the realm will pay homage, one by one, at the feet of King George VI, then rise, one by one, to touch His Majesty's crown and then kiss his left cheek.'

The Archbishop first, then the Dukes of Gloucester and Kent as well as the Duke of Norfolk – the Earl Marshal – each first removing their own coronets.

Now came the turn of Queen Elizabeth to be anointed and crowned. She paid homage to her husband, and took her own throne; then the King and Queen took Holy Communion at the altar, and entered St Edward's Chapel, where King Edward's Crown was replaced by the lighter Imperial State Crown. Then came the final procession of the King, followed by his Queen, out of the Abbey and into the Imperial State Coach for the long drive back through London to Buckingham Palace. The component parts now made up a procession so long that, as the Imperial State Coach left the Abbey, the front of it was more than 4 kilometres away at Piccadilly Circus.

After the King and Queen arrived back at Buckingham Palace, they took to the balcony to greet well-wishers and were joined by their attendants and family, including the young princesses, who worked their way to the front and tucked in with their parents before giving the crowd regal waves.

In contrast, the Duke of Windsor and his now-fiancée Wallis Simpson listened to a radio broadcast of proceedings from their exile in Paris. Three weeks later, on 3 June 1937, the pair married at the Chateau de Cande in the Loire Valley. The ceremony was attended by just twenty guests, none of them from Edward's family. His equerry 'Fruity' Metcalfe served as his best man. In line with French custom, the couple had a civil marriage performed by the Mayor of Monts, followed by a religious ceremony officiated by Reverend R. Anderson Jardine. They honeymooned at Schloss Wasserleonburg in Southern Austria.

Controversially, in October, the Duke and Duchess took a twelve-day trip to Germany. The Duke claimed he was interested only in the German working man. But in Britain, the tour was viewed with suspicion. Many within the establishment, personal friends and family of the Duke included, worried that Edward's affection for Germany might extend to Nazism. In 1934, 'Fruity' had attended meetings of Mosley's January Club and was a member of the British Fascist Blackshirts. The FBI believed that Wallis was pro-Nazi and, in 1933, Edward had told Prince Louis Ferdinand – grandson of former Kaiser Wilhelm II – that it was 'no business of ours to interfere in Germany's internal affairs re Jews or re anything else. Dictators are very popular these days, we might want one in England before long.'

It helped little that, in 1935, Edward had addressed the British Legion to propose that a deputation of ex-servicemen go to Germany on a mission of reconciliation and prevent conflict.

Now it was feared that the Windsors' tour would simply feed the Nazi propaganda machine. British diplomats in Germany were instructed to have no contact with the couple.

For Edward, though, it was finally a chance to give Wallis the VIP 'royal' treatment that she had not received in the United Kingdom. Everywhere they went, they were greeted by the National Anthem, as well as by Nazi salutes. They were wined and dined by the Nazi hierarchy – Göring, Goebbels, Speer, and von Ribbontrop (with whom

Wallis was later rumoured to have had an affair). The visit ended with a highly publicised tea with Hitler at Berchtesgaden. The Führer made a great fuss of Wallis and later noted what a good queen she would have made. Finally, after a private dinner at the home of Rudolf Hess, the Windsors returned to France via Berlin.

In the early days of the Second World War, Edward would tell Alexander Weddell, American ambassador to Spain, that the war was bound to result in a catastrophic defeat for Britain: 'The most important thing to be done now was to end the war before thousands more were killed or maimed to save the faces of a few politicians.'

Whether anything more than social contact was made was unclear. But, in 1957, secret Nazi papers were released by the United States which revealed that Hitler, at least, had a plan – 'Project Willi' – that would see Edward restored to the throne, should Britain succumb to Nazi control. The papers proved only Nazi intentions, not Windsor cooperation. But wartime Prime Minister Winston Churchill installed Edward as Governor of the Bahamas, safely out of Europe for the duration.

In the days after the Coronation of King George VI, Stanley Baldwin had announced that he would resign as Prime Minister. Baldwin made his final statement to the House of Commons on 27 May 1937. Harold Nicolson recorded that 'his final words are to give us all £200 a year more. This means a lot to the Labour members and was done with Baldwin's usual consummate taste. No man has ever left in such a blaze of affection.' In 1939, the Lord Baldwin Fund for Refugees would raise £500,000 (more than £36 million in 2022) for the Kindertransport and other relief schemes.

Chapter 17

Voting Only for Peace or War

'I could not make out easily whether Mr Lloyd George wants us to resist the dictators by disarmament or to give up rearmament because they have beaten us already. I am afraid there was no solution to the sorry plight in which he finds us.'

Birmingham Daily Gazette's
'Our London Letter'

After Neville Chamberlain took over from Stanley Baldwin as Prime Minister in the National Government in May 1937, his immediate focus was on domestic issues. His Factories Act that year was designed to provide better and safer conditions for workers. The following year, the Coal Act opened the way for the nationalisation of coal deposits, and there was also the Holidays With Pay Act. The Housing Act was aimed at maintaining fair rents and encouraging the clearance of the slums that blighted so many British towns and cities throughout the 1930s and before. The problem, of course, was not building more houses, especially semi-detached suburban homes; it was finding enough people who could afford to buy them. A weekly mortgage repayment of 25s (£1.25) was beyond the means of a man earning less than £3 a week.

And then, of course, there was Nazi Germany. Few people in Britain were unaware of how events there were affecting people who now lived under the Third Reich. You only had to read your morning newspaper.

In October 1936, a German refugee, 31-year-old author Heinz Max Liepman, had appeared before Marylebone police court charged with attempting to obtain morphine from a doctor, contrary to the Dangerous Drugs Act. Liepman told the court that he had to have the drug to deaden the pain caused by Nazi beatings in a concentration camp. He told the court that he had taken no interest in politics but in March 1933, because he was a Jew, he was put into the camp. As a result of the beatings, he received twelve open wounds and serious injuries to his kidneys.

In August 1933, he managed to escape and made his way to Paris. He had come to England with thirty other German authors in September 1934, then sailed to the United States to work as a lecturer before his health broke down and he returned to England in 1935. When arrested, he had said, 'I am suffering kidney trouble and I must have morphia. Shall I kill myself as this is the end of my career?' Sentence was postponed until 5 January, and Liepman was bailed in the surety of £25. If he gave up the habit, the magistrate told him, he would be treated leniently. In March 1937, he was sentenced to six months' imprisonment so that he could continue medical treatment for his craving. Magistrate Ivan Snell told him, 'I believe that at the end of that period you will come and thank me.' Whether he thanked Mr Snell or not, Heinz Max Liepman lived to become a prolific author. He died in Switzerland in June 1966.

Liepman's story, harrowing though it was, was no more remarkable than that of thousands of others who sought refuge in the UK during the latter half of the 1930s, but the reporting of even this relatively minor court case meant that the British public were being made more and more aware of events in Nazi Germany, and that some institutions at least were prepared to act. In April 1937, Oxford University reversed its previous decision to send a delegate to the Göttingen University bicentenary celebrations in June that year. Not one British university had accepted an invitation to join in similar celebrations at Heidelberg University in 1936 because of 'a reluctance to associate with a university at which the pursuits of learning were subjected to political purposes where a number of professors had been dismissed on political grounds'.

Wherever one looked in the newspapers, there was reaction to the Hitler regime. In January 1936, in response to a letter from an 'An Aberdonian in Germany', someone signing themselves 'Truth' wrote to the *Aberdeen Press and Journal* claiming that 'Germany isn't so very terrible'. 'Truth' felt that the letter was 'new proof that it is possible to live in Germany and see only very little of the surface of things, even being misled in very important points', especially when it came to Jewish people:

> How little 'Aberdonian' grasps the real conditions is obvious from her statements about the Jews. Admitting that not everything is lovely for them, she maintains that their position is now better than two years ago. The facts prove just the opposite. Two years ago, the position of

the Jews was very uncomfortable; today they are utterly desperate. Two years ago, the Jews were driven out of the Civil Service and various professions, but there were some exceptions allowed. Now these exceptions have practically all been withdrawn, and the Jews have been driven out of every possible occupation. They are treated in every respect untouchable. Law courts have ruled that non-Jews must break off even old established personal friendships with Jews. Things are made almost unbearable for the Jews, even in commercial life. More and more of them are forced to sell their businesses to Nazi competitors at ridiculously low prices. Jews are expelled from the health resorts; they are not allowed to use public swimming pools. In some places they are even unable to obtain milk for their children. Yet 'An Aberdonian in Germany' maintains that their position is now better, because they are 'encouraged to pursue their own culture as a separate entity'. Not even this quite true, although the Nazi propagandists boast of it to foreigners whom they want to deceive. Although the Jews were allowed to form their own cultural organisation, the Nazi Commissioner, in agreement with the secret police, appointed as chairman of this organisation a man who is suspected of being a secret agent of the Nazi police, and is distrusted by the Jews themselves. The Jews are not allowed to produce, for instance, Mozart's operas on their own stage, because the police allege that the Jews are incapable of understanding the real German art of Mozart (the bitter irony of this lies in the fact that Bruno Walter, who is recognised as one of the greatest living conductors of Mozart's music, is a Jew). I have gone into details in order show how a person, living in Germany and seeing only the clean streets and the outward order, can get entirely wrong impression, and to show how skilful the Nazi propaganda is in deceiving even those foreigners who go to Germany with the best intentions of learning the truth.

Yet it appeared that the German people themselves believed it was all necessary. In October 1937, Sir Thomas Cook, the MP for Norfolk Northern, told a constituency meeting, 'The German masses desired peace with the rest of the world, particularly with Britain. They believed that Germany's rearmament was solely for the purpose of defence and that labour camps and Nazi policy in industry were necessary to make Germany self-supporting.'

So, Britons were alive to the plight of the Jews in Germany, and the average German seemed to think that it was all for their greater good. But what about the danger that Nazism posed to the rest of Europe? In January 1936, Joseph Goebbels read, over the wireless, Hitler's New Year's message to the German people. Rearmament was a key point:

> The new Germany is celebrating the New Year for the third time. Twelve months ago, the imminent breakdown of the National Socialist regime was prophesied for the third time. Now, for the third time, Germany has grown out of this regime stronger and healthier in every part of her national life ... The coming year will be a further year of National Socialist determination and energy ... as the country has grown stronger and finds the visible expression of its strength in the restoration of the armed forces, so do we become more conscious of the responsibilities which the possession of the new weapon lays upon us ... In the coming year it will be our zealous endeavour to remain a bulwark of European discipline and culture against the Bolshevist enemy of mankind.

As for the British government, there appeared to be indecision about whether to re-arm or not. In November 1936, Winston Churchill 'severely reproached' Stanley Baldwin for having failed to keep his pledge to see to it that in air strength Britain would 'no longer be in a position inferior to any country within striking distance of its shores'. 'The Government simply cannot make up their minds, or they cannot get the Prime Minister to make up his mind,' he complained. They go on 'deciding only to be undecided', he said.

Baldwin's response was that there was a stronger pacifist feeling running through Britain than at any time since the Great War, and so he had to tread carefully. The Peace Ballot, or the National Declaration on the League of Nations and Armaments, to give it its proper title – five questions attempting to discover what the public's attitude was to rearmament – held in 1934–1935 saw 11.64 million adults, 38.2 per cent of the population aged 18 and over, vote. Leaflets explained to voters:

> In this Ballot you are asked to vote only for peace or war – whether you approve of the League of Nations or not, whether you are in favour of international disarmament or not. And by voting for the League of Nations you are helping not only your country, but the other countries of the World to maintain Peace and abolish war with all its horrors.

The overwhelming majority, more than 90 per cent, were in favour of Britain remaining in the League of Nations and in favour of a reduction in rearmament by international agreement. The only question that brought a 'yes' majority (58.7 per cent in favour) for military action was 5(b) that asked, if one nation attacked another, should others combine militarily if economic and non-military measures failed.

According to his son, A. Windham Baldwin, writing in 1955, Stanley Baldwin had been planning rearmament from 1934 but had to proceed cautiously to avoid antagonising public opinion. Baldwin himself had already replied to Churchill's criticism, arguing that had he gone to the country and said that because Germany was rearming, then Britain must too, then the loss of the 1935 General Election would have been certain.

Baldwin referred to Britain as a 'pacific democracy' and there were movements to oppose rearmament. By 1937, the Peace Pledge Union, created in 1934 by a passionate pacifist orator, Dick Sheppard, a former Dean of Canterbury Cathedral, boasted 133,000 members organised into 725 groups aimed at creating a warless world. Its message of 'War will cease when men refuse to fight' subscribed to the theory that, if men refused to fight, then others would too.

By 1938, Moral Re-Armament, the nondenominational revivalistic movement that had evolved from American churchman Frank N. D. Buchman's Oxford Group, held that the roots of all problems were fear and selfishness. In May that year, Buchman, a former Lutheran minister, would tell a meeting at East Ham Town Hall, 'The crisis is fundamentally a moral one. The nations must re-arm morally. Moral recovery is essentially the forerunner of economic recovery. Moral recovery creates not crisis but confidence and unity in every phase of life.' Moral Re-Armament appealed to those who found

Dick Sheppard's pacifism just too simple. Its adherents were opposed to political solutions that communism and fascism offered, and during the 1930s it championed French-German reconciliation and a European integration with strong moral foundations. Moral Re-Armament made some progress in Germany after the Second World War. In May 1949, the *New York Times* reported, 'German industrialists and employers in the Ruhr area have been more than usually receptive to the activities here of the Moral Rearmament group, which currently has a hundred representatives living with families of workers.'

Lord Beaverbrook, whose *Daily Express* had ridiculed the Peace Ballot, wrote later that, by 1936, Baldwin had been badly damaged in public life by his approach to rearmament: 'He was believed by many to have behaved with cynicism and dishonesty.'

When it came to re-equipping Britain's military forces, in 1919 the government had drafted the 'Ten Year Rule'. Another great war was not expected for at least a decade and so the UK made no investment in new armaments. In 1928, Winston Churchill, the Chancellor of the Exchequer, made the rule permanent, thus setting the clock back each year to year one. The problem with this was that the end of the ten-year period would never be reached, which pleased the Treasury but was deeply worrying for the armed forces, especially the Royal Navy. And with orders for warships at an all-time low, that also adversely affected shipbuilding and steel, and engineering because weapons and ammunition were not needed either.

The collapse of the Geneva Disarmament Conference in June 1934 was the key to Britain seriously considering rearmament. Germany had withdrawn from the conference two years earlier, and there was also disagreement over the definition of 'offensive' and 'defensive' weapons. During 1936, the Defence Requirements Sub-Committee doubled its projection for the Royal Navy's fleet to bring it equal with the combined strength of the world's two largest navies, which happened to be those that Germany and the increasingly aggressive Japan were moving towards.

Despite the loss of skilled men during the period of disarmament, by 1937, the UK's shipbuilding was at full capacity, although it would take some years to achieve the target set by the Defence Requirements Sub-Committee. The needs of the RAF, which was also chasing parity with Germany, were given priority, and in 1938, the emphasis moved from heavy bombers to fighter defence, although continual delays meant that the supply of modern aircraft was not keeping up with demand. When it came to rearmament, the army was bottom of the pile and, again, defence was the key. The chances of having to send a land army to Europe were considered limited, and the emphasis was on coastal defence and anti-aircraft guns. It would be the spring of 1939 before the Cabinet came round to agreeing that Britain would probably have to send troops to fight on the Continent. Only then would conscription be introduced, and the Territorial Amy would be doubled in size.

The time was coming. In December 1937, writing in the *Nelson Leader*, Vincent Myles wanted to know why 'Germany is spending three quarters of its income on armaments when still her people are in a far worse plight since Hitler came to power'.

Chapter 18

A Terrible Transformation

> 'The threat of war now, or in the immediate future, has been averted ... and for that the whole country will be deeply thankful ... but peace has not yet been established.'
> Sir Archibald Sinclair MP

More rumblings in Europe. On Tuesday, 1 March 1938, Britain's newspapers reported that in Graz, the capital of the Austrian province of Styria, troops were standing by, awaiting a visit in the next two days by Arthur Seyss-Inquart, the country's pro-Nazi Minister of the Interior. Seyss-Inquart's visit, said a Reuters correspondent, was 'likely to be a fateful one as testing the strength and feeling in the most strongly Nazi city in Austria ... The more extreme Nazi elements may decide to defy his counsels of moderation'.

Trouble was also feared in Linz, the capital of Upper Austria. Nazis there were resisting a ban on the celebration – arranged by the National Political Department of a new organisation, the Fatherland Front – for 'German Day' the following Sunday. They would accept the ban only if three posts in the provincial government, including that of deputy governor, were given to Nazis.

In Berlin, Field Marshall Hermann Göring was addressing members of the armed forces: 'When the Führer, in his Reichstag speech, said that we could not tolerate the ill-treatment of the ten million Germans living beyond our frontiers, you must be ready to sacrifice all for this idea, if the day should come.'

That day was very close. The previous month, Hitler had invited the Austrian Chancellor, Kurt von Schuschnigg, to Berchtesgaden where he forced him into agreeing to give Austrian Nazis what amounted to a free hand. Schuschnigg had little choice. In 1934, after the murder of his immediate predecessor as Chancellor, Englebert Dollfuss, by Nazis, the Austrians could count on Mussolini for support. Now, after invading Abyssinia, Mussolini needed Hitler's support. And when the Führer gave Il Duce a personal assurance that he would not press for the return of Italian territories that had once been ruled by Austria, that led, in 1937, to the formation of the Rome–Berlin Axis, a military coalition between Germany, Italy, and Japan.

Schuschnigg soon reneged on his agreement with Hitler, announcing instead a plebiscite on the question of 'Anschluss', the political union of Germany and Austria. The vote would be held on 13 March 1938. On 11 March, Hitler sent Schuschnigg an ultimatum: hand power to the Austrian Nazis or face invasion. Schuschnigg looked around for support from fellow members of the League of Nations. None was forthcoming. Britain and France had no appetite for interfering. On 12 March, German troops crossed the border into Austria. It was claimed to be in response to a telegram from Seyss-Inquart requesting German military aid:

> The provincial Austrian Government, which after the resignation of the Government of Schuschnigg sees as its task the restoration of peace and order in Austria, addresses the German Government the urgent request to help it in its task and to help it in preventing bloodshed. For this purpose it asks the German Government for the despatch of troops at the earliest possible time.

In fact, the wire had been drafted for some time and when it was eventually sent, by a Nazi agent in Vienna, the Wehrmacht were already on their way. If those troops were not best organised then it did not matter. Austria's armed forces had been ordered not to resist.

The Germans were greeted with cheers and were garlanded. Nazi flags lined their progress. The *News Chronicle*:

> In Vienna, in the strongly Nazi cities of Graz, Linz and Innsbruck, the long-forbidden uniforms of Storm Troopers and Black Guards appeared in hundreds and thousands on the streets. Vast torchlight processions marched through the capital ... Fifty thousand Nazis swept through Graz, shouting German songs and raising the swastika banner. Police withdrew from the streets and working-class people remained behind closed doors.

That afternoon, Hitler, with a bodyguard reported to number around 4,000 soldiers, entered Austria at his birthplace, Braunau am Inn. By evening, he was in Linz, and when he reached Vienna on 15 March, there were 200,000 Austrians in the Heldenplatz (Square of Heroes) to hear him announce that 'the oldest eastern province of the German people shall be, from this point on, the newest bastion of the German Reich'. Hitler's original intention had been to leave Arthur Seyss-Inquart, who had been appointed Chancellor of Austria at midnight on 12 March, as the head of the satellite state, but the enthusiasm that greeted the invasion provided all the encouragement the Führer needed to absorb Austria directly into the Third Reich. Seyss-Inquart's time as Chancellor of his country lasted all of two days. Austrians now saluted Adolf Hitler. On 10 April, a referendum throughout the entire Reich had, it was claimed, seen 99.75 per cent of Austrians vote in favour of their fate. Seyss-Inquart would serve as governor of what was now a provincial administration.

At one stroke, Hitler had added to the Third Reich 7 million people, an army of 100,000 men and had access to vital resources such as iron ore and steel. Moreover, he now had a clear run at Yugoslavia and Hungary – and, yes, Italy – as well as practically encircling the new democratic state of Czechoslovakia, which he had come to hate during his days in Vienna. The ease with which he had swallowed up Austria was most encouraging. Who would stand in his way now?

Journalist Norman Ewer wrote:

> Hitler has achieved his greatest aim. From now on Austria is, in fact, a part of the German Reich. To effect 'reunion of the two German States,' to bring about 'the return of German Austria to the great German Motherland' – these are the first objectives proclaimed in the opening chapter of *Mein Kampf*. Desire for reunion was not peculiar to the Nazis. In the days when both Germany and Austria were democracies it was the ardent wish of the majority of both nations. It would have come about in 1918 if the Allies had not forbidden it. But the union of two democracies was one thing, the bringing of Austria under the heel of the Third Reich and under the Nazi terror was another.

Faced by a dictator taking another country's land by force, the rest of Europe had again done nothing. Criticism from across the Atlantic prompted the former editor of the Liberal newspaper the *Westminster Gazette*, J. A. Spender, to write:

> I own some slight irritation on reading the comments of some American newspapers and the observations of certain American public men on our crisis. Let them say, if they will, that they have chosen the better part in standing aloof from the wicked and quarrelsome continent of Europe but let them spare us their homilies on our supposed lack of spirit.

Britain was having her own political problems. In February 1938, Anthony Eden had resigned as Foreign Secretary over Neville Chamberlain's appeasement policy towards Mussolini. Eden had been replaced by Lord Halifax, a major ally of Chamberlain's pursuit of appeasing Hitler too, and it has to be said that the reaction of most people in Britain to the Anschluss was one of indifference, apathy, one might say self-delusion. No one wanted another war, and, anyway, many shared the view that Germany had been badly served by the Treaty of Versailles, and who could blame the Germans if they became restless? The general view was perhaps best summed up by the politician and diplomat Lord Lothian, whose reaction to Germany marching back into the Rhineland in 1936 was that the Germans were doing 'no more than walking into their own back garden'. Lothian would be another leading advocate of appeasement throughout, the 1930s.

Others saw the mounting danger. On 24 March 1938, Winston Churchill, in the House of Commons, spoke of Britain's failure to respond to the Nazi menace: 'Now the victors are the vanquished, and those who threw down their arms in the field and sued for an armistice are striding on to world mastery. That is the position – that is the terrible transformation that has taken place bit by bit.'

So, no one wanted war. But throughout 1938, British towns and cities prepared for it. In Derby, the Air Ministry bought 55 acres of land to establish a £100,000 barrage balloon depot to defend against aerial attack. In April, the town marked 'Protection Week' – a drive to make locals aware of the air-raid precautions that would be implemented if war came. Some 26,000 leaflets were distributed and films encouraging new recruits to the Civil Defence authority were shown. More than 100,000 households received a booklet entitled *The Protection of Your*

Home Against Air-raids. On 7 August, an area of the Midlands covering more than 160 kilometres was subject to an experimental 'blackout' for two hours between 1.00 am and 3.00 am to allow home defence exercises by the RAF.

Czechoslovakia was now the hot spot. After Austria was handed to Hitler, the Czechs, surrounded on three fronts, were most at risk. The state had emerged in 1918, from the collapse of Austria-Hungary. Its territories, which included the valuable industrial areas of those vanquished Central Powers, were inhabited mostly by 7 million Czechs and 2 million Slovaks. But there were other nationalities such as Magyars, Poles, and Ukrainians. Most significantly, predominantly in the west – in the Sudetenland – lived 3.25 million German-speakers who had had Czech nationality thrust upon them at the birth of the new state. Here was the problem. Despite its disparate make-up, Czechoslovakia enjoyed a relatively high standard of living, but the Sudetenland, with high unemployment, did not fully share in that. And because it shared a border with Germany, it was subject to oppressive security measures.

It was a situation that Hitler manipulated to his fullest advantage. In 1934, the German minority formed the German Home Front Party. The following year, its name was changed to the Sudeten German Party, and in 1937, financed by Hitler, it was demanding the right to form an autonomous National Socialist state. The Anschluss had left the Sudetenland exposed to the might of the German army, which meant that the rest of Czechoslovakia was also laid bare to invasion. The day after Germany entered Austria, Churchill told the House of Commons that although the name of Czechoslovakia might sound 'outlandish' to British ears, 'they are still a virile people, they still have their rights ... and they have a strongly manifested will to live, a will to live freely'.

There were so many complications. In the event of an invasion, if France, which had guaranteed Czechoslovakia's independence, went to the aid of the Czechs, then Russia had offered to do the same. The French, meanwhile, wanted to know, if they went to war, what Britain's reaction would be. And as the overriding mood in the United Kingdom was that the British did not want to go to war at all, least of all over this 'outlandish' sounding country, France rejected Russia's offer of support because it would never be needed. There was also the popular view that Hitler was Europe's defender against the 'Red Peril' of communism. Indeed, for several years now he had been declaring himself as such.

A Terrible Transformation

Throughout the summer of 1938, Germany conducted what today would be called a campaign of false news against the Czechs. Goebbels's Nazi Propaganda Ministry poured out stories of Czech atrocities against the Sudeten Germans. The Czech president, Dr Edvard Benes, became the target of a stream of threats and insults from Berlin. In August, German troops were moved to the border.

Neville Chamberlain was convinced that the only hope for peace in Europe was to concede to German demands for the Sudetenland being granted autonomy. On 15 September 1938, for the first time in his life, he travelled by aircraft. His destination was Munich. When he arrived at Berchtesgaden, he discovered that, while he was en route, Hitler had upped his demands from Sudetenland autonomy to, just like Austria, its complete absorption into the Third Reich. Chamberlain agreed, feeling that 'here was a man who could be relied upon when he had given his word'.

Back in London, Chamberlain met with the French Prime Minister, Edouard Daladier, and his Foreign Minister, Georges Bonnet. There was no discussion about trying to persuade Hitler to conduct a plebiscite to ascertain how enthusiastic the majority of Sudetens were at the prospect of becoming citizens of the Third Reich. It was certain that it would produce the same overwhelming 'yes' vote as the Austrian referendum on the same question. So the French were persuaded to abandon their former allies. The only concern now was how best to break it to Edvard Benes and his government that Chamberlain and Daladier accepted the outright incorporation of the Sudetenland.

On the day after the Anschluss, Churchill had reminded Parliament that the 'virile' people of this 'outlandish' country had a line of fortresses. And the entire line of these defensive fortifications upon which the rest of Czechoslovakia depended for protection lay within the Sudetenland.

Elsewhere, life was going on as usual for a group of fifty-three medical students and lecturers from Edinburgh University, who told *The Scotsman* about the lovely trip they had just enjoyed while visiting clinics in Germany. They were met by a 'jovial white-haired professor' and were able to pull in a visit to Berchtesgaden 'where a few days later, Neville Chamberlain was to pay his historic visit to the Führer'.

Historic indeed. In the small hours of 21 September, British and French ministers in Prague told Dr Benes that all areas of his country containing more than 50 per cent of Germans should be handed over to Hitler 'before producing a situation for which France and Britain could take no responsibility'.

Clement Attlee asked for Parliament to be recalled, but Chamberlain told him that to do that when he was engaged on 'difficult and delicate negotiations with the object of finding a peaceful solution to a problem which, if not handled with the utmost care, might have the most serious consequences for this country' would make his task impossible.

Chamberlain again flew to Germany, apparently full of optimism. As he boarded his aircraft, he told reporters, 'European peace is what I am aiming at. I hope that this journey will open the way to get it.'

On 23 September, the *Belfast Telegraph* reported that the postponement of talks between Chamberlain and Hitler had 'caused a sensation, and newspapermen feared an entirely new situation had arisen'. The Berlin-based *Tageblatt* was more optimistic: 'We are convinced that the English people will finally sanction the policy of Mr Chamberlain, who looks further ahead than his opponents.' *Jour Echo de Paris* felt, 'It remains for Hitler to be persuaded that from our side he has obtained the maximum.'

The delay was temporary. On 24 September, Chamberlain met Hitler at the Rheinhotel Dreesen in Bad Godesberg, a suburb of Bonn on the banks of the Rhine. He told the German leader that Britain and France had recommended to Dr Benes that the Czechs should agree to Hitler's demands. Hitler thanked the British Prime Minister very much but said that he was afraid that this would not now be enough. Other nations, bordering parts of Czechoslovakia in the east, now wanted areas that contained their kinfolk – Poles and Hungarians, for instance – handing back to them. Czechoslovakia would be dismembered.

Hitler's proposal – the so-called Godesberg Memorandum – was that if the Czech government had not agreed by 2.00 pm on 28 September to his terms, then the German army would march into the Sudetenland on 1 October.

The 28 September would be a momentous day: Czechoslovakia rejected the Memorandum and her army waited behind the fortress line; France ordered the mobilisation of more than half a million men; Belgium mobilised 270,000; Britain mobilised the Royal Navy. At 3.00 pm, Hitler sent a message to Chamberlain and Daladier, proposing yet another meeting. Mussolini would also be there. The Soviet Union would not be invited. And the Czechs could come but would have to wait outside before leaning their fate.

Two days later, in Munich, Chamberlain and Daladier signed an agreement that confirmed their willingness to pay Hitler's price for, so they thought, peace in Europe. German troops would move into the

Sudetenland from 1 October, and an international commission would decide Czechoslovakia's new borders. Poland was happy because she would get back land where her people now lived on the Czech side of a new border that had been inflicted upon her. Less than a month later, the German Foreign Minister, Joachim von Ribbentrop, would be telling the Polish ambassador to Germany that the free port city of Danzig must be handed back to Germany and that Germans must be given extraterritorial rights in the Polish Corridor.

On 30 September 1938, Neville Chamberlain was greeted by cheering crowds as he alighted from an aircraft at Heston aerodrome, to the west of London, and stood before a microphone, waved a piece a paper that he had taken from his wallet, and announced, 'Here is the paper which bears his [Hitler's] name on it as well as mine.' The paper, he said, was symbolic of the desire of 'our two peoples never to go to war with one another again'. Chamberlain and Hitler had agreed that 'the method of consultation shall be the method adopted to deal with any other questions that may concern our two countries ... and thus contribute to the assurance of peace in Europe'.

Even before he left Munich, Chamberlain had enjoyed a taste of the reception that was in store for him back home. The *News Chronicle*'s Vernon Bartlett wrote, 'by ten o'clock there was a crowd calling for him outside his hotel. When he appeared on the balcony he received such an ovation as no other British statesman has ever had in Germany.'

From Heston, the Prime Minister, together with Lord Halifax, was driven straight to Buckingham Palace. As his car, already covered in red, white, and blue streamers thrown by well-wishers, was driven at walking pace into the forecourt, people cheered, motorcar horns blared, and members of the King's household and their friends ran forward, waving their hats and cheering. In the palace's private quarters, Chamberlain was greeted by his wife before stepping out on to the balcony with the King and Queen. When the King motioned for him to move forward, he fumbled with his handkerchief and, for a moment, seemed overcome with emotion before acknowledging more cheering crowds with a wave and a broad smile.

Then it was off to 10 Downing Street, where police struggled for twenty minutes before they could make a path wide enough for his chauffeur-driven car to pass. A girl leapt onto the top of the car, with Chamberlain still in it, screaming at the top of her voice as she waved a Union Flag. While they were waiting, the crowd sang 'Rule Britannia',

'O God Our Help in Ages Past', and 'For He's a Jolly Good Fellow' before the Prime Minister could be squeezed out of the car and into the house. Almost immediately, he appeared at the centre window on the first floor. He then put his hands on the sill, leant slightly forward and, according to the *Daily Mirror*, 'talked to the crowd like a man telling his neighbour good news': 'This is the second time in our history that there has come back from Germany to Downing Street peace with honour [a reference to Disraeli's return from Berlin in 1878]. I believe it is peace in our time. We thank you from the bottom of our hearts.'

'We thank you, you have saved us,' someone in the crowd shouted back.

'Now I recommend you go home and sleep quietly in your beds,' Chamberlain told the crowd before turning and disappearing back into the house. In the street below, a man with a foreign accent began shaking hands with everyone around him. 'I am German. Three cheers for England!' he shouted. 'Three cheers for Germany!' shouted an Englishman.

All evening, crowds of rejoicing Londoners streamed up and down Whitehall. Bouquets and telegrams continued to arrive at Number 10. That weekend, relief swept throughout Britain. The nation's pubs were full, and one minute's silence was held at football matches to give thanks for that promised peace that had seemed to have been slipping away. Almost everyone was celebrating – and grateful. *Paris-Soir* opened a subscription to buy Neville Chamberlain a house in France, near a river so that he could indulge in his favourite pastime of fishing. It would be called 'Maison de le Paix', the 'House of Peace'. In Geneva, the authorities announced that a city street would be renamed 'Neville Chamberlain'. Birmingham University was offered £10,000 to provide a Neville Chamberlain Scholarship, and at the North Staffordshire Royal Infirmary in Stoke-on-Trent, a local worthy donated £1,000 to endow a bed in the name of the Prime Minister.

For the moment, newspaper headlines were all about that piece of paper signed by Neville Chamberlain and Adolf Hitler.

There were, however, already pockets of disaffection. Two leaders of a march protesting against Chamberlain's policy were allowed to hand in a petition at 10 Downing Street. And when everyone had settled down and began to consider another piece of paper, the one to which Daladier and Mussolini had added their signatures, the one that agreed to hand over the Sudetenland to Germany, the one that had been signed in the

A Terrible Transformation

face of a threatened invasion of Czechoslovakia, then the country's mood began to change. Euphoria gave way to the realisation that Britain had stepped not away from another war, but towards the possibility of it – that 'terrible transformation' that Winston Churchill had warned had 'taken place bit by bit'.

The digging of trenches for air-raid protection continued, and it was announced that in the event evacuation from larger cities proved necessary, the counties of Derbyshire, Lancashire, and Cheshire could provide emergency accommodation for 611,400 people from Liverpool, Bootle, and Manchester. In Hull, another forty-six ARP (Air-Raid Precautions) wardens were recruited, and the city's consignment of gas masks for civilians was almost complete.

Now Britain could not take her eyes off Hitler.

Chapter 19

Asylum and Sanctuary on Our Doorsteps

> 'Whosoever rescues a single soul is considered by scripture to have saved the whole world.'
>
> *The Talmud*

On the night of 9 November 1938, violent anti-Jewish demonstrations broke out across Germany, Austria, and the Sudetenland. They were portrayed by the Nazis as a justifiable reaction to the assassination of a Foreign Office diplomat at the German embassy in Paris earlier that day. Ernst vom Rath had been shot five times by Herschel Grynszpan, a 17-year-old Polish Jew. Grynszpan's family had been among the thousands of Jews of Polish citizenship expelled from Germany. In the forty-eight hours following vom Rath's murder, Jewish homes, shops, and synagogues were attacked. The violence became known as 'Kristallnacht', 'Crystal Night', or 'The Night of Broken Glass', referring to the shards from thousands of broken windows that littered the streets.

Five days after Kristallnacht, a delegation of Jewish, British, and Quaker leaders met with Neville Chamberlain. They had an urgent request for the Prime Minister: that the British government temporarily permitted the admission of unaccompanied Jewish children fleeing from the Third Reich. Chamberlain, only too aware of the increasingly precarious situation for German, Austrian, and Czech Jews, discussed the issue with his Cabinet the following day. On 21 November, a Bill to waive visa requirements was presented to Parliament and quickly passed, enabling what would be one of the world's biggest rescue operations. But would Jewish families send their unaccompanied children to the United Kingdom, away from everything familiar – and with no guarantee that they would ever see them again?

When Hitler came to power five years earlier, the answer would probably still have been a resounding 'no'. But now, with the ever-worsening persecution faced by Jews living under Nazi rule, it was clear that thousands of families saw this option, while utterly heart-breaking, as the only sensible one. There were still difficulties. Although the British government had made a rescue effort of Jewish children from Nazi territory a legal possibility, it was the organisational work and financial generosity of individuals, organisations, and charities that would make it happen.

But just where would Britain house what could be tens of thousands of young refugees? The original intention was first to get them to safety in the UK, and then to relocate them across the Empire to begin their new lives. British Guiana, Northern Rhodesia, and Tanganyika were among the places considered. It was doubted that the traditional 'Jewish homeland' of Palestine could yet cope with the number of refugees anticipated. And there was another problem: in the words of the *Yorkshire Post:* 'Most of the new refugees are townsmen, whereas most of the available places for settlement are agricultural.' It was clear that, for the time being at least, any refugees coming through the 'Kindertransport' ('Child Transport') would have to be cared for in Britain.

On 24 November, the BBC Home Service broadcast an appeal for fosterers. Five hundred families came forward immediately and volunteers began visiting homes to report on suitability. With time short, and need great, the emphasis was on finding clean houses and respectable families, whether or not they were Jewish.

Meanwhile, the agencies which made up the Movement for the Care of Children from Germany (later known as the Refugee Children's Movement) began to raise funds for the rescue operation. Since it was assumed that each child's stay in Britain would be only temporary, a sum of £50 per child had to be guaranteed to pay for their eventual onward relocation. Home Secretary Sir Samuel Hoare reassured the public that Jewish and other organisations had already promised to cover the costs and that the refugees would not become a financial burden on the country.

The congregation of St Matthew's Church in Worthing announced plans to adopt two Jewish children. They had guaranteed £70 per year for three years to secure education and to 'give a start in life'. Parish curate Reverend Rowland S. Smith told the local newspaper, the *Worthing Gazette*, that although the children would be chosen by the Church of England Committee for non-Aryan Christians (children with some Jewish blood, although Christian by faith), he had received many letters from refugee Europeans from all across England nominating their brother or sister for the scheme.

As undeniably enthusiastic and kind as most of the people of Britain were, the idea of adopting, even temporarily, an unlimited number of Jewish children into the country did not meet with universal approval. Even Reverend Smith received a number of anonymous letters condemning the plans. One correspondent suggested that, since there were many Britons unemployed and struggling, perhaps it might be preferable to help them first?

Representatives from the organising charities were sent to Germany and Austria to establish a system for selecting and processing the children, with some cooperation from the Germans who seemed happy to assist any scheme that would leave them fewer Jews with which to deal. Priority was given to those considered in most peril – children from Jewish orphanages, or living in poverty, or with at least one parent already in a concentration camp – as well as teenagers themselves held in concentration camps or at risk of arrest.

The first transport comprised 196 children, most of whom came from a Jewish orphanage in Berlin that had been destroyed on Kristallnacht. The remainder were from Hamburg. They left Berlin on 1 December 1938 and arrived aboard the TSS *Prague* at Parkeston Quay, Harwich, the following day. The children had been accompanied by eight adults, who were not permitted to join them in Britain, and who returned to Germany with the grim realisation of the fate that awaited them – like that of Irma Zanker, who was eventually deported to Auschwitz.

A few members of the press were there to witness the sad little crocodile of young refugees stepping ashore. The children carried with them small rucksacks and suitcases which contained what now represented all their worldly goods. Before they had been permitted to cross from Germany into the Netherlands, their neatly packed bags had been searched aggressively by the SS to ensure they contained no valuables, and no more than the equivalent of one shilling (5p) in money. In contrast, as they passed through British Customs at Harwich, they were greeted with encouraging smiles. Some of the children arrived with nothing but the clothes they were wearing; others carried treasured belongings like the small boy who had told reporters that he was from Breslau. In a battered case, he was carrying a violin, and he wanted, one day, to be a musician, he said.

Each youngster emptied their pockets of childhood ephemera – propelling pencils and fountain pens, small torches, and the like. Some clutched their identity cards and small photographs. Each was issued with a manila tag bearing their name and an identifying number. They were taken first to the nearby Dovercourt Bay holiday camp, then owned by Butlins, which was used as a refugee reception centre. There the children were given a breakfast of porridge, bread, butter, and jam, as well as a cup of tea or cocoa – their first meal for more than twenty-four hours. A Press Association reporter observed some writing home to their loved ones, others splashing around in the camp's swimming pool or helping out in the kitchen, while some of the older girls comforted the youngest children. One room was piled to the ceiling with donated clothing. It would certainly be needed – hundreds more children were expected within days.

In January 1939, accompanied by Lady Marion Philipps, Nancy de Selincourt visited Dovercourt on behalf of the Women's Voluntary Service. Mrs Selincourt's report noted, 'The camp leaders are very keen, full of human kindness, vitality and emanating a cheerful atmosphere. Great efforts are made to stress the hopes of the children, and so help them forget the past. They seemed wonderfully happy, considering all they had been through.'

She was somewhat less convinced by the catering arrangements provided by Butlins: 'The one glaring defect appears to be the profiteering on catering, which should be remedied. The excuse for this would seem to be the difficulty of finding suitable accommodation in a short time, which necessitated using the easiest available.' Soon the youngsters would be placed in their foster homes. Some to live with families, others to hostels of varying sizes, or housed in schools, like the Quaker Ayton School in North Yorkshire, where dozens of youngsters would spend the rest of their childhoods.

On 8 December, former Prime Minister Stanley Baldwin made a stirring radio appeal urging the British government to do more for Jews living under the Nazis. He spoke of 'thousands of men, women, and children, despoiled of their goods, driven from their homes ... seeking asylum and sanctuary on our doorsteps'. Few listening could have failed to be moved when he reminded:

> They may not be our fellow subjects, but they are our fellow men. Tonight, I plead for the victims who turn to England for

help ... Thousands of every degree of education, industry, wealth, position, have been made equal in misery. I shall not attempt to depict to you what it means to be scorned and branded and isolated like a leper. The honour of our country is challenged, our Christian charity is challenged, and it is up to us to meet that challenge.

On the same day, the *Midland Daily Telegraph* published a letter signed by notable local figures including the Mayor of Coventry, Alderman S. Stringer, the local MP, William Strickland, and religious leaders of several faiths, asking for the citizens of Coventry to do their bit. Coventry's Jewish community were already preparing to accept twenty-five children into their homes, and now the wider population of the city was being asked to provide accommodation for a further fifty. German-speaking locals were being drafted in to work as translators.

Sixty-four kilometres away, in Derby, the vicar of St Alkmund's Church, local Quakers, and the local Soroptimist Club had organised a public meeting to decide how best that town could help out. The following May, the *Derby Evening Telegraph* revealed that officials from Victoria Street Congregational Church had rented a small house in nearby Mount Street to provide temporary shelter for refugees. While some furniture had also been provided, beds and bedding were still needed.

In early February 1939, the people of Leicester, too, were asked to provide homes, as well as jobs in local industry, for those aged 15 and 16 who would soon be arriving. Meanwhile, some 200 refugees were taken to Whittingehame House in East Lothian, the former home of Lord Balfour. There a 'farm school' had been established to prepare Jewish child refugees for a potential new life in Palestine.

While the infrastructure was there to receive them, all the Kindertransportees faced two common challenges. Firstly, whether toddler or teenager, all had experienced the tremendous upheaval and separation from mums, dads, and older siblings without proper explanation or any understanding of how long this might last. The older ones also bore the burden of some knowledge of what might now be happening back home. Secondly, each refugee had to try to fit in somewhere where they were undeniably different. Different from their new families, their new schoolmates, their new neighbours. Most had to learn English from scratch. And it was not easy to blend in when many British children had been taught to mistrust all things German.

Indeed, at the outbreak of war, the many refugees from Germany would be regarded as security threats, and susceptible to Nazi propaganda. It was a painful irony that the older Kindertransportees fell into this grouping. In 1940, when 'enemy aliens' would find themselves interned on the Isle of Man, their number included some 1,000 older Jewish children.

The first three months of the scheme had concentrated on rescuing children from Germany and Austria. As the months went by, and Nazi control stretched over more of Europe, so the rescue operation was extended, expanding into the rest of Czechoslovakia and eventually into Poland, although generally using the same route. The Nazis would not agree to any evacuation that might block German ports, and so, although some children travelled by air into Heston where, in September 1938, Neville Chamberlain had waved the piece of paper that confirmed 'peace in our time', or by boat into Dover, most travelled by train to the Hook of Holland near Rotterdam and then by ferry to Harwich. Those with pre-organised foster families were taken to London by train to meet them at Liverpool Street Station. Over nine months, some 10,000 predominantly Jewish children were brought to safety in the United Kingdom. No upper restriction had been placed on the number of refugees who could be rescued. The only limit was time. And that was fast running out.

Some of the last to escape arrived in Leicester in the late summer of 1939. One local family who opened their doors to two Jewish refugees was that of Frederick and Mary Attenborough, who lived at College House. Frederick was the principal of University College in the city – an establishment that had welcomed a number of fleeing Jewish academics for several years. In the late summer of 1939, Irene and Helga Bejach, the youngest daughters of a Berlin public health official, joined the Attenboroughs and their three sons, Richard, David, and John. Richard, who would become the actor and director Lord Attenborough, remembered them as

> two pale waifs with their pathetic little cases, aged ten and 12. They looked sad and ill. They were nervous wrecks ... Their house in Germany had been smashed by Nazis with guns and their father taken away ... After the girls had been with us for three weeks, my brothers David, John and I were called into the study by our parents. Our mother said, 'We absolutely love you boys, but we will have to show even

more love to these girls because they are here on their own and without their parents. It is entirely up to you, darlings, if they stay.'

The girls had expected to move quickly on to family in the United States. However, the outbreak of war put paid to that. Middle Attenborough son, the naturalist Sir David, remembered his mother saying to the five children, 'Well, now we are one family.'

The girls would spend the next seven years with the Attenboroughs before joining an uncle in New York. In an interview with the *Daily Mail* in 2009, Richard said that the Bejachs did indeed become very much a part of the family: 'They helped shape our lives ... we loved and cherished them ...We really did see them as sisters, virtually from the time we were told they were going to live with us.' Like most of the refugees, Irene and Helga never saw their parents again.

The last transport left Germany on 1 September 1939. A party that departed Prague on 3 September was sent back. The line between being rescued or being left behind was simply that fine. The declaration of war meant it was no longer possible to evacuate any more refugees from Nazi-held territory.

Kindertransports from other parts of Europe continued for a while but ended as the Nazis rampaged through Europe. Britain had done its best for its young neighbours, but now had more pressing matters at home.

Chapter 20

A Period of Danger More Acute...

> 'Gas masks have suddenly become part of everyday civilian life, and everybody is carrying the square cardboard cartons that look as though they might contain a pound of grapes for a sick friend.'
>
> Mollie Panter-Downes in the *New Yorker* magazine

On 17 March 1939, Neville Chamberlain announced that he had changed his opinion. Adolf Hitler was no longer 'a man who could be relied upon when he had given his word'. Three days earlier, the province of Slovakia had declared its independence from Czechoslovakia. Then German troops marched into Prague. The Slovaks' independence had lasted all of two days. On 16 March, Hitler accepted Slovakia as a protectorate of the Third Reich.

For some time, Chamberlain had been reluctantly abandoning his policy of appeasing Hitler. It had been a slow and painful process but his visit to Rome in January had dashed hopes of keeping Mussolini out of the picture and increased fears of where the dictators would strike next. As far as Hitler was concerned, the obvious answer was Czechoslovakia. Mussolini's next target was Albania, which he invaded in April 1939, absorbing the country into the Italian Empire.

The day after the dismemberment of Czechoslovakia began, Lord Halifax, the Foreign Secretary, told the House of Lords that the situation there was 'a shock to the confidence that had begun to spring up in Europe'. Halifax told the Lords that

> it would appear that the state of Czechoslovakia has ceased to exist and the territory over which the Government was formerly responsible has been divided ... having regard to the effect on general conditions in Europe which these events are bound to exert, the Government feel the present moment to be inappropriate for the proposed visit of the

President of the Board of Trade, and the Secretary for Overseas Trade, to Berlin, which has accordingly been postponed. The German Government has been so informed.

Yet, overall, the immediate reaction of the British government was muted. Chamberlain told the House of Commons that in the opinion of the government, the situation had radically altered since the Slovak Diet declared the independence of Slovakia. The effect of this declaration of independence, he said, put an end by internal disruption to the state whose frontiers Britain had proposed to guarantee, and His Majesty's government could 'not accordingly hold itself any longer bound by those obligations'. There was no sympathy for the Czechs, and no word of reproach for Hitler.

Hitler's march into Prague, however, brought about a sea-change in British public opinion. No longer could the fate of this country with the 'outlandish' name be ignored. A policy of isolation towards central Europe was not going to avoid conflict. Public anger had been aroused, and Chamberlain now felt obliged to acknowledge it. On 17 March, in a speech at Birmingham Town Hall to a crowded annual meeting of the local Unionist Association, he warned Germany that 'acts of violence and injustice bring, sooner or later, their own rewards'.

Chamberlain asked if this was the end of an old adventure, or the beginning of a new one. Was this the last attack on a small state or was it to be followed by others? Was this, in fact, a step in the direction of an attempt to dominate by force? To most people, the question was rhetorical.

Chamberlain continued, 'Every one of these incursions raises fresh dangers for Germany. I venture to prophesy that in the end she will bitterly regret what her Government has done ... One thing is certain: public opinion in the world has received a sharper shock than has ever yet been administered to it, even by the present regime in Germany.'

Chamberlain reminded his audience of a speech that Hitler had made in the Sports-Plast in Berlin, after the Prime Minister's second visit to Munich the previous September, when the Führer said, 'This is the last territorial claim I will make in Europe.' Chamberlain said, 'I am convinced that after Munich the great majority of the British people shared my hope, and ardently desired that the policy [of appeasement] should be carried further. Today, I share their disappointment and indignation that these hopes have been so wantonly shattered.'

According to a proclamation read out in Prague the previous day, Bohemia and Moravia had been annexed to the German state. Non-German inhabitants now found themselves in a German protectorate, subject to the political, military, and economic needs of the Third Reich.

Where next? On 31 March, sixteen days after Hitler had entered Prague, Chamberlain told the Commons:

> I now have to inform the House ... that in the event of any action which clearly threatened Polish independence ... His Majesty's Government would feel themselves bound at once to lend the Polish Government all the support in their power. They have given the Polish Government an assurance to this effect. I may add that the French Government have authorised me to make it plain that they stand in the same position as do His Majesty's Government.

In reply to Arthur Greenwood, for the Labour opposition, Chamberlain said that his statement was meant to cover 'an interim period' and that other powers, including the Soviet Union, were being consulted.

'HITLER FURIOUS AT BRITISH PLEDGE' screamed the front-page headline in the following day's *Daily Mirror*.

The paper's lead story read:

> For the first time since 1914, Britain told the world yesterday that she was ready to fight in Europe to stop further German aggression ... It enraged Hitler who tore up the speech he had prepared to make today at Wilhelmshaven ... Hitler sent for his secretary, says Reuters, and redirected entirely those passages of his speech dealing with foreign affairs.

Part of it now read:

> If British statesmen today demand that every problem concerning vital German interests should first be discussed with England, then I could make precisely the same claim and demand that every British problem must first be discussed with us. Admittedly, this Englishman would answer,

'Palestine is none of your business!' But just as Germany has no business in Palestine, so England has no business in the German Lebensraum! ... One says we had no right to do this or that. I would like to ask a counter-question: what right, just to quote one example, has England to shoot down Arabs in Palestine, only because they are standing up for their home? Who gives England the right to do so?

By the end of April, Hitler would have denounced the Anglo-German Naval Treaty of 1935 and the German–Polish non-aggression pact of 1934.

The official German news agency of course reflected the anger of the Nazi leadership, and a violent anti-British campaign was soon in full flow: 'It is absolutely incomprehensible how Mr Chamberlain came to make such a statement out of the blue. One can only regard this statement as a laughable attempt to stir up unrest and show mistrust of Germany in the concert of nations.'

On 6 April, Chamberlain announced that the British and Polish governments had decided to enter into an agreement 'of a permanent reciprocal character'. The *Daily Record and Mail*'s 'The Lights of London' column commented, 'Mr Chamberlain has cleared the air very considerably. As a citizen of Britain you are now committed to fight for the Poles. The Poles have agreed to fight for Britain should Germany attack us. You may agree or disagree as you like. But the promise has been undertaken solemnly by both sides.'

As news spread through Warsaw that Poland would not be fighting alone, there was general rejoicing. A government spokesman said, 'The matter is simple. If Germany does not respect our frontiers, we will fight.'

Poland was now the major concern. The Poles had come down on Germany's side when part of the Munich agreement gave them land on their frontier with Czechoslovakia. Indeed, they had enjoyed that non-aggression pact with Germany since 1934.

But the Treaty of Versailles had provided the newly formed Second Republic of Poland with access to the Baltic, and economic rights to Danzig, historically one of the Germanic Free Ports of the Hanseatic League. West Prussia and East Prussia were separated by the Polish Corridor, a thin strip of land around the River Vistula. It meant that large numbers of German-speakers fell under Polish rule and East

Prussia become an enclave. Shortly after Munich, Poland was being quietly told by von Ribbentrop that Danzig must be handed back to Germany. From early in 1939, Hitler was openly demanding the city's reunification within the Third Reich. His diplomatic strategy for settling Germany's eastern front in preparation for an attack on the west was complex and, although he did not want to drive Poland into the arms of Britain, diplomacy was never going to settle the issue. In late March, the Polish Foreign Minister, Colonel Józef Beck, announced that any attempt by Germany to unilaterally alter Danzig's status would lead to war. Statements from Berlin said that reports of demands and ultimatums to Poland were 'exaggerated'. But it was not just Danzig and the Polish Corridor but the whole country that Hitler wanted. In early April, he ordered the German military high command to begin planning for 'Fall Weiss' ('Case White'), the codename for the invasion of Poland. In early May, Colonel Beck told the Polish Parliament, 'We in Poland do not know the conception of "peace at any price"; the one thing without price is honour.'

On 28 June, addressing members of London's Carlton Club, Winston Churchill warned:

> We are entering a period of danger more acute with ugly facts than we have ever known in the hard and disturbed period in which we have lived our lives. I take a serious view of the position in which we find ourselves today. It is very similar to what happened last year, but with this difference – this very important difference – that this year no means of retreat are now open. We had no treaty obligations to Czechoslovakia; we had never guaranteed their security ... But now we have given an absolute guarantee to Poland that if she is the object of an unprovoked attack by Nazi Germany, we, in company with our French allies, will be forced to declare war ... If my words could reach him – as indeed, they may – I would say to Herr Hitler, 'Pause, consider well before you take the plunge into the terrible unknown. Consider whether your life's work, which may even now be famous in the eyes of history is raising Germany from frustration and defeat to a point where all the world is waiting for her actions; consider whether all this may not be irretrievably cast away.'

Hitler was considering only one thing. In Berlin, the fine details for 'Fall Weiss' had already been settled. He just needed to be sure that the Soviet Union would not interfere, and, in late August, Germany and the Soviets would sign a non-aggression pact. Neither would attack the other, and neither would they support a third power against the other or join a group of powers that aimed at the other. The USSR also insisted on a secret protocol that effectively partitioned Eastern Europe, the northern border of Lithuania providing a dividing line between German and Soviet spheres of interest. Latvia, and Poland up to the Vistula, would be Soviet.

The summer of 1939 saw diplomats bluff, bargain, and threaten, and Britain prepare for war. Under the Military Training Act of 27 April 1939, all British men aged 20 and 21 who were fit and able were required to take six months' military training. At the Labour Party conference at Southport in June, there was a resolution that 'deplored the action of the National Executive in affording support to the scheme and the national register and called for the complete cessation of all further support of all National Service schemes, with the exception of air-raid precautions, initiated by the National Government'. Mr J. Morris, moving the motion on behalf of Lambeth Borough Labour Party, told conference that the National Service scheme by the 'pro-Fascist National Government' would inevitably lead to military and industrial conscription. The motion was defeated by 1,766,000 to 729,000.

The French were quite keen on Britain making military service compulsory. *Le Matin* commented, 'The voluntary system causes delay and is no longer compatible with modern warfare ... Only conscription can give Britain a powerful army which could be mobilised at a moment's notice.' When war broke out, the British Army still numbered only 897,000 men, compared to France's five million. By the end of 1939, however, more than 1.5 million men had been called up, just over 1.1 million in the British Army, the rest split between the Royal Navy and the RAF.

Civilians, too, were being prepared. In the typically English Midlands industrial town of Derby, by August 1939, the borough's air-raid precautions committee had delivered almost 9,000 air-raid shelters to private houses. Public shelters were adapted under railway arches, and trenches, each holding 740 people, were dug in public recreation grounds. Passengers on Corporation buses found the windows painted blue and the internal lights now dull amber. A mock air-raid was made on one factory and 700 workers were evacuated to the shelters.

The effectiveness of the lighting blackout was tested as part of a huge ARP exercise that covered the southern half of Britain. On 19 June, a nationwide campaign to educate the public in air-raid precautions began with a daytime experiment in London. Between 12.30 pm and 12.45 pm, in Chelsea, all traffic was brought to a standstill. The 'raid' was announced by police sirens and everyone in the streets was told to go to the shelters. Drivers were ordered to pull their vehicles in to the roadside to make way for ambulances and fire engines, and then themselves proceed to the nearest public shelter.

Throughout Britain, local council workers prepared to evacuate municipal archives and arts treasures, while rare museum exhibits were prepared for underground storage. All manner of official leaflets appeared: 'What to Do on a Train Journey'; 'What to Do with Your Pets'; 'Advice to Householders taking in Unaccompanied Children'.

The chief constable of Manchester, John Maxwell, said that air-raid precautions had claimed so much police time that there had been a sharp increase in crime in the city. Owing to the call to provide personnel for other essential services, he said, it had not always been possible to maintain the full strength of the preventative branch of the police. The *Daily Record and Mail* reported, 'Small tradesmen in London complain that customers are not paying their bills. It really is wicked to take advantage of the international situation to avoid paying dues and demands locally. Yet there are unscrupulous and unpatriotic people who are doing it.'

In Bristol, 'examination fright' was said to be the reason why there was a shortage of air-raid precautions recruits in the city. Mr R. H. Swainson, general secretary of Bristol YMCA, told the *Bristol Evening Post* that he thought that many people had an idea that the examinations were difficult, and feared that they would not be able to meet their requirements: 'It should be known that there was no difficulty in an ordinary man passing the examinations, which are nothing to be afraid of.' Warden training, he said, did not take up a tremendous amount of time or make severe demands on the individual. Special constable work was very interesting, and so was the training of the auxiliary firemen.

Birmingham City Council proposed to spend £11,866 on the provision of 420 warden posts for communicating reports of bomb damage, £2,622 on constructing air-raid shelters under shops at Digbeth, and £13,500 on a survey of basements. Trenches would provide accommodation for 50,000 citizens taking refuge from bombing raids. The city required 15,662 air-raid wardens and by June had enlisted 12,027. The auxiliary fire service had recruited 9,341 of the 10,338 it needed.

Not everyone was immediately worried about the prospect of war. Some had more immediate concerns. To publicise their grievances over the local council's differential rating scheme, municipal tenants in Birmingham went on a tour of housing estates. A correspondent writing to the *Birmingham Mail* said:

> We are certainly a queer people. Not only did the Corporation allow them to spend on buses a goodly portion of the rent they say they cannot afford to pay ... but also permitted them to plaster their vehicles with slogans declaring their undying defiance of their landlords. What would Hitler say to such good-natured tolerance, I wonder?

Meanwhile, Leicester City Council advertised for a 'temporary woman' instruction organiser for the transport section of its Air Raid Precautions Department. Applicants for the £2 10s-a-week (£2.50) post had to be expert drivers of heavy-type vehicles and be able to execute running repairs.

A meeting of ARP volunteers in Blyth was told by the mayor, Alderman A. W. Mather, that nothing that had arisen in the last few years had been so unmercifully criticised as air-raid precautions, and the critics were, in the main, people who should have known better: 'It is not reasonable to expect that something new and untried, which touches the lives of millions of people, would go swimmingly right from the start. The criticism has been levelled against those endeavouring to do their best under the most difficult circumstances.'

Nine days before the Second World War began, Britain was already familiar with enemy action. At 2.30 pm on 25 August 1939, a bomb placed in the carrier basket of a bicycle exploded in the heart of Coventry. By June that year, an IRA campaign known as the 'S Plan', devised to sabotage the economic, civil, and military infrastructure of the United Kingdom, had launched fifty-seven bomb attacks in London and seventy in the provinces. On 16 January, 27-year-old railway porter Albert Ross was killed when a 5lb bomb – one of three – was detonated in the centre of Manchester. That day, there were also bombs planted in London, Liverpool, and Birmingham. The orchestrated attacks continued through the spring and summer. In London, in June, a 22-year-old kitchen porter, Joseph Malone, appeared at Bow Street police court charged with causing an explosion after a gas bomb went off at the New Victoria Cinema on Vauxhall Bridge Road. There were between 1,500 and 1,700 people in the cinema at the time, and some were affected by fumes. Appearing in court with his left hand heavily bandaged, Malone said, 'I want you to understand that I am in this alone … the thing went off in my hand a bit too quick.' Malone, a native of Belfast, was later sentenced at the Old Bailey to five years' penal servitude.

In the small hours of 3 July alone, bombs exploded at railway stations in Birmingham, Coventry, Derby, Leicester, Nottingham, Stafford, and Warwick. On 26 July, Dr Donald Campbell, a 36-year-old lecturer in Latin at Edinburgh University, was killed when a bomb was detonated at London's King's Cross railway station. He was returning with his wife from their honeymoon.

The following month, the bombers returned to Coventry, and as Elsie Ansell, a 21-year-old shop assistant, paused to look in the window of a jeweller in the busy shopping area of Broadgate, the bomb in the bicycle went off. Elsie could be identified only through her clothes and her engagement ring; she had been due to marry in two weeks' time. The bomb claimed four more victims: John Arnott (15) and Rex Gentle (30), who both worked for W. H. Smith & Son; James Clay (82), who was a former president of the Coventry and District Co-operative Society; and Gwilym Rowlands (50), a road sweeper. Seventy others were injured. On 12 December, five people appeared before Birmingham Assizes, charged with Elsie's murder. Husband and wife Joseph and Mary Hewitt, and Brigid O'Hara, were found not guilty, but 32-year-old Peter Barnes and 29-year-old James McCormack, who used the alias of James Richards, were found guilty and sentenced to death. They would be hanged at Winson Green prison in Birmingham on Wednesday, 7 February 1940. Later that year, Coventry would have more horrors unleashed upon it, this time from the skies.

On 1 September 1939, writing in the *Daily Record and Mail*, Ian Coll raised the spectre of 'the war after next':

> Supposing the 'Peace powers' win this war it may be deferred but not for long – what are the chief considerations in the drafting of the victory treaty? Are they to be similar to those which motivated the gentlemen who formulated and imposed the Versailles Treaty? If so, we need not think we shall prevent the next war by winning this one. Peace is not imposed by rendering the loser impotent and trying to keep it in subjection for ever.

Chapter 21

Adolf Hitler Stepped In, Didn't He?

> 'I wound up my personal affairs, cursed Hitler and all his works, and, occasionally, sat down to think of what had been, and what might have been.'
>
> Tommy Lawton, Everton and
England footballer

Two German cars were entered for the late September 1939 motor-sport meeting at the Castle Donington circuit in Leicestershire. One of the drivers scheduled to appear was the star of Mercedes-Benz's famous 'Silver Arrows' Grand Prix team, Manfred von Brauchitsch, a relative of a German general. By then, however, von Brauchitsch would be busy elsewhere.

On Friday, 1 September, the front pages of the nation's evening newspapers broke the news. The *Gloucestershire Echo* was typical: 'War has begun. A German offensive along the entire Polish front has started and several towns have been bombarded. An official at the Polish embassy said, "I think the European war will start today. Poland will fight to the end for victory." Poland has now invoked the treaty with Britain.' The *Liverpool Echo* reported, 'Air-raid system in operation. Ban on ordinary hooters.'

At 5.40 am that day, Hitler had broadcast to his troops:

> I have no other choice than to meet force with force. The German army will fight the battle for the honour and vital rights of reborn Germany with hard determination. The Polish state has refused the peaceful settlement of relations that I desired and has appealed to arms. Germans in Poland are persecuted with bloody terror and driven from their houses. A series of violations of the frontier, intolerable to a great power, prove that Poland is no longer willing to respect the frontier of the Reich. I expect every soldier,

mindful of the great traditions of eternal German soldiery, will ever remain conscious that he is a representative of the National Socialist Greater Germany. Long live our people and our Reich.

A few minutes after Hitler's early-morning attempt to justify what had just happened, in Danzig, bands of Nazis attacked Polish shops, smashing their windows. The Nazi Party, which had been dominant in the city since the elections of 1933, proclaimed Danzig part of the Third Reich. In July 1938, Sir Geoffrey Mander, the Liberal MP for Wolverhampton East, had asked Rab Butler, the Under-Secretary of State for Foreign Affairs, 'Is it not a fact that Herr Forster is the real ruler of Danzig, under the German Government?' Now Albert Forster sent Hitler a telegram informing him that Danzig was his, and the Führer replied, 'I accept the proclamation. The law for reunion is ratified forthwith.'

The British Cabinet met at 11.30 am and sat for almost two hours. The King held a Privy Council meeting and signed orders for the full mobilisation of Britain's land, sea, and air forces. That afternoon, Britain's town centres were full of military uniforms as soldiers, sailors, and airmen mingled with the housewives who were snapping up all remaining blackout material and first-aid requirements.

It would be the strangest of weekends, typically reflected in the nation's sporting calendar. On Saturday, 2 September, there should have been plenty to talk about as football supporters all over Britain headed for the exits. Yet on the trams and buses taking supporters home for their tea on that stifling, brooding afternoon, no one said very much. At Arsenal's Highbury, where the kick-off of the game against Sunderland had been put back for two hours due to traffic congestion as the first of London's children were evacuated from the capital, the atmosphere was especially subdued. It was almost eight o'clock and dusk was setting in by the time the Arsenal players left for home, the sight of a barrage balloon moored on the club's training pitch leaving them in little doubt that their victory that afternoon would ultimately count for nothing. For once, the result of a football match seemed unimportant.

At eleven o'clock the following morning, Sunday, 3 September 1939, in the lobby of the Russell Hotel – half a mile from King's Cross railway station and 'made of reinforced concrete', the establishment boasted, not all that reassuringly – the defeated Sunderland team gathered around a wireless set ready to hear the Prime Minister's broadcast to the nation. When Neville Chamberlain reached the bit that everyone would remember word for word, England international Raich Carter's first thoughts were of how they would get back to Sunderland. Would the trains still be running now there was a war on? The Leicester City players who had beaten West Ham United at Upton Park the previous day were already safely home, but they had arrived back in Leicester late on Saturday evening to find the city's blackout already in force. Despite the inconvenience, they noticed that there were still plenty of people about. It appeared that no one wanted to go home, despite a fierce thunderstorm.

The nation's footballers could hardly be surprised that their livelihood was being interrupted by war with Germany. Unlike the world situation five years earlier, when Derby County's players had been in a privileged position to see what was happening in Germany, now no one had needed a holiday on the Rhine before they understood the dangers.

Two Lincolnshire teachers, Mr J. H. Sharpe and Miss A. M. Pick, cut it fine, arriving home from a holiday in France and Germany a few days before Germany invaded Poland. 'We'd made plans for our holiday long ago,' said Mr Sharpe,

> but probably should not have gone to Germany at all. There was some talk of war when we left, but we'd grown accustomed to such scares in the last few months that we made light of it. Even a fortnight ago we were struck by the preponderance of military vehicles ... but German civilians were friendly and hospitably inclined, and we tried to be as courteous to the people we met as they were to us. At one hotel we visited the manager said to me, 'You English think there will be a war, but there will be no war.' The general opinion was that Danzig would return to the Reich. It was only when we were travelling through France some days later that it was brought home to us how much the position had deteriorated.

Two young Scots, Peter Gibson and Robert Kinning, both from Kirkintilloch, were among the last Britons to leave German soil before war was declared. Arriving at Euston railway station on 1 September, Gibson told reporters:

> I must say that the Germans were exceedingly pleasant to us. They didn't seem to bear us the slightest ill-will ... none

of the Germans we spoke to appeared to be out-and-out Nazis ... they paid lip service to the party although in every case their allegiance to the cause seemed to be qualified.

We had one amusing experience at a place called Weindor, a sort of wine village restaurant in Koblenz. Every evening the master of ceremonies welcomes visitors to its tables and mentions by name each country ... On this occasion he asked if he had omitted to pay his respects to any foreigner present. A young man immediately stood and said, 'Yes.' The master of ceremonies asked where he came from. 'Danzig,' he said. There was a lot of laughter, after which the master of ceremonies replied, 'Never mind. You may not be a foreigner for long.'

As late as 20 August 1939, a British track and field athletics team had competed against a German team in Cologne, although that same month, when British heavyweight boxing champion Tommy Farr was due to meet a German opponent, Arno Koeblin, at St Helen's rugby football ground in Swansea, the Welsh branch of the British Boxing Board of Control intervened 'in the best interests of the sport' and refused to recommend to the Ministry of Labour that Koeblin be granted a work permit. Instead, it was planned that Farr would face the West Hartlepool heavyweight, Jack London. That fight did not take place either. This time, a contractual problem, not Adolf Hitler, was to blame.

Nine hundred miles away, the 1939 Polish football championship had been whittled down to a four-club play-off between Slask Swietochlowice, Smigly Wilno (from what is now Vilnius, the capital of Lithuania), Junak Drohobycz (now part of Ukraine), and Legia Poznan, but the title was never decided. In Warsaw the city was preparing itself for war. Trenches were being dug, power stations sandbagged, and people had started to carry gas masks. On 1 September, as the Luftwaffe bombed the Polish capital, and German tanks crashed their way over the country's border, in Britain theatres were closed, cricket matches abandoned, greyhound racing cancelled, and the BBC wireless service changed to two wavelengths only. The first Saturday of the new football season had attracted a total of 600,000 spectators to forty-four Football League games; seven days later, the figure had slumped to well under 400,000. Everywhere clubs struggled to find enough players.

Adolf Hitler Stepped In, Didn't He?

Liverpool's Territorials managed to persuade colleagues to stand in for them on sentry duty so that the players could travel to Anfield for the match against Chelsea. The Brentford match programme for the game against Huddersfield Town contained a cartoon of a man entering a turnstile, scowling over his shoulder at a storm cloud which bore the word 'Crisis'. The caption read: 'Let us forget our troubles for a while and see an honourable fight.'

On Merseyside, Norman Greenhalgh was going to be annoyed for several years to come. His club, Everton, were due to meet Portsmouth in the traditional FA Charity Shield game: 'We won the League and Portsmouth won the Cup, and we were supposed to play them. And what happened? Bloody Adolf Hitler stepped in, didn't he, and the bloody war was on, and I lost a medal. That was always a bone of contention with me.'

In the early evening of Saturday, 2 September, the nation's streets were still unusually crowded as people came out to walk and talk. Pubs everywhere were full to overflowing. Holidaymakers returning home after the Bank Holiday weekend were confronted by sandbagged railways stations and the sinister shapes of those barrage balloon defences. Buckets and spades were accompanied by a chilling reminder of the times – gas masks in their containers.

That night, Jim Phelps, a 9-year-old boy from Derby, went to bed wondering what the morning would bring. That Sunday, at 11.15 am, the Phelps family switched on their wireless, already tuned to the Home Service. They listened as Neville Chamberlain told the nation:

> This morning the British ambassador in Berlin handed the German Government a final note, stating that unless we heard from them by 11 o'clock that they were prepared at once to withdraw their troops from Poland, a state of war would exist between us. I have to tell you now that no such undertaking has been given and that, consequently, this country is at war with Germany.

Young Jim ran into the street to find his pals. 'Then I saw some of the neighbours. They could remember the last war. They were weeping. Suddenly I realised what it meant.' Jim spent the remainder of the day helping to fill sandbags. That evening, the family gathered around their wireless set again, this time to listen to the King's broadcast to the Empire: 'For the second time in the lives of most of us, we are at war...'

Jack Wheeler, a young goalkeeper on the books of Birmingham FC, was not too worried, though. On that Sunday morning, as was his custom, he left his digs and went down to the St Andrew's stadium to take a shower and then enjoy a game of snooker with some of the junior players. On his way back home at lunchtime, someone told him that war had been declared: 'I wasn't really bothered. I was young, single and, let's face it, it would all be over by Christmas.'

Bibliography

Beaverbrook, Lord, *The Abdication of King Edward VIII* (London, Hamish Hamilton, 1966)
Boothby, Robert, *Recollections of a Rebel* (London, Hutchinson, 1978)
Channon, Henry (Robert Rhodes James, ed.), *'Chips': The Diaries of Sir Henry Channon* (London, Weidenfeld and Nicholson, 1993)
Churchill, Winston S., *The Gathering Storm* (London, Cassell, 1948)
Cross, Colin, *The Fascists in Britain* (London, Barrie & Rockliff, 1961)
Grosshans, Henry, *Hitler and the Artists* (New York, Holmes & Meier, 1983)
Hitler, Adolf, *Mein Kampf* (English edition) (London, Hurst & Blackett, 1933)
Niemöller, Martin, *From U-Boat to Pulpit* (English edition) (London, William Hodge, 1936)
Klemperer, Victor, *I Shall Bear Witness: The Diaries of Victor Klemperer 1933–41* (London, Weidenfeld and Nicholson, 1998)
Nicolson, Harold, *Diaries and Letters 1939–45* (London, William Collins, Sons and Co Ltd, 1967)
Rippon, Anton, *Gas Masks for Goalposts: Football in Britain During the Second World War* (Stroud, Sutton Publishing, 2005)
Rippon, Anton, *Hitler's Olympics: The Story of the 1936 Olympic Games* (Barnsley, Pen & Sword, 2006)
Rippon, Anton, *How Britain Kept Calm and Carried On: True Stories from the Home Front* (London, Michael O'Mara, 2014)
Seger, Gerhart Heinrich, *A Nation Terrorized* (English edition) (Chicago, Reilly & Lee, 1935)
Shirer, William, *Berlin Diary: The Journal of a Foreign Correspondent 1934–1941* (Baltimore, Johns Hopkins University Press, 2002)
Shirer, William, *The Rise and Fall of the Third Reich* (New York, Touchstone, 1981)
Shirer, William, *The Nightmare Years, 1930–1940* (New York, Bantam, 1985)

Snyder, Louis L., *Encyclopaedia of the Third Reich* (New York, Paragon House, 1989)
Snyder, Louis L., *Hitler and Nazism* (London, Bantam Books, 1967)
Symons, Julian, *The Angry 30s* (London, Eyre Methuen, 1976)
Wheal, Elizabeth-Ann & Pope, Stephen, *The Macmillan Dictionary of the Second World War*, second edition (London, Macmillan, 1997)
Wilkinson, Ellen, *The Town That Was Murdered* (London, Victor Gollanz, 1939)

Newspapers and Journals

Aberdeen Press and Journal, Bedfordshire Times and Independent, Belfast Telegraph, (Birmingham) Evening Despatch, Birmingham Daily Gazette, Deutsche Zeitung, Birmingham Mail, Bristol Evening Post, Coventry Evening Telegraph, Coventry Standard, Daily Chronicle, Daily Dispatch, Daily Express, Daily Herald, Daily Mail, Daily Mirror, Daily News (London), Daily Record and Mail, Daily Telegraph, Daily Sketch, Daily Worker, Derby Evening Telegraph, Dover Express and East Kent News, Dundee Courier, (Exeter) Express and Echo, Gloucestershire Echo, Hull Daily Mail, Illustrated, Illustrated London News, Illustrated Sporting and Dramatic News, Isis, Jour Echo de Paris, Lancashire Evening Post, Larne Times and Weekly Telegraph, Leicester Evening Mail, Liverpool Daily Post, Liverpool Echo, Liverpool Evening Express, Manchester Guardian, Manchester Evening News, Midland Daily Telegraph, Morning Post, Motherwell Times, Muenchener Zeitung, Nelson Leader, New York Herald Tribune, New York Sun, New York Times, New Yorker, Newcastle Evening Chronicle, Newcastle Weekly Chronicle, News Chronicle, News Review, North-Eastern Daily Gazette, North Herald and County Down Independent, Northern Daily Mail, Northern Whig, Nottingham Evening Post, Nottingham Journal, Oxford Magazine, Penrith Observer, Portsmouth Evening News, St Pancras Gazette, Sheffield Star, Sheffield Daily Telegraph, Staffordshire Sentinel, Sunday Illustrated, (Birmingham) Sunday Mercury, Sunday Pictorial, (Newcastle) Sunday Sun, Sunderland Echo, Tageblatt, The Bystander, The Clarion, The People, The Shields Gazette, The Scotsman, The Sketch, The Sphere, The Times, West Sussex Gazette, Western Daily Press, Western Morning News, Westminster Gazette, Völkischer Beobachter, Vorwärts, Yorkshire Evening Post.

Index

Aberdare, Lord, 78, 79, 83
Abrahams, Harold, 84
Allan, Maud, 9
Allen, William E., 48
Anderson, Sir John, 63
Ansell, Elsie, 173
Arnott, John, 173
Asquith, Herbert, viii, 12
Asquith, Margot, 9, 45
Athol, Duchess of, 124
Attenborough, Sir David, 163, 164
Attenborough, Frederick, 163
Attenborough, John, 163
Attenborough, Lord, 163
Attenborough, Mary, 163
Attlee, Clement, 61, 80, 111–113, 121, 125, 154
Auden, W. H., 125

Baldwin, A. Windham, 145
Baldwin, Stanley, 11–12, 24–25, 27–28, 30, 43, 45, 60, 97, 106, 111–113, 121, 129–131, 133–134, 140–141, 144–146, 161
Balfour, Lord, 162,
Bankhead, Tallulah, 6
Barnes, Peter, 173
Barney, Elvira, 9–10
Bartlett, Vernon, 155

Bates, Alfred 'Cosher', 108, 110, 112
Baumgartner, Edumund, 80
Beaverbrook, Lord, 130–131, 146
Beck, Colonel Józef, 169
Beckles, Gordon, 38–39
Beaton, Cecil, 5–6
Bejach, Helga, 163–164
Bejach, Irene, 163–164
Benes, Dr Edvard, 153–154
Berber, Anita, 2
Bergmann, Gretel, 86
Bevin, Ernest, 24
Billing, Noel Pemberton, 9
Billinger, Karl (see Massing, Paul), 70
Bismarck, Otto von, 40, 66
Bismarck, Prince, 80
Blakeney, Brigadier-General Robert, 51
Blunt, Alfred, Bishop of Bradford, 131
Boardman, Harold, 57
Bonar Law, Andrew, viii, 11–12
Bonnet, Georges, 153
Bottomley, Horatio, vi, viii
Boothby, Robert, 35
Borchardt, Ludwig, 89–90, 92, 93
Brauchitsch, Manfred von, 175
Brockway, Fenner, 61
Brüning, Heinrich, 31, 34–36

Broome, Frank, 78
Buchman, Frank N.D., 145
Bulmer-Thomas, Ivor, 41
Burghley, Lord, 78, 83
Burn, Sir Charles, 51
Butler, 'Rab', 176
Butt, Sir Alfred, 108, 110, 112
Byron, Robert, 5

Calvo Sotelo, José, 121
Campbell, Dr Donald, 173
Carnarvon, Lord, 90–93
Carter, Howard, 90–93
Carter, Horatio, 'Raich', 177
Cassidy, Sir Maurice, 127
Chamberlain, Neville, 46,
    107–108, 110–112, 141, 151,
    153–156, 158, 163, 165–168,
    177, 179
Chamberlayne, Arthur, 43
Channon, Sir Henry 'Chips', 75,
    105, 112
Channon, Lady Honor, 75
Churchill, Clementine, 124
Churchill, Winston, 24, 30, 43, 48,
    81, 113, 124, 131, 134, 140,
    144–146, 151–153, 157, 169
Chuter Ede, James, 117
Ciano, Count Galeazzo, 101
Citrine, Walter, 25, 79, 81–82
Clay, James, 173
Clegg, Sir Charles, 82
Clemenceau, Georges, x
Clive, Robert, 13
Coll, Ian, 174
Collin, George, 76
Conze, Dr E., 100–101, 106
Cook, Arthur J., 25,
Cook, Sir Thomas, 143

Cooney, Bob, 125
Curtis-Bennett, Sir Noel, 78–79, 83
Curtius, Dr Julius, 44
Curzon, Lady Cynthia (see
    Mosley, Lady Cynthia)
Cripps, Sir Stafford, 125

Daladier, Edouard, 153–154, 156
Danchik, Bernard N., 85
Darwin, Charles, 95
Dawson of Penn, Lord, 127
Day-Lewis, Cecil, 125
De Winton Wills, Mrs Ernest, 7
Deakin, Miss, 19
Dean-Paul, Brenda, 7
Diem, Carl, 81
Dietrich, Marlene, 67
Disraeli, Benjamin, 156
Dixey, Neville, 111
Doherty, Peter, 77
Dollfuss, Englebert, 96, 148
Doret, Catherine, 34
Dormer, Dr P. A., 114
Duckham, Marion, 34
Dudgeon, Cecil, 48

Ebert, Friedrich, 3, 14, 20,
Eden, Anthony, 83, 85–86, 104,
    107, 151
Einstein, Albert, 67, 69
Erman, Adolf, 89
Ewer, Norman, 104, 150

Fairbanks, Douglas, 45
Farr, Tommy, 178
Forgan, Robert, 53
Forster, Albert, 176
Franco, Francisco, 86,
    121–122, 125

Index

Freud, Sigmund, 67
Frick, Wilhelm, 38, 71
Fritsch, Werner von, 126
Furness, Thelma, 129
Furness, Viscount, 129

Game, Sir Philip, 62
Garraty, John A., 31
Geddes, Sir Eric, ix
Gentle, Rex, 173
Gerard, James, 22
Gibson, Peter, 177–178
Glenconner, Baron, 5
Gloucester, Duchess of, 137
Gloucester, Duke of, 138
Goebbels, Joseph, 3, 23, 63, 69, 97, 139, 144, 153
Göring, Hermann, 38, 70, 126, 139, 149
Gough, Annie, 137
Graeme, Kennedy, 20, 26
Gratton-Doyle, Sir Nicholas, 117
Greenhalgh, Norman, 179
Grender, Mrs, 136
Greenwood, Arthur, 121–122, 167
Gropius, Walter, 67, 93
Grosshans, Henry, 89
Guinness, Bryan, 7
Grynszpan, Herschel, 158

Halifax, Lord, 151, 155, 165
Hall, Clark, 59
Hamilton Piercey, Eric, 55
Handel, George Frederic, 138
Hanfstaengel, Ernst, 13
Hapgood, Eddie, 77
Harris, Henry Wilson, 36
Hartley, Lister, 34
Hartnell, Norman, 7

Hastings, Sir Patrick, 10
Henderson, Arthur, 29
Henderson, Sir Neville, 77
Hess, Rudolf, 14, 17, 140
Hewett, Sir Stanley, 127
Hewitt, Joseph, 173
Hewitt, Mary, 173
Himmler, Heinrich, 69, 74
Hindenburg, Paul von, 21, 22–23, 26, 31, 33, 36–38, 65
Hitler, Adolf, viii, ix, xi, xii, xiii, 3, 10–19, 21–23, 26–28, 31–40, 45, 48–50, 58, 60–63, 65, 69, 72–77, 79, 81, 83–85, 87, 89, 94–98, 100, 105–107, 119, 122, 125–126, 128, 32, 140, 142, 144, 147–158, 165–170, 172, 175–179
Hoare, Sir Samuel, 103, 105–107, 159
Holford, Dave, 76
Hoesch, Leopold von, 81
Holme, Christopher, 120, 122
Hossbach, Colonel Friedrich, 126
Houghton, Mr F. S., 119
Howard, Bryan, 8
Howard, Peter Dunsmore, 48

Iddon, E. F., 95

Jardine, Reverend Robert Anderson, 139
Jeffress, Arthur, 9
Jobey, George, 86
Jokl, Ernst, 67
Joyce, William, 48

Kahr, Gustav von, 13–16, 74
Kaiser Wilhelm II, xi, 139

Kenworthy, Joseph, 54
Kessler, Count Harry, x
King Alfonso II, 120
King Alfonso XIII, 120–121
King Edward VIII, 127–140
King George V, 24, 29, 51, 87, 127–129
King George VI, 41, 135–136, 138, 140
King Henry VIII, 132
King Manuel II, 121
Kinning, Robert, 177
Kitchener, Lord, 53
Kirby, Jack, 77
Klemperer, Otto, 67
Klemperer, Victor, 66, 86, 88
Knilling, Eugen Ritter von, 14–15
Koeblin, Arno, 178
Kroner, Friedrich, 13

Lang, Cosmo Gordon (Archbishop of Canterbury), 128
Lang, Fritz, 67
Laval, Pierre, 105–106
Lawton, Tommy, 175
Leese, Arnold, 51–54
Lewald, Dr Theodor, 81
Lewis, Ted 'Kid', 48–49
Liepman, Heinz Max, 141–142
Lintorn-Orman, Rotha, 50–52, 54
Lloyd George, David, vi, vii, viii, x, 22, 29, 42, 141
Locker-Lampson, Commander Oliver Stillingfleet, 28, 32–33
London, Jack, 178
Londonderry, Lord, 97
Lossow, General Otto von, 14–15
Louis, Joe, 86

Lubbe, Marinus van der, 64–65
Lucas, Frank, 105
Ludendorff, Erich von, 13, 15–16, 18, 21–22, 26–27, 33
Ludendorff, Margarethe, 26–27
Lunn, Sir Arnold, 84

McCormack, James, 173
MacDonald, Ramsay, 11–12, 19, 28–31, 45, 47, 60–61, 97
MacEachean, Captain Neil, 6
Malone, Joseph, 173
Mander, Sir Geoffrey, 86, 176
Mann, Thomas, 67
Marchioness of Carisbrooke, 7
Margesson, David, 54
Marx, Wilhelm, 22
Massey, Raymond, 107
Massing, Paul, 64, 69–70
Mather, Alderman A. W., 172
Maxwell, John, 171
Melly, Andre, 103
Mendelsohn, Erich, 94
Metcalfe, Edward Dudley, 'Fruity', 139
Miller, Jacob, 59
Minniti, Tito, 103
Mitford, Diana (see Mosley, Lady Diana)
Mitford, Nancy, 5
Moore, Lieutenant Colonel Thomas, 86
Morris, Hugh, 45
Morris, J., 170
Morris, Sir William, 48
Mosley, Lady Cynthia, 44–48, 63
Mosley, Lady Diana, 56, 7, 63
Mosley, Sir Oswald, 5, 41–63, 118, 139

Mozart, Wolfgang Amadeus, 6, 143
Müller, Hermann, 31, 35, 37
Mussolini, Benito, xiii, 12, 34, 39, 50–51, 55, 58, 96, 100–107, 121–123, 148–149, 151, 154, 156, 165
Mussolini, Bruno, 101
Mussolini, Vittorio, 101
Myles, Vincent, 147

Neithardt, Georg, 17
Neurath, Baron von, 97, 99
Nichols, Beverley, 1, 6
Nicolson, Harold, 35–36, 49, 54, 98, 140, 181
Niemöller, Martin, 72, 181
Noel-Baker, Philip, 122
Norfolk, Duke of, 138
Novello, Ivor, 7

Oliver, Roland, KC, 112
Orwell, George, 125
Owens, Jesse, 87

Panter-Downes, Mollie, 165
Papen, Franz von, 36–38, 72, 96
Parry, Sir Hubert, 137
Phelps, Jim, 179
Philipps, Lady Marion, 161
Picasso, Pablo, 124
Pick, Miss A. M., 177
Pöhner, Ernst von, 14
Ponsonby, Arthur, 7
Ponsonby, Elizabeth, 7
Portal, Viscount, 78, 83
Porter, Mr Justice, 112
Pownall, Lieutenant-Colonel Sir Assherton, 109

Primo de Rivera, José Antonio, 121
Primo de Rivera, General Miguel, 120–121
Prince of Wales (see King Edward VIII)
Princess Elizabeth, 128, 135, 137
Princess Margaret Rose, 128, 135, 137
Princess Lalita of Burdwan, 7
Preston, Harry, 108

Queen Elizabeth (wife of George VI), 41, 132,
Queen Mary, 127, 128,

Raeder, Admiral Erich, 125–126
Ranshofen-Wertheimer, Egon, 45
Rath, Ernst vom, 158
Rathenau, Walther, 73
Ratzel, Friedrich, 95
Rayner, John, 7
Redmonds, F. H., 4
Reichberg, Arnold, 26
Reith, Sir John, 134
Ribbentrop, Joachim von, 155, 169
Richards, James (see McCormack, James)
Röhm, Ernst, 13, 74
Romilly, Colonel Bertram, 124
Romilly, Esmond, 124
Ross, Albert, 173
Rous, Stanley, 77, 82
Rowlands, Gwilym, 173
Runciman, Walter, 117

Sassoon, Sir Philip, 51
Schafer, Heinrich, 89
Schleicher, General Kurt von, 37
Schmeling, Max, 86
Schuschnigg, Kurt von, 148
Seelenbinder, Werner, 87
Segar, Gerhart, 69
Seisser, Colonel Hans Ritter
    von, 14–15
Selincourt, Nancy de, 161
Seyss-Inquart, Arthur,
    148–150
Sharpe, J. H., 177
Sheppard, Dick, 145–146
Shirer, William L., 13, 75
Silva-White, Mrs Clare, 118
Simon, James, 90, 93
Simon, Sir John, 61–62, 80–81
Simonds, Gavin, KC, 112
Simpson, Ernest, 129
Simpson, Wallis, 129, 130–131,
    139–140
Smith, Eleanor, 7
Smith, F. E., 1st Earl of
    Birkenhead, 7
Smith, Herbert, 22
Smith, Reverend
    Rowland S., 159
Snell, Ivan, 142
Snowden, Phillip, 29, 35, 47
Spender, John Alfred, 151
Spender, Stephen, 125
Sprague, Oliver, 35
Spray, Leonard, xii, xiii, 11
Stephen, Michael Scott, 9
Strachey, Lytton, 6
Stresemann, Gustav, 15
Strickland, William, 162

Stringer, Alderman S., 162
Swaffer, Hannen, 2, 73
Swainson, R. H., 171
Sweeney, Joseph, 42

Tauber, Richard, 67
Temple, Dr William, 79
Tennant, David, 5
Tennant, Stephen, 5–6
Thutmose, 90
Thomas, J. H. 'Jimmy',
    107–113
Thomas, Leslie, 119
Thompson, Alderman J. W., 114
Thomson, Lord, 53
Todt, Fritz, 73
Torgler, Ernst, 65
Trevelyan, Sir Charles, 47
Tsar Nicholas II, 53
Tschammer und Osten,
    Hans von, 81
Turnour, Edward, 119

Vansittart, Sir Robert, 104
Vincent, Sir Percy, 82

Walter, Bruno, 143
Walton, William, 5
Ward, John, 47
Ward-Jackson, Major Charles,
    44–45
Waugh, Evelyn, 5
Webb, Beatrice, 45
Weddell, Alexander, 140
Weill, Kurt, 67
Wells, H. G., 11, 18
Wheeler, Jack, 180
Wigram, Ralph, 81

Index

Wilkinson, Ellen, 34, 114, 117, 119
Whitehead, Walter, 51–52
Whistler, Rex, 5
Windsor, Duke of (see King Edward VIII)
Willans, Sir Frederic, 127
Wilson, Woodrow, 18

Wise, Rabbi, 85
Wreford Brown, Charles, 77

York, Duke of (see King George VI)

Zinoviev, Grigori, 19, 46, 50
Zweig, Stefan, 2